TRUSTING GOD WHEN LIFE IS HARD
A FRESH LOOK AT THE LIFE OF JACOB

PAUL W. DOWNEY

JOURNEYFORTH

Greenville, South Carolina

Library of Congress Cataloging-in-Publication Data
Downey, Paul W., 1957-
  Trusting God when life is hard : a fresh look at the life of Jacob / Paul W.
Downey.
    p. cm.
  Includes bibliographical references.
  Summary: "A look at the life of Jacob" —Provided by publisher.
  ISBN 978-1-59166-987-6 (perfect bound pbk. : alk. paper)
  1. Jacob (Biblical patriarch) 2. Bible. O.T.—Biography. I. Title.
  BS580.J3D69 2009
  222 .11092—dc22
                          2009012506

Cover Photo Credits: Paper iStock; Grungy Old Paper iStock

Trusting God When Life Is Hard: A Fresh Look at the Life of Jacob

Design and page layout by Craig Oesterling

© 2009 by BJU Press
Greenville, South Carolina 29614
JourneyForth Books is a division of BJU Press

Printed in the United States of America
All rights reserved

ISBN 978-1-59166-987-6

15 14 13 12 11 10 9 8 7 6 5 4 3 2 1

Contents

Introduction

Jacob: Saint or Scoundrel?

everal years ago, while reading a commentary in preparation for teaching the book of Genesis, I came across a statement describing Jacob as "a man of faith, to whom God's plans and promises meant far more than physical pleasure."[1] I was startled, because this conflicted with my preconceptions concerning Jacob's character. In Bible story books, Sunday school quarterlies, commentaries, and study Bibles, Jacob is typically presented as a scoundrel always looking out for himself. Having grown up using a Scofield Reference Bible, I was used to seeing Genesis 27 entitled "The Stolen Blessing."

God's having chosen to bless Jacob instead of Esau is usually considered a mystery—evidence of inexplicable grace toward Jacob, to Esau's detriment. That is, the only explanation typically offered for Jacob's elevation is the sovereignty of God. Of course, no further explanation is needed, and Paul specifically and explicitly attributes the blessing of Jacob to God's sovereign authority to bless whomever He chooses (Rom. 9:10–24). Those who write commentaries and other instructional materials have often assumed that God used Jacob despite the ungodliness of his heart. Theodore Epp says, "Although Jacob continued to abase his life with his fleshly actions, God continued to work with him in patient love. . . . If we had been choosing a man to head a nation, I am sure we would not have chosen Jacob. He was a schemer and crooked in so many ways as he sought to gain both material and spiritual blessings."[2]

There is, of course, a sense in which this is true. Since all men are corrupt by nature, every man God ever uses is blessed despite the ungodliness of his heart. However, to describe Jacob as a man who continually "abase[d] his life with fleshly actions" is a charge that neither Paul nor God ever lays against him. Paul speaks only of Jacob and Esau before they were born. He does not describe their character as men. Paul's point is that God's choice was made without consideration of what kind of men they would become. He never denies that they acted according to God's plan. As a matter of fact, it seems implicit in Paul's statement that Jacob and Esau became the men they were because of God's choosing, not that God's choosing was in some way based on what they became, much less that it in some way set aside what they became. We cannot appeal to Paul as a critic of the character of Jacob—he says nothing negative about him.

Still, my presuppositions being what they were, I found myself disputing Morris's statement describing Jacob as a man of faith. I set out in my study to prove him wrong. "If Jacob was a man of faith," I reasoned, "then I'd expect to find God saying so somewhere." I was well aware that there were many places where God identified others as men of faith. Sometimes God called Himself "the God of . . . " an individual, or called a person "my servant" or "friend." As I searched the Scriptures for references that tied God to Abraham, to Isaac, or to Jacob, I began to compile lists that you may find as surprising as I did (see appendix). Bear with me for a few minutes. I realize statistics can be boring, but I don't think these facts are trivial if we are to understand what the Bible actually says about Jacob.

I began by considering how often God identifies Himself with Abraham. I discovered that God is never called "the God of Abram," using the patriarch's given name even though Abram's name is not changed to Abraham until several years after we are told that "he believed in the Lord; and he counted it to him for righteousness" (Gen. 15:6). After God changed Abram's name, God is called "the God of Abraham" a total of twenty-two times. In sixteen of those, He is also called the God (or the fear) of Isaac, and twelve include Jacob's name as well. In the four of those in which Jacob's name is not included, twice God is speaking to Jacob and did not need to include his name, once Jacob is speaking about God in relation to his father and grandfather, and once Jacob's father-in-law, Laban, is speaking to Jacob about God in relation to Abraham and to Nahor and "the god of their father."[3] God is called "the God of Abraham" only six times in a "stand-alone" statement. Four of those are found in Genesis 24 and were spoken by Abraham's servant when he was sent to find a bride for Isaac. One is from the mouth of God when He was speaking to Isaac about the promise He had made to Abraham (Gen. 26:24), and once is in a context where He is called "the excellency of Jacob, whom he loved" just five verses prior in the same passage (Ps. 47:4, 9). Therefore, my attempt to show that God often identified Himself with Abraham proved surprisingly weak, since Jacob is either named or involved in all but five contexts in which such a statement is made, and four of those occurred twenty years before Jacob was born.

So I decided to run a parallel check of references in which God is called "the God of Jacob," using the patriarch's given name. I found that expression twenty-seven times. Remember, God never used Abram's given name to identify Himself. In nine of these instances, the phrase is used in conjunction with Abraham and Isaac. The other sixteen times are all "stand-alone" uses, mostly in Psalms, but also in Genesis, 2 Samuel, Isaiah, Micah, and Acts.

After God changed Jacob's name to Israel, He is also called "the God of Israel" a staggering 204 times. Three of those clearly refer to Israel the individual, using the name in conjunction with Abraham and Isaac. The remaining 201 times are scattered throughout the Old Testament (besides one each in Matthew and Luke), with Jeremiah using the name 49 times. I assumed that this is overwhelmingly a reference to God's identity with Israel the nation rather than Israel the man but found that in most contexts that is impossible to determine with certainty. The harder I tried to make that case, the more it seemed to be a distinction without a difference. God gave Jacob the patriarchal name Israel, then chose to name the nation after the patriarch. He then chose to use that patriarchal name to identify Himself throughout the Scriptures. Even if one could prove that God is identifying Himself with Israel the nation most of the time, it would make little difference to the argument in support of the high spiritual character of Jacob/Israel. The fact that God calls His chosen people "the children of Israel" or "the descendents of Israel," not "the children of Abraham," gives added significance to Israel the man. I know that Abraham and Isaac had other sons not included in "God's people," so identifying His people in either of their names would have been impossible. However, that merely serves to emphasize that God stopped narrowing the line of promise with Jacob, not Abraham or Isaac, and chose to bless all Jacob's sons in a way that He did not for the other sons of Abraham and Isaac.

I also found that God frequently identified Himself with Jacob/Israel in other, similar ways. God is called "the excellency of Jacob/Israel," "the mighty one [or God] of Jacob/Israel," "the glory of

Jacob/Israel," "the Holy One of Jacob/Israel," "the King of Jacob/Israel," and "the portion of Jacob" fifty-three additional times. None of these designations is ever used for Abraham.

To summarize, God identifies Himself with Jacob/Israel personally or with his descendents in his name a total of 284 times. By contrast, He identifies Himself in similar terms with Abraham only 22 times. You could say that God identifies Himself with Abraham only 7.7 percent as often as He does with Jacob/Israel, or that for every time God identifies Himself with Abraham, He identifies Himself with Jacob/Israel thirteen times.

This in no way diminishes Abraham's special relationship with God. He is called the "friend" of God three times—in 2 Chronicles 20:7; Isaiah 41:8; and James 2:23—but it should be noticed that even one of those includes references to Jacob by both his names and the emphasis is on God's relationship with Jacob, not Abraham—"But thou, Israel, art my servant, Jacob whom I have chosen, the seed of Abraham my friend" (Isa. 41:8). Still, besides these times, the title "friend" of God is applied only once to Moses (Exod. 33:11) and never to Jacob.

Another title of relationship to God that is reserved to only a few is that of "servant" of God. Most significantly, several Old Testament prophecies use that title for the coming Messiah, the clearest references being Isaiah 53:11 and Zechariah 3:8. The title is used seventeen times for the prophets collectively. It is even used three times for King Nebuchadnezzar of Babylon, who would punish Judah. David is the Old Testament figure most commonly referred to as the "servant" of God—sixty-six times in all (which would be reduced by about a dozen if we eliminate times when one passage is quoting another). That number includes twenty-five times that David calls himself God's servant and nineteen times that others refer to him that way. God calls David "my servant" twenty times. The second person most frequently referred to by this title is Moses, of whom it is said forty-two times. That number includes three times when Moses applies it to himself, seven times when Joshua calls Moses "the servant of the Lord," and twenty-four times when others are speaking or writing. God calls Moses "my servant" eight times and uses the title for Job six times. It is used five times for Abraham, but only once when God is speaking—twice Moses uses it for "Abraham, Isaac, and Israel"[4] and it is used twice in Psalm 105. The title "servant of the Lord" (or some form thereof) is also used four times for Nehemiah, three times for Joshua, twice each for Daniel and Elijah, and once each for Caleb,

Samson, Samuel, Jonah, Isaiah, Eliakim, Zerubbabel, James, and Paul.[5]

Jacob, however, is called the "servant" of God a surprising twenty times, making Jacob the person third most frequently referred to as God's servant. That ranking moves up to second, ahead of Moses, if we count only the times God is speaking. Jacob uses the title once for himself, Moses uses it for Jacob twice, and David does so once. God calls Jacob "my servant" sixteen times. Significantly, all but two of those instances use his birth name, Jacob, rather than his God-given name, Israel.

I was faced with the dilemma of conflicting evidence. On the one hand, I had a lifetime of teaching on Jacob in which he was presented as one who sneaked and connived to gain advantage over his brother, to fool his father, and to cheat his father-in-law. But opposed to that were the repeated statements of Scripture that God was the God of Jacob, the King of Jacob, the Mighty One of Jacob, the Excellency of Jacob, the Glory of Jacob, the Holy One of Jacob, and the Portion of Jacob, along with God calling Jacob "my servant" twice as often as He had Moses. Either I could teach Jacob the way he'd been taught to me, as a sneaking, lying scoundrel, or I could work my way through the text of Genesis, seeking to reinterpret the events in his life in the light of the repeated statements of Scripture about Jacob's strong, positive relationship with God. The former would be easier. It would allow my presuppositions to remain undisturbed and would not require a great deal of thought to prepare—I could simply reiterate the bulk of the material others had written before me. The latter would be a challenge. I was not at all sure it could be done, let alone that I was able to do it.

A study of Jacob's life must wrestle with the apparently conflicting testimony of the texts mentioned above and other texts that are highly critical of Jacob. While the testimony of every citation of Jacob's name from Exodus to Revelation is virtually unanimous in its identification of Jacob as a great man of God, passages within his biography in Genesis seem to present a different picture. Some of the things said about him cause us to wonder, "How could God love Jacob?" (see Rom. 9:13). For instance, Genesis 27:35 describes Jacob as a sneaky thief who took away a blessing that was rightfully his brother's. Genesis 27:36 describes him as one who supplanted his brother twice, taking away first his birthright and then his blessing. In Genesis 31:26–30 Jacob is described as an ungrateful son-in-law who stole from his father-in-law, Laban, and tried to slip away with the loot, the family, and the heirlooms. In Genesis 31:43–53 he is accused of threatening harm to his family and needing his father-in-law to invoke the name of God to keep an eye on Jacob when Laban couldn't be there.

While these accusations are damaging, we must remember that none of them are made by God or the narrator of the Bible text. Who is speaking in each case? In Genesis 27:35, where Jacob is accused of subtlety and taking his brother's blessing, the speaker is Jacob's father, Isaac. As we will see when we examine that text, Isaac himself was behaving less than honorably or forthrightly in that situation, so his testimony is tainted. In the verse that follows, where Jacob is accused of twice supplanting his brother, the speaker is none other than the aggrieved Esau, whose testimony is highly questionable since his character is less than sterling. In the final texts in which Jacob is criticized for being a dishonest and dishonorable son-in-law (Gen. 31:26–30, 43–53), the speaker is his father-in-law, Laban, whose testimony is impeached by the fact that for twenty years he had done everything he could to cheat Jacob out of his living.

Jacob is certainly not without his faults. There are a couple of situations in which we see him behaving badly, but there are no other texts in Scripture that accuse Jacob of wrongdoing. None. In every case, the accusations are leveled by men whose own motives and behavior are at least as doubtful as Jacob's.

We must be committed to the basic principle of Bible interpretation that says we have to let the Bible mean what it says. The problem was that I had found God to describe Jacob in terms that conflicted with what I believed the Bible revealed about Jacob. Since there was no honest way around what God said to and about Jacob, I was forced to reevaluate what I thought I knew about him. In doing so, what emerged was a portrait of a man deeply committed to obeying God despite the manifold injustices with which he was treated—a man who learned to trust God when life was hard.

In studying the biography of Jacob in Genesis, you will find that on the seven occasions in which God speaks to Jacob He never speaks a word of rebuke or censure (Gen. 28:13–15; 31:3, 11–13; 32:28; 35:1, 9–12; 46:3–4). In each case, God has a message for Jacob of blessing and promise. Every time. This certainly does not excuse Jacob's lies on the one occasion he deceived his father (Gen. 27:18–30). Of course, the fact that Abraham is called "the friend of God" does not excuse him for the two occasions in which to save his own life he sold his wife to a pagan king—once to the king of Egypt (Gen. 12:14–16) and once to the king of the Philistines (Gen. 20:2–14). Nor does David's being described as a "man after God's own heart" excuse him for impregnating his friend's wife and then having her husband killed to cover up his sin (2 Sam. 11:1–27). Yet writers persist in saying things such as

> Jacob's grandfather Abraham is remembered as a very righteous man, and his father Isaac as a somewhat righteous man, [and] Jacob is largely regarded an unrighteous man. . . . Oh, he doesn't stand in the rogue's gallery of Scripture with notorious figures like King Saul, King Ahab, and Judas Iscariot. But Jacob was no saint, at least until God got hold of his life. . . . For most of his life, he was determined to have his way. If necessary, he would lie, cheat, and steal to accomplish that.[6]

For some reason Jacob is consistently thought of as a scoundrel while Abraham and David are considered heroes of the faith, despite the fact that their sins were far more egregious than Jacob's.

As I've studied the Scripture, as well as several representative commentaries, I've been forced to conclude that commentators, preachers, and writers of Sunday school materials have been almost unanimous in treating Jacob far more harshly than does the Bible itself. Therefore, you will find that this study does not do a very thorough job of reporting what others have written about Jacob. I found those commentaries I've studied to be somewhat enlightening but not particularly helpful for my primary task. They provide a good deal of background help on the text and information on Jacob's contemporary culture but are more or less uniform in their treatment of Jacob's character. Most persist in what I believe to be the error of allowing Jacob's critics—Isaac, Esau, and Laban—to tell us what to think of him. This study will try to interpret the events in the life of Jacob in the light of what God has to say about him.

1

What's in a Name?

Gen. 25:19–34

was speaking with a friend recently who was approaching his eightieth birthday. Since he is from a generation that preceded mine, I enjoy listening to him reminisce about his childhood growing up in early-twentieth-century rural Georgia. His father came from a large family, and his grandfather had trouble keeping track of who all the grandchildren and great-grandchildren were. Being elderly and feeble and unable to see very well, he liked to stop any of the children who came near him to talk briefly. He often had to ask, "Now, who's your daddy?" He wanted to be able to connect the child to the right member of the clan.

Even such a seemingly insignificant act illustrates the fact that information about a person's family background and connections is vital if one is to understand an individual. Late-twentieth and early twenty-first century Westerners are prone to think of history as beginning with themselves and their life stories as beginning when they became adults. However, much that goes into making people what they are happens during childhood or even before. To present an accurate picture of a person's life, biographers routinely start by examining the subject's family roots, paying special attention to significant events related to his birth and childhood.

I could spend a great deal of time and space describing the lives of Jacob's father, Isaac, and his grandfather, Abraham. I'm sure it would help us place Jacob in his historical context. However, a study of Abraham and Isaac is not my purpose, and I'll assume you are familiar with their stories. Take heart. I promise not to digress far in our study of Jacob. However, we do need to consider his life from the time just before his conception.

The Conception of Jacob and Esau (Gen. 25:20–23)

Who was Jacob's father? His name was Isaac, the only son of Abraham and Sarah. He was the son through whom God's promises to Abraham would be fulfilled (Gen. 21:1–3; cf. Rom. 9:10–13). When he was a young man, possibly as old as thirty, he went with his father to Mount Moriah and cooperated with the presentation of himself as a sacrifice to God. Being released at the last moment, he was returned to Abraham as if from the dead (Gen. 22:1–19; cf. Heb. 11:17–19). When Isaac was forty years old, Abraham sent a trusted servant to find Isaac a bride. That servant returned with a cousin of Isaac's named Rebekah, who had been willing to trust the Lord to give her a future with a man she had never met (Gen. 24). Years later, after Abraham died, Isaac "dwelt by the well Lahai-roi" (Gen. 25:11; cf. 16:14), located about fifty miles southwest of Beer-sheba, which is apparently where he was living when Jacob and Esau were born.

Going through a trial similar to that endured by Abraham and Sarah, Isaac and Rebekah were childless for the first twenty years of their marriage.[1] When Isaac took his supplication to God, the Lord permitted Rebekah to conceive. Martin Sicker points out that the Hebrew phrase translated "for his wife" (Gen. 25:21) can be "read more literally as 'opposite his wife' suggesting that they both prayed together."[2] Clearly, they were praying within the will of the Lord, since God had promised that His covenant with Abraham would be fulfilled through Isaac's offspring. The previous twenty years had apparently been a test of Isaac's faith. "The seed of the promise was to be prayed for from the Lord, that it might not be regarded merely as a fruit of nature, but be received and recognized as a gift of grace."[3] To his credit, Isaac had not responded to two decades of barrenness the way his father, Abraham, had, by taking another wife.

As would normally be the case, Rebekah did not immediately know that she was carrying twins. However, the text tells us that "the children struggled together within her" (Gen. 25:22), which caused Rebekah great distress. This was more strenuous than normal movement of children within the womb. The verb means "to abuse or crush" and is often linked with the word "to oppress" (cf. 1 Sam. 12:3–4; Hosea 5:11; Amos 4:11).[4] Because of her distress, she asked,

"If this be so, why am I thus?" (Gen. 25:22). She may have meant simply, "Why is this happening to me?" (HCSB). It's also possible that she meant, "Why am I alive?"[5] The latter suggestion finds some support in Rebekah's later expression of a similar sentiment in frustration over conflict with Esau's wives (Gen. 27:46). Another possibility is that Rebekah may have understood the conflict in her womb as signifying lifelong contention between two children that might endanger the fulfillment of God's promise, or even the attempt of one to kill the other before birth. God's reply, that there were "two nations in thy womb and two manner of people" (Gen. 25:23) confirmed her fears. The intensity of the conflict between the twins was fierce. The promise that they "shall be separated from thy bowels," though, gave her confidence that she would deliver them alive.

We should not miss the fact that while Jacob and Esau were still "fetuses" the Bible refers to them as "children." This is one of several biblical texts that present life beginning at conception. The Bible teaches that a "fetus" is a person, bearing God's image and possessing a soul. In this case, twins in the womb were distinguishable from one another and from their mother. The text deals with this situation as involving three distinct individuals—the mother and the twins within her. This alone should silence those who try to present abortion as a mother's exercise of control over her own body.

Notice that when Rebekah was in distress she turned to the Lord, not to Isaac. This is significant for at least three reasons. First, we see that men and women alike have direct access to God in prayer without the need for a human mediator. Isaac had earlier entreated the Lord on her behalf that she might conceive, and she may have been involved in praying too. Now we have a clear statement that Rebekah herself went to God with her concerns about her pregnancy. Second, the incident implies that Rebekah may have had a closer relationship with the Lord than did Isaac. It strikes me as odd that this point is so often overlooked in this text, while commentators routinely make much of Hannah's begging the Lord for a son (1 Sam. 1:1–11). Unlike Hannah's case, in which the Lord's reply to her was through the corrupt priest Eli, the Lord replied to Rebekah directly. In fact, Rebekah is one of the very few women to whom God ever spoke directly, and she may be the only woman in Scripture to receive a verbal message directly from God in response to her prayer. Other women who heard from God directly include Miriam, in rebuke for her criticism of Moses (Num. 12:4–9), Huldah the prophetess (2 Kings 22:14–20; cf. 2 Chron. 34:22), and Deborah (implied in Judg. 4:6–7).

If "the Angel of the Lord" is identified as God, He also spoke directly to Hagar (Gen. 16:9–13) and the wife of Manoah and mother of Samson (Judg. 13:3–5). There is no evidence that Sarah ever heard directly from God, and neither did Mary (Gabriel was the messenger who announced her conception, and later dream revelations were made to Joseph, not Mary).

This leads to the third reason this incident is significant. In reply to her question, the Lord provided information that would impact Jacob and Esau and their offspring for generations, and this information was given to Rebekah rather than to Isaac. It was Rebekah who was told that the twins in her womb would grow to become two nations, that one would be stronger than the other, and that the elder would serve the younger.[6] She understood that her family would not be peaceful and unified, but contentious and ultimately divided. She also understood that the continuity of the promise made to Abraham through Isaac would proceed through the second-born twin, not the first-born.

At this point in history the right of primogeniture was assumed, and it would later be established by the Law of Moses—the first-born son was to become the clan leader, or patriarch, upon the death of the father, with responsibility for leading family worship and maintaining the family property. For this reason, he was to receive a double portion of the estate as his inheritance. However, the law would also make provision for a father to transfer the birthright from the eldest son if another were more deserving (1 Chron. 5:1–2).

In several examples in the Messianic line the promise passed through someone who was not the first-born, starting with the very first generation. The line of promise passed from Adam through Seth, not Cain, and from Noah through Shem, not Japheth. At least one of Abraham's brothers, Haran and Nahor, was older than he. Isaac was the younger brother of Ishmael. Jacob, being only minutes younger than his twin brother, Esau, was closer to the age of the first-born than any of these others. The line would then pass from Jacob to his fourth-born son, Judah. Later, the promise would continue from Jesse to his seventh son, David, and from David through Solomon, his second son by Bathsheba, when he already had other sons by other wives. As a matter of fact, while many of the men in the Messianic line may have been first-born sons, it is impossible to prove from the biblical record that a single individual in the line of Christ prior to Jesus Himself was actually a first-born son. God has always reserved the right to bless whomever He chooses, and He often extended His blessing "to those who have no other claim to it" so they "received what they did not deserve."[7]

In the case of Jacob and Esau, God told Rebekah in advance that He intended to bless the younger twin. Given the typical expectation of the father to pass his estate on to his first-born son, along with the special revelation to the mother that "the elder would serve the younger," we should not be surprised to find that "Isaac loved Esau . . . but Rebekah loved Jacob" (Gen. 25:28). What is disappointing is that Isaac did not seem to share Rebekah's discernment of or commitment to the word of the Lord in this matter.

The Birth of Jacob and Esau (Gen. 25:24–26)

When the twins were born, each had something remarkable about him. The first boy came out covered with reddish-brown ("earth-colored"[8]) hair, "all over like a hairy garment" (Gen. 25:25) or like a "fur coat" (HCSB), so he was named "Esau," which probably means "the hairy one."[9] Exactly what this signifies is not clear. It may be just a description of the physical characteristic that distinguished the two boys. C. F. Keil suggests that this "was a sign . . . of excessive sensual vigour and wildness."[10] Esau's brother, continuing the struggle that had been going on in the womb, latched onto Esau's heel. Apparently with a grip that was not broken during the birth, the second son was born hanging onto Esau's heel. He was called "Jacob" (*ya'qob*). The text uses a wordplay on the name Jacob because it sounds so much like *aqeb*, "heel-grasper" or "heel-holder." Jewish scholar Nahum M. Sarna says, "By folk etymology, the name is here derived from the Hebrew *'akev*, 'heel.' In reality, Hebrew *ya'kov* stems from a Semitic root *'-k'v*, 'to protect.' It is abbreviated from a fuller form with a divine name or epithet as its subject, *Ya'akov-'el*, 'May El protect.' "[11]

Esau would later give the rhyming word for heel-holder a new shade of meaning, saying it signifies a "supplanter," or "one who takes the place rightfully belonging to another" (Gen. 27:36). Over a thousand years later, Jeremiah uses the word heel-holder in the sense that Esau gives it, warning Israel to "Take ye heed every one of his neighbour, and trust ye not in any brother: for every brother will utterly supplant, and every neighbour will walk with slanders" (Jer. 9:4). However, the idea of supplanting is not intrinsic to the word. When *heel-holder* is used in Job 37:4, a text that is roughly contemporaneous with the lives of the patriarchs, it is given the meaning "to restrain, stop, hold back, guard, or protect"—"He will not stay them when his voice is heard."

It is significant that when the prophet Hosea uses this word when speaking of Jacob, he assumes the positive connotation given the word in Job, not the negative one of Jeremiah.

> He took his brother by the heel in the womb, and by his strength he had power with God: yea, he had power over the angel, and prevailed: he wept, and made supplication unto him: he found him in Bethel, and there he spake with us; even the Lord God of hosts; the Lord is his memorial." (Hosea 12:3–5)

Hosea interprets this heel-holding "as an evidence of strength and power with God."[12] Summarizing several events yet to be considered in Jacob's life, Hosea concludes with high praise—"the Lord is his memorial." Speaking of this passage, Charles L. Feinberg says,

> Those who have interpreted the account of the life of Jacob in the book of Genesis in such a manner that no good thing could be said of him, will find it difficult to understand the words of Hosea concerning the illustrious patriarch, with whose name God links His own—'the God of Jacob.' It is easily discernible in the life of Jacob that he ever sought spiritual blessings throughout his life.[13]

It is vital to note that the popular notion that Jacob's name means "supplanter" is false. Getz admits that the name "initially had a positive meaning—perhaps 'to protect,'" then adds, "Later, however, the name came to mean 'take by the heel, trip up, to engage in fraud,' . . . it also came to mean to 'usurp' or 'deceive.'"[14] He fails to state that it is Esau who gives the name that new, negative nuance of meaning and that commentators adopted Esau's "definition." For instance, Joyce C. Baldwin says that Jacob's name means "he deceives or supplants," then states in a footnote, "The name Jacob has been found in cuneiform and Egyptian texts dating from the early second millennium, in a form which meant 'may God protect.' The Hebrew for 'heel' and 'to take by the heel' or 'supplant' have the same consonants, and therefore lend themselves to puns on the already current name, Jacob."[15] She fails to mention that the naming of Jacob in Genesis 25 is at least contemporaneous and perhaps earlier than those cuneiform and Egyptian records.

Furthermore, the word for heel-holder doesn't necessarily mean supplanter, despite the common assumptions, and Jacob's name doesn't even mean heel-holder; it just rhymes or puns with it. "Scholars are agreed that the name Jacob is an abbreviated name, of which the longer form is 'Jacob-el.'"[16] Hamilton explains that there are three ways this name could be understood. If taken as an imperfect, it could be a prayer, "May God protect [him]." That is the way Sarna understands it, saying, "The name Jacob is thus, in origin, a plea for divine protection of the newly born. Most appropriate for the one who was to live his entire life in the shadow of danger."[17] Alternatively, it could be understood as a future tense statement, "God will protect [him]," or even as a past tense statement, "God has protected [him]." Hamilton considers the third "particularly appropriate, in view of the painful and uncertain pregnancy Rebekah had to endure. Jacob has survived that ordeal."[18]

Whoever may be right about the best way to understand the expression, it is undeniable that Jacob's name signifies God's protection, not what has been popularly interpreted as "Jacob's scheming." The name may imply that it was divine intervention that caused him to survive the struggle with Esau in the womb, or that God will protect him throughout his life, or both. Since that name is tied to his "heel-grasping" at his birth, it seems necessary to reject the negative connotation Esau gives the name in favor of Hosea's positive interpretation—Jacob's birth name signified that he had "strength with God." God's changing his name to Israel years later will simply reinforce and expand on the meaning of his birth name, as is typical when God changes a name.

Unfortunately, much of what has been written about Jacob interprets his life through Esau's negative application pronounced when he was furious with Jacob. Since we should be committed to allowing God's statements concerning Jacob to overrule the statements of his critics, we must reconsider the significance of his name being linked to the word *heel-holder*. The writer of Hebrews describes Esau as a "profane," or "godless," person (12:16), but Jacob is described as a servant of the Lord twenty times.[19] Paul says that "being not yet born, neither having done any good or evil, that the purpose of God according to election might stand, not of works, but of him that calleth; it was said unto [Rebekah], The elder shall serve the younger. As it is written, Jacob have I loved, but Esau have I hated" (Rom. 9:11–13). God had determined that even in the womb, Jacob was to be blessed and Esau was not. Hosea says that Jacob's grabbing of Esau's heel in the womb was evidence of his strength with God. Therefore, we should see Jacob's grasp on Esau's heel as positive, not negative. It did not signify that Jacob "went through life taking advantage of others—tripping them up so he could get ahead."[20] That is Esau's view, not God's.

What, then, does it signify? Jacob's grasp on Esau's heel, and his name meaning "May God protect [him]," "God will protect [him]," or "God has protected [him]" and its being linked with heel-holder, must mean that Jacob went through life enduring mistreatment yet acting as a restrainer of evil, especially his brother's, and enjoying the special protection of God. God used Jacob even in the womb to struggle against Esau's sensual selfishness, grasping his heel to signify that even though Esau managed to emerge from the womb first, he would not be permitted to disrupt God's program. Describing Jacob as "something of a grabber, an exploiter, a manipulator and a cheat"[21] grows from what seems to be a fundamental misunderstanding of this event, coupled with a profound misinterpretation of a key word in the next verse—"plain."

The Maturing of Jacob and Esau (Gen. 25:27–28)

This passage provides only a brief summary of Isaac's twin sons' growth to maturity. It begins by simply saying, "And the boys grew," and then gives us a glimpse of their character. Esau is described in terms that our culture considers admirable—"a cunning hunter, a man of the field." On the other hand, Jacob is described in terms that are interpreted to mean something that our culture treats scornfully—"a plain man, dwelling in tents." These statements are usually taken to mean that Esau was a sportsman, an outdoorsman, while Jacob was a "sissy" or a "nerd," someone who was quiet, was unremarkable, and stayed inside. This image is reinforced by the fact that we see Jacob cooking when Esau comes in from the field. From all this, we tend to visualize Esau as rugged and tough, and Jacob as weak, even effeminate. Esau's daddy loved him, so he must have been a "man's man." Jacob's mommy loved him, so he must have been a "momma's boy."[22] But is that what the text means?

Let's start with Esau. What good is being a "cunning hunter"? No one in Scripture is ever praised for that. "Hunting as a way of life was held in low esteem in Israel."[23] While there are others in the Bible who hunted, only two men are identified as "hunters" and both are described as being skilled at it—Esau and Nimrod. "No Israelite or Judean king is ever mentioned as indulging in the sport."[24] The fact that the narrator calls Esau a "cunning hunter" and "a man of the field [the open country]" is understood by Jewish scholar Benno Jacob to mean that he had an undisciplined and disorderly way of life.[25] Nimrod is called a "mighty hunter" in the context of being identified as a rebel against God (Gen. 10:9), who claimed for himself an authority not authorized by God. This characteristic is probably mentioned here in order to prepare us for Esau's willing participation in Isaac's scheme to confer the blessing of Abraham on Esau when God had ordained Jacob to be the next patriarch. At the very least, we should understand the narrator to intend this as a critical evaluation, not praise.

Hunting is not wrong, but for Esau it was not necessary. The family's persons and property were not endangered by wild beasts, so there was no need to hunt down predators for safety. They were extremely wealthy with extensive flocks and herds, so hunting for meat or any other animal product was unnecessary. Isaac was the first person since Cain to be known as a farmer, since you can find him planting crops (Gen. 26:12), but there is no evidence that deer or other animals were destroying the crops. There would be no need to be "cunning" in one's hunting. The text suggests that Esau hunted because he and/or his father preferred venison. However, we find later that his father couldn't tell venison from goat meat when it was properly prepared, so that reason falls a little flat.

It seems that the real reason Esau became a cunning hunter was for the sport of it. Hunting was not just a hobby for Esau—it was his life. The text, then, does not present Esau as a rugged outdoorsman but implies that he was a self-absorbed goof-off, unconcerned about the family, the business, or God. The fact that Isaac loved him for it says more about Isaac than it says about Jacob.

What about the description of Jacob? He's called a "plain man, dwelling in tents." For all the times this word (*'is tam/tam/tamim*) appears in the Hebrew text, it is translated "plain" only here. The word is usually translated "perfect." Besides Jacob, it is used to describe the character of two other individuals. In Genesis 6:9 it describes Noah—"Noah was a just man and perfect in his generations, and Noah walked with God." In Job 1:1 and 8 it describes Job—"There was a man in the land of Uz, whose name was Job; and that man was perfect and upright, and one that feared God, and eschewed evil. . . . And the Lord said unto Satan, Hast thou considered my servant Job, that there is none like him in the earth, a perfect and an upright man, one that feareth God, and escheweth evil?" In Genesis 17:1 it's applied to a third individual, stated as a command describing the character God expected Abram to develop or display—"The Lord appeared to Abram, and said unto him, I am the Almighty God;

walk before me, and be thou perfect." Speaking of this word's use in Genesis 17:1, Victor Hamilton says, "Blamelessness was first applied to Noah (6:9). The difference between 6:9 and 17:1 is that for Noah blamelessness is an accomplished fact . . . while for Abraham it is a goal."[26]

Commenting on this word's use in Genesis 9:6, Hamilton says, "The word blameless [NIV] means free from defect, as may be observed from the many passages describing the unblemished animal presented to God (Exod 12:5; Lev. 1:3, 10; 3:1, 6; etc.)."[27] Sarna says,

> These cardinal terms of biblical Hebrew, *tsaddik* [just] and *tamim* [perfect], are used here for the first time without definition, thus presupposing a clearly recognizable quality of virtue favored by God. . . . The term *tamim*, which is mostly found in ritual contexts, describes a sacrificial animal that is without blemish. . . . As applied to human beings, *tamim* acquired a moral dimension connoting 'unblemished' by moral fault—hence a person of unimpeachable integrity. Such an individual enjoys God's fellowship, according to Psalms 15 and 101:6.[28]

Speaking of this word's use to describe Job, Layton Talbert translates it "integrity" and says, "Integrity (*tamah*) has come to imply ethical morality, especially honesty."[29] He adds, "The Hebrew word means wholeness, completeness, soundness. Job's integrity signified that he was 'whole-hearted in his commitment to the person and requirements of God.' No ulterior motive lurked behind his morality."[30]

In each of these contexts we understand the word to mean "mature and complete" and to be connected with godliness. We find that is, in fact, what this word means when we consider some of the other contexts in which the word is used. In contrast with the things that the Canaanites did that were "abomination unto the Lord" (Deut. 18:12), it describes how God expects His people to behave before Him—"Thou shalt be perfect with the Lord thy God" (Deut. 18:13). The word also describes God's dealings with men—"He is the Rock, his work is perfect" (Deut. 32:4), and "As for God, his way is perfect" (2 Sam. 22:31). Most tellingly, the word is used to describe the only kind of animal that was acceptable for sacrifice—"If his offering be a burnt sacrifice of the herd, let him offer a male without blemish" (Lev. 1:3) and "whosoever offereth a sacrifice . . . in beeves or sheep, it shall be perfect to be accepted; there shall be no blemish therein" (Lev. 22:21).

So we find the word *'is tam/tam/tamim* to have been used to describe God's words and works, man's responsibility to live righteously before God, and the physical perfection of animals acceptable for sacrifice. It is also used to describe the character of Noah, Abraham, and Job as men of unimpeachable integrity. To substitute the word *plain* or *quiet* in any of these contexts would grossly distort the meaning of the texts.

I am baffled by the fact that so few writers seem to attach real significance to this same word's being used to introduce Jacob in Genesis 25:27—"And Jacob was a plain ['*is tam*] man, dwelling in tents." That Jacob's possession of this quality is stated as an "accomplished fact," as in the cases of Noah and Job, rather than as "a goal," as in Abram's case, should not go unnoticed. That is, Jacob is not commanded to be blameless. Rather, we are told from the start that he is a blameless man.

It is beyond dispute that the Lord wants us to understand that Noah, Abraham, and Job are described as men of blameless, godly character. One of the few commentators who even acknowledges that this word is used to describe Jacob is Victor Hamilton. He says, "Normally in the OT *tam* means innocence or moral integrity (i.e., 'blameless'), as in Job 1:1, 8; 2:3; 9:20–22, and is connected with the verb *tamam*." Then he adds, "But one may argue that this would be a poor translation here for two reasons. First, Jacob is anything but blameless; second, it would provide a puzzling and meaningless contrast with Esau as an outdoorsman, a hunter."[31] The reasons Hamilton suggests for redefining this word in this context are unconvincing—he makes an a priori assumption that Jacob is "anything but blameless," and he has misunderstood the significance of Esau's being described as a "cunning hunter." He apparently rejects his own arguments, since a few lines later he adds, "I am persuaded, however, that we should give the same meaning to '*is tam* in Gen. 25:27 as we do to '*is tam* in Job 1:8."[32] Martin Sicker is another who acknowledges this word's use in connection with Jacob, but he says without justification that in this context it should be translated "whole-hearted" and that it signifies "that Jacob was a self-assured young man."[33]

I've already explained why I believe the description of Esau to be intended as a moral condemnation in contrast to Jacob's moral integrity. I'm not willing to concede that we must reinterpret this word in this verse alone on the basis of what we've always assumed the rest of Jacob's life story indicates about his character. We must not allow what is essentially a traditional mistranslation in Genesis 25:27 to obscure the point the narrator is making regarding Jacob. Jacob is introduced as a blameless man, and the rest of his story should be interpreted in that light. In a classic case of understatement, Henry Morris says, "The translators have done Jacob a disservice by calling him a 'plain' man, or a 'quiet' man."[34]

That brings us to the second phrase used in Jacob's introduction. Is there any significance to his being described as "dwelling in tents" rather than being a "man of the field"? In one sense, Jacob is presented as a man interested in civil order—"with a simple, well-regulated way of life"[35]—while Esau is presented as a man disdaining the social order—"roving about like the animals of the field which he chased."[36] That is, Jacob is presented as staying with the family and assisting in the livestock business enterprise, while Esau irresponsibly neglects home and business and goes his own way for fun.

In a more important sense, though, Jacob is compared favorably with two other tent-dwellers—his grandfather Abraham and his father, Isaac, as an indication of faith in God's promise: "By faith [Abraham] sojourned in the land of promise, as in a strange country, dwelling in tabernacles with Isaac and Jacob, the heirs with him of the same promise: for he looked for a city which hath foundations, whose builder and maker is God" (Heb. 11:9–10).

The writer of Hebrews links Abraham, Isaac, and Jacob as "tent dwellers" and ties this to their faith in God's promises of redemption. For Jacob to be identified as a "tent dweller" when he is introduced is not an accident. God intends us to get the point that Jacob is a righteous man who trusted God's promises, while Esau was a godless man who cared nothing for God and His promises. Understanding this foundational point profoundly influences our interpretation of the lives of these two men.

The Birthright of Jacob and Esau (Gen. 25:29–34)

Before Genesis 25 closes, we are provided with an anecdote from the lives of these brothers that is intended to illustrate the prior statements concerning their character. Again, how we read this is colored by how we understand the previous descriptions.

While they were still relatively young, a day came when Jacob was boiling lentils ("sod pottage"). Esau came in from "the field," or "the open country." I've often heard this text treated as if Esau came in from a manly day's work while Jacob had stayed home helping his mommy in the kitchen. Such a warped interpretation is foreign to the text and merely reveals the preacher's bias against Jacob. It is much more consistent with the narrator's descriptions to assume that this event illustrates their characters: Jacob is hard at work at home while Esau has been off hunting all day. It would seem that part of Jacob's responsibilities in the running of the estate involved food preparation. Mature, responsible, trustworthy Jacob had been cooking supper while immature, irresponsible, unreliable Esau played.

We don't know how old the boys were when this occurred. An ancient tradition found in the Midrash claims that this happened on the day that their grandfather Abraham died.[37] The boys would have been fifteen years old at that time. If so, it may be that the solemnity of the occasion had something to do with why Jacob, and not a servant, was preparing the meal. It would also reflect very badly on Esau that he'd been out hunting all day and came in demanding something to eat. It is possible that while Jacob prepared the soup he was thinking about his grandfather's legacy and what would become of it if it were handed over to Esau. Sicker suggests that it may be that "Jacob's primary concern was to preserve that heritage, which meant preventing Esau from replacing Isaac."[38]

Esau had been out goofing off all day. If hunting, he was obviously unsuccessful on this occasion. Nevertheless, he came home at the end of the day expecting to be fed. Exaggerating his weakness, Esau demanded "Let me eat some of that red stew, for I am exhausted!" (Gen. 25:30 ESV). This event was noteworthy enough in the history of this family that Esau came to be known as "Red" ("Edom"). Of course, we've also been told that the furlike hair that covered his body was reddish, so the name fit. Still, it was this event that gave him the name. One Jewish writer comments on the phrase translated "let me eat," saying it carries the connotation of "let me gulp." He explains, "The Hebrew expression is taken from the feeding of animals and characterizes the uncontrolled gluttony as well as the vulgar language of Esau."[39] It actually implies that one has his mouth open for food to be poured down his throat. Esau apparently expected Jacob to feed him since that was the verb he used: "Feed me."

Jacob's response is usually understood to mean that Jacob said he'd give Esau some lentil soup if Esau would sell him the birthright. The text isn't clear about the price of the birthright. It is usually assumed that Jacob was offering to trade bread and soup for the birthright. It is also possible that he offered the food for the promise to negotiate a price for the birthright. After reaching an agreement, they sealed the deal with an oath, then Esau finished his meal and went his way. However, there is yet another way this text could be read. Sicker maintains that the clause translated "then Jacob gave Esau bread" should be translated "And Jacob had given Esau bread."[40] If correct, this would at least imply that the sale of the birthright was not a condition of Jacob's giving Esau something to eat but was a separate transaction discussed over the meal.

A couple of things are implied by the fact that Jacob offered to buy the birthright. First, it tells us something about the young men's desires. Esau had proved by his lifestyle that he had no desire for family leadership or responsibility—it was clear that he didn't want the birthright. The one who held the birthright would receive two shares (presumably two-thirds, if there are only two heirs) of the estate, but he would also be expected to manage the estate, care for the parents, and lead the family in worship as well as business. Esau would rather take one share and go his own way, responsible only for himself. To have the birthright was not necessarily a financial advantage—it carried a great burden of responsibility. Esau's willingness to sell it proves that his ambition was self-satisfaction. Jacob's willingness to buy it tells us his ambition was to shoulder the responsibility of spiritual and financial care for the family. Scofield has no basis other than his own prejudice for his statement that "Jacob's conception of the birthright at that time was, doubtless, carnal and inadequate."[41] He is right, however, in noting that "his desire for it evidenced true faith."[42]

Second, Jacob's offer implies that he may not have trusted his father to obey God in the distribution of the inheritance. Remember that even before they were born, God had told Rebekah that the birthright would be Jacob's (Gen. 25:23). His father's favoritism of Esau, despite Esau's godless self-absorption, was already apparent. Future events will indicate that such fear was well founded. Even though God had said the birthright would be his, Jacob may have wanted this transaction to seal a contract between himself and his brother. If Isaac and Esau tried at a later time to appoint the birthright to the impious Esau, Jacob could claim it by right of previous purchase, sealed by Esau's oath.

Many believe that this transaction demonstrates a weakness in Jacob's character. Getz says, "Jacob had been looking for an opportunity to trap Esau in a moment when his fleshly appetites were excited," then calls his offer to buy the birthright a "sneaky proposition."[43] Baldwin calls Jacob an "opportunist" who recognized "the moment" and prepared an appetizing dish so that Esau "fell into the trap."[44] Those who take this position seem to do so on the basis of tradition more than text, since there is nothing in the text to even imply that Jacob did something evil here. The story is a commentary on Esau's disdain for the responsibilities of the birthright, not Jacob's grasping for it.

Others who are a little more charitable find evidence of a weakness of Jacob's faith—that he was attempting to obtain by human means something God had promised to provide. While their case is stronger, such a charge is still questionable for a couple of reasons. First, the text itself makes no such accusation, saying that the story shows how Esau despised the birthright, not how Jacob obtained it. Second, the charge ignores that many of God's promises are fulfilled through human means. The promise made to Abraham that Sarah would have the son God promised required the very human action of sexual intimacy. For Abraham to wait for Sarah to conceive without expecting to participate in the process would have been absurd, and the same is true at the beginning of this very text in the case of Isaac and Rebekah. God had promised the birthright to Jacob. If Esau and Isaac conspired to reassign the birthright, as Jacob had reason to suspect, the obvious means God might use to give it to Jacob instead could be to kill his brother Esau. If Esau were dead, Jacob would inherit. It is possible that Jacob reasoned that a contract to purchase the birthright might forestall God's judgment upon Esau.

The text does not describe Jacob's motive. Everyone, including me, can only guess at his motive. If others are correct, and Jacob was conniving to trap his brother into a bad deal in a moment of weakness for Jacob's financial gain, then Jacob was guilty of great sin. However, given the lack of censure in the text here or in the future, and the positive assessment of Jacob's character that introduced it however often that's been misunderstood, I prefer to give Jacob the benefit of the doubt. Whether or not Jacob's purchase of the birthright accomplished God's purpose, it certainly coordinated with it. It demonstrated a heart that longed for spiritual things and God's blessing in contrast with Esau's disdain for the same. At worst, Jacob employed a human means to achieve a divine end—and he did it through the legitimate means of purchase, not theft or deceit.

When Jacob made his offer to buy the birthright, Esau didn't hesitate. The KJV reading, "I am at the point to die: and what profit shall this birthright do to me?" (Gen. 25:32), implies that Esau feared he was dying at that moment and without food would not live to enjoy the birthright. However, it's probably better to understand Esau's reply as indicating that he "cared for nothing but the momentary gratification of sensual desires."[45] Since the text says that Esau "despised" the birthright, it is more likely that he meant "I'll soon be dead. What would I want with this birthright?" If so, he was probably mocking Jacob for being so concerned about it. Jewish talmudic writers believe that Esau's statement constitutes a denial "of the revival of the dead"[46] because he assumed the birthright would cease to have value when he died. Esau was certainly not near death, since after eating and drinking, he "rose up and went his way." Before doing so, he sealed the pact with an oath, selling his birthright to Jacob.

The point of the entire incident is summarized in the final statement—"thus Esau despised his birthright" (Gen. 25:34). Jacob did not steal it, trick him out of it, nor manipulate Esau deceptively. Esau threw the birthright away because he cared nothing for God and His promises. Jacob bought it because he believed God's promises and was willing to take responsibility for leadership. The narrator specifically tells us that this story is told to illustrate weakness in Esau's character, not in Jacob's. We must not interpret it through Esau's eyes. The story also gives us insight into the injustice Isaac and Esau tried to work on Jacob in Genesis 27.

So what has this introductory text said about the character of Jacob and Esau? Far from Jacob being plain or quiet, God actually said that Jacob was "a perfect [blameless] man," indicating a sincere, undefiled integrity. He called him a man who lived in tents, indicating Jacob's interest in perpetuating the family estate and his expectation of the promise of God. By contrast, Esau was a man who spent his life away from the family estate, having no desire for personal responsibility and having nothing but disdain for the future promise. Esau despised any birthright, desiring nothing beyond his current enjoyment. Jacob understood the value of the birthright and the potential damage to the promise of God if responsibility for leadership were left in the hands of a man who despised it.

Lesson

The primary lesson for us from this section is that God wants us to believe His promises. Even as a young man, Jacob ordered his life with God's promises in view. God had told Abraham and Isaac that He would make of them a nation through whom all families of the earth would be blessed. He had told Rebekah that His promises would be passed on to Jacob. Jacob desired the blessing of seeing those promises fulfilled, or at least perpetuated, in him.

You and I do not have the same promise of earthly prosperity that God gave Abraham and his descendents. We have no right to demand the same blessings from God that He gave them. However, God has promised us spiritual blessings beyond value. He has promised to make us His children (John 1:12–13), to give us eternal life (John 3:16), to forgive our sins (Eph. 1:7), to transform us into the image of His Son (Rom. 8:29), and to work through all life's circumstances to bring us to ultimate glory in His presence (Rom. 8:18–30). None of these blessings can be purchased; they have been paid for by the blood of Christ Jesus our Savior (Acts 20:28; Eph. 1:7; 2:13; Col. 1:14, 20; Heb. 9:12, 22; 1 John 1:7; Rev. 5:9).

What impact do the choices you make have on the work of God in you? Rather than moving contrary to God's purposes, and caring nothing for God's will, we must set our hearts on Him. When we make personal comfort, pleasure, ease, and wealth our most important goals, we have sold our spiritual birthright for the equivalent of a bowl of beans. We must make choices now that will coordinate with God's work in us.

2

A Father's Influence

Gen. 26:1–33

ave you ever noticed how two people can go through the same experience but respond to it differently? Some Holocaust survivors live out their lives and go to their deaths in bitterness of soul over the atrocities they witnessed or endured. Others live and die joyously, grateful for having survived and risen above their trials. Children from the same family sometimes respond differently to the death of a parent. While one becomes bitter and rebels against God for taking the parent, another learns to accept God's timing and the mystery of God's purpose and goes on to a joyful Christian life of submission to God's will. Two children of an alcoholic or abusive father may respond differently as well. One may grow up to be just like Dad, drunk and mean. The other learns from his father's bad example, avoids alcohol, and treats his family with loving kindness. The difference is not in the environment but ultimately is in the grace of God. As people go through life, the distinctions become apparent in the contrasting characters of the individuals.

The events described in this chapter present striking parallels with similar events in the life of Isaac's father, Abraham, and some that foreshadow later events in the life of his son Jacob. Commentators have questioned how Isaac's sojourn among the Philistines fits in the chronology of his life. During his stay in Philistia, Jacob and Esau are not mentioned. Further, Isaac's attempt to convince the Philistines that Rebekah was his sister might have been compromised by the presence of the children. Therefore, some have suggested that these events must have occurred before the birth of the twins. However, the narrative seems to flow chronologically. Jacob and Esau were adults by the end of Genesis 25, and Esau's marriage at age forty is mentioned immediately after the family returns from Philistia. It is best to assume that the twins were adults by the time Genesis 26 opens. Jacob has a well-established pattern of involvement in maintaining the household and the estate, and Esau has a well-established pattern of disinterest and absence. It may have been easy for the Philistines to make no connection between them and their parents.

Doubtless, the events recorded here would have had a profound impact on the dynamics of the family's relationships with one another, with the neighboring people groups, and with the Lord. In the chapters that follow, we can see the ripple effects of Isaac's actions here and the different ways his twin sons responded.

Isaac in Gerar (Gen. 26:1–11)

Another famine had come to the region. This had truly been a land of bounty since this is the first famine in the region in over one hundred years—"beside the first famine that was in the days of Abraham" (Gen. 26:1). In the earlier famine, mentioned here to draw our attention to the parallels in the stories, Abram had left the land God promised him and traveled to Egypt. It seems that on this occasion Isaac was planning to do the same. Isaac traveled to the coastal region around Gerar, occupied by the Philistines. While on his way or once he arrived, the Lord appeared to him and specifically told him not to go down into Egypt. As far as the biblical record reveals, this is the first time the Lord appeared to Isaac, unless we count that day on Mount Moriah about fifty years before when the Lord interrupted Abraham's sacrifice of Isaac and provided a ram in his place (Gen. 22). The only other time God would appear to Isaac would be with another message of promise later in this chapter (Gen. 26:24).

The Lord restates to Isaac His earlier promise to Abraham. Telling Isaac to "sojourn in this land," as opposed to seeking refuge in Egypt, God promised to be with him, to bless him, and to "give all these countries" (Gen. 26:3) to Isaac and his progeny. This phrase is used to make it clear that the promise was not limited to the territory in which Isaac and his father had lived, but it would include the land of the Philistines as well. God tells Isaac that the reason He would do this is that He had sworn an oath to Abraham that He intends to keep. God also restates the parts of the promise that included a multitude of offspring and the ultimate blessing of all nations of the earth through Isaac's "seed." God ends the reiteration of the promise by reminding Isaac of his father's faithfulness—"Abraham obeyed my voice, and kept my charge, my commandments, my statutes, and my laws." God did not say that Abraham never sinned—we know that was not the case—but that Abraham's heart inclination and habitual practice was to obey God comprehensively. No mention is made of Isaac's obedience.

Ironically, the text tells us that Isaac obeyed the initial command—he "dwelt in Gerar" rather than going to Egypt—then immediately describes how Isaac failed to trust God. Apparently not convinced that God would really be with him and bless him, Isaac put self-preservation ahead of obedience. He lied to the Philistines to protect his own life. Fearing that the Philistines would kill him so they could have his beautiful wife, Rebekah, he told them she was his sister.

Granted, Isaac was imitating Abraham, who had told the same lie about Sarah twice, but a few factors make Isaac's lie more blatant. First, Abraham's lie was easier to rationalize, since Sarah was, in fact, his half sister. Isaac's lie was further removed from the truth since Rebekah was his cousin.

Second, in Abraham's case Sarah was actually taken from him on both occasions—once by the Pharaoh of Egypt and once by King Abimelech[1] of the Philistines. Apart from what was probably polite inquiry as to Rebekah's identity, the fact that none of the Philistines made any move on her, even after Isaac "had been there a long time" (Gen. 26:8), indicates that Isaac's fears were more imaginary than real.

Third, the first time Abraham tried to pass Sarah off as his sister he did not have the advantage of history—no earlier example of failure from which to learn—and the second time followed immediately on the heels of the destruction of Sodom and Gomorrah, in which he had reason to fear that Lot and his family had perished. In his discouragement and fear, with no word from God on the fate of his loved ones, he fell prey to doubt and fear. Isaac had decades of the history of God's work in his family from which to learn. Not only were there two prior examples of identical failures in the life of his father, but there were the decades of God's faithfulness to his family even when things looked bleak.

Finally, the last thing to happen before Isaac's lapse was not something to cause fear but something to inspire hope. God had spoken to him and renewed the promise He had made to Abraham. Isaac had been given full assurance of God's blessing on himself and his family. With God's words ringing in his ears, he walked into Gerar and lied about his wife's identity, putting her at risk out of fear for his own safety.

Did Isaac's lie prove any more effective than Abraham's? No. In Abraham's instances, God protected Sarah, revealing to the foreign kings that she was Abraham's wife and was under God's protection. In Isaac's case, God did not intervene directly. Isaac's own actions gave him away—Abimelech saw him "sporting with Rebekah" (Gen. 26:8) and realized she must be his wife. The fact that Abimelech immediately concluded this indicates that this "sporting" did not mean that they were merely "laughing together" (NEB, ESV), which one might do with his sister, but at least "caressing" (NASB, NIV, HCSB), "fondling,"[2] or even "making love."[3] This could be interpreted as another mark against Isaac's character. Not only was God's promise of companionship inadequate to inspire his trust, but he was so indiscrete as to behave intimately with his wife in public.

Abimelech's response represents a role reversal that should have been shameful to Isaac. "The picture of the Philistine king that emerges at this point in chapter 26 is that of a righteous, even pious, Gentile, one who did what was right and, by contrast, showed Isaac to be less righteous than he."[4] Jacob would later face a similar interrogation by his father-in-law, Laban (Gen. 31:26–31). While presenting a clear parallel, the scene would be quite different. Jacob would be falsely accused by a vindictive man while Isaac was justly accused by a gracious man. Jacob would respond to Laban's charges directly and forthrightly. Not surprisingly, in this context Isaac responds only indirectly to Abimelech's charges, "Because I said, Lest I die for her" (Gen. 26:9).

The Philistine king becomes the defender of the truth, while Isaac pleads fear for his life. Abimelech was more interested in obeying God, or at least in seeing Isaac obey God, than was Isaac himself. Isaac had proved himself willing to risk his wife and family, as well as God's blessing, for his personal safety, never thinking about what God might do to the Philistines to protect him. Abimelech protested that Isaac's lie could have caused one of the men of Gerar to do something that would "have brought guiltiness upon us" (Gen. 26:10). Abimelech was not just concerned about guilt, which is a rather weak rendering of the word, but about retribution. "A whole city was put in jeopardy because one man wanted to escape jeopardy."[5]

Abimelech could have taken vengeance on Isaac, at least ordering him out of the country. Instead, he extended mercy to Isaac, allowing him to stay. To make sure no one provoked God's wrath, Abimelech even decreed that anyone who molested ("toucheth") either Isaac or Rebekah would be executed. "Rebekah deserves protection, but Abimelech is also merciful to a two-faced deceiver like Isaac."[6] The Philistines obviously honored the decree, because they were able to say to Isaac later, "we have not touched thee" (Gen. 26:29).

Isaac Enriched (Gen. 26:12–16)

Even though Isaac had behaved disgracefully, both Abimelech and God treated him with grace. Abimelech allowed him to settle in the land long enough to plant and harvest crops. At the same time, God blessed Isaac materially despite his earlier unbelief and shameful treatment of his wife and his host.

This is the first time anyone in Scripture is described as sowing seed and may imply that prior to this time neither Abraham nor Isaac had been involved in the cultivation of crops. Isaac's success is remarkable, reaping a harvest a hundred times as great as that sown, and is attributed to God's blessing. Such a great harvest for an inexperienced farmer was especially significant since all the land within a few miles of him was experiencing famine.

A reliable water supply was critical to Isaac's farming and herding. Surface water being inadequate, Isaac had to rely on wells for his water. Apparently he still held water rights in the wells that Abraham had dug a generation before and was using them. Isaac quickly became so prosperous and powerful that the Philistines began to see him as a threat. While the Philistine populace continued to honor Abimelech's edict of protection for Isaac and Rebekah, they began to retaliate by trying to disrupt his prosperity. Filling his wells with dirt, they cut off his water supply, causing a grave threat to his livestock's survival. Then Abimelech came and announced a policy change—Isaac was no longer welcome in Gerar.

Isaac in Beer-Sheba (Gen. 26:17–25)

Assuming Abimelech was correct, and Isaac was in fact "much mightier than we" (Gen. 26:16), it is conceivable that Isaac could have resisted the Philistines and stayed by force as an occupying power.

Instead, without disputation, Isaac did as he was asked. He did not, however, immediately return to his homeland. The famine presumably persisted in Canaan, so Isaac moved only a short distance to the Valley of Gerar. Wadi Gerar was "a water course running between hills . . . whose water amounts may vary from a swift-flowing and deep stream to a completely dry bed of river mud, depending on the amount of rainfall."[7] This stream would provide a temporary water supply for his flocks and herds until new wells could be dug. Isaac immediately launched a project to reopen old wells dug by Abraham and stopped up by the Philistines when Abraham died. Apparently when Abraham had lived among them, the Philistine population was sparse enough that they had no need of Abraham's wells. Wanting to maintain their claim on the land, they filled in the wells to discourage other tribes from settling there.

In addition to redigging old wells and giving them their old names, Isaac's servants also looked for new sources of water. The first new well was dug in the Wadi Gerar and is described as "a well of springing water," literally "living water" (Gen. 26:19). Such a well was especially valuable because the water came to the surface under pressure without having to be hauled up in jars. When the Philistine herdsmen in the region realized what Isaac's servants had found, they claimed the water rights as their own. Rather than fighting for the well, Isaac merely named this well "Contention" ("Esek," KJV) and moved to another site at which he had another well dug. When the Philistines claimed that one, too, Isaac named it "Hatred" ("Sitna," KJV) and moved on. Finally reaching a place where the Philistines were content to leave him alone, they dug another well and named it "Room" ("Rehoboth," KJV), saying, "The Lord hath made room for us, and we shall be fruitful in the land" (Gen. 26:22).

Like Abraham before him and the history of the Jews ever since, Isaac enjoyed God's blessing despite the jealousy of and bitter contention with the people among whom they lived. The fact that Isaac has now learned to trust God despite the abuse of others is a lesson that will not be lost on Jacob. He will be misused by his father-in-law and will have to demonstrate great patience and godly character to endure it patiently.

Eventually, Isaac moved to Beer-sheba, the site of another well dug by Abraham. This was also a place where Abraham made a covenant with Abimelech and where he built an altar. Abraham's well had been contested by the Philistines, but the Abimelech of Abraham's day had transferred permanent title to Abraham. The agreement was sealed by a vow and the sacrifice of seven female lambs on the altar he built. Abraham named it Beer-sheba, which means either "well of the oath" or "well of seven" (Gen. 21:22–34). The very night that Isaac arrived, the Lord appeared to him a second and final time. Identifying Himself as "the God of Abraham thy father," God told Isaac he had no need to be afraid. God renewed the promise confirmed earlier, to be with him and to multiply his offspring "for my servant Abraham's sake" (Gen. 26:24). Early in the account, Isaac had "entreated the Lord" on behalf of Rebekah because she was barren. For the first time since that day nearly forty years before, we read of Isaac's calling on God. This is the only time the text says that Isaac built an altar and "called upon the name of the Lord" (Gen. 26:25).

On both occasions that the Lord spoke to Isaac, He confirmed the promise made to Abraham, specifically tying His faithfulness to the oath to Abraham, not Isaac. The first time, He said He would keep His word "because Abraham obeyed my voice, and kept my charge, my commandment, my statutes, and my laws" (Gen. 26:5). The second time, He said it was simply "for my servant Abraham's sake" (Gen. 26:24). Significantly, on the seven times God will speak to Jacob, He makes specific promises to Jacob without ever tying them to Abraham—the promises to Jacob are for Jacob's sake, not Abraham's or Isaac's.

Isaac's Treaty with Abimelech (Gen. 26:26–33)

While Isaac was at Beer-sheba, Abimelech came to visit him, accompanied by one of his friends and his top military commander. Rather than greeting them with hospitality and grace, Isaac met them with hostility and suspicion—"Wherefore come ye to me, seeing ye hate me, and have sent me away from you?" (Gen. 26:27). Granted, he had been forced from wells that were arguably his by right of inheritance, having been given to his father, Abraham. Still, it doesn't seem to have occurred to Isaac that Abimelech has little reason to trust him or treat him as a friend. In his first contact with Abimelech, he had shown himself to be a craven, selfish liar. Despite that, God had blessed him with such prosperity that the Philistines justifiably feared that their own security was threatened by his presence. If mustering his servants would have been sufficient to challenge the Philistine army, he had nothing to fear. A visit from what was apparently a three-man entourage—the king and his two closest associates—was not a threat but a sign of their great respect for Isaac. Isaac should have greeted them graciously rather than saying, "Why have you come to see me? You hate me and even drove me away from you."

Abimelech again acts with better grace than Isaac. Acknowledging the Lord's hand of blessing upon Isaac, Abimelech says that they came to ask Isaac to participate with them in an oath of peace. They wanted him to agree to a nonaggression treaty with them similar to the one made a generation earlier between the Philistines and Abraham. In a subtle reminder of Isaac's duplicity, Abimelech makes his appeal for Isaac to agree to a peace treaty with them on the ground that "we have not touched thee," adding, "we have done unto thee nothing but good" and have "sent thee away in peace" (Gen. 26:29). In another contrast between Abimelech's dealings with Isaac and Laban's future dealings with Jacob, Abimelech recognizes the true source of Isaac's prosperity—the blessing of the Lord—while Laban will falsely accuse Jacob of dishonesty and theft.

As an important part of the covenant process, Isaac prepares a meal, the idea being that "the individual offering the meal admits the other individual to his family circle."[8] Isaac was extending to Abimelech the same protection his family would expect. By partaking of Isaac's covenant feast, Abimelech acknowledged Isaac as his superior. After the meal, they all sleep. Arising early in the morning, the oath of peace is pronounced and the guests depart in peace. Later that same day, Isaac receives word that the servants who had been working to reopen Abraham's old well had struck water. Again giving it the historic name given it by Abraham, he called it Beer-sheba. The narrator, presumably Moses, adds that the city that grew up on that site still bore the same name at the time that he wrote some five hundred years later.

Isaac's Character Revealed

When faced with a famine, Isaac has followed his father in his sin against his wife and his neighbors, distrusting God's protection. Isaac's lies about Rebekah's identity were further removed from the truth than had been Abraham's lies about Sarah. Isaac lied in full knowledge of his father's sin and the consequences, and he lied in a situation in which his fears proved to be unfounded. While God twice confirms to Isaac His promise to Abraham, on both occasions He stresses that He will keep His word for Abraham's sake. Though Isaac is never commended for personal obedience, Isaac was clearly a believer, for he builds an altar and worships the Lord; and the Lord later identifies himself to Jacob, saying "I am the Lord God of Abraham thy father, and the God of Isaac" (Gen. 28:13). However, Isaac demonstrates the he is not particularly committed or faithful.

The events described here would surely have had a profound impact on Isaac's sons, Jacob and Esau. Isaac's willingness to put Rebekah at risk for his own safety may explain what seems to be tension between Isaac and Rebekah as the narrative progresses. It may also explain a lot about the way their sons related to each parent. The young men witnessed Isaac's ambivalence toward the Lord and His promises, and they saw how even God's blessing could be fraught with conflict. Esau apparently decides that God's will doesn't matter much, and he rebels. On the other hand, from the same set of circumstances Jacob seems to decide that God's will matters a great deal and that the blessing of God is worth whatever conflict comes with it. Jacob also learns that his father, Isaac, could not be trusted.

Lessons

One of the primary lessons from this chapter is for us to learn to trust God even when mistreated and abused. Isaac's actions sometimes demonstrated trust and sometimes did not. At the start, he was so afraid of possible mistreatment that he put his wife and family at risk by lying about her identity. Yet later, even while being shoved around the countryside by the Philistines and their fickle welcome, he remained peaceable. He moved from place to place as circumstances required with no apparent bitterness or anger. His sons are not mentioned in this chapter at all, yet they must have been present and observing. We'll see in the next chapter how they each seem to take away different lessons from these experiences. Esau, emulating his father's early mistrust and bad choices, will decide to put himself first and do whatever he wants. Jacob, practicing his father's later patience while being cheated out of his property and forced to move, will patiently work the estate for his father without thanks or reward and will then move on to work for his father-in-law the same way.

We must commit ourselves to being faithful in what God gives us to do. Rather than being afraid to do right because of what might happen to us, we should determine to obey God regardless of the consequences. When we are mistreated by the world, we should still trust God. He alone is our true provider. Our enemies in this world can take nothing from us that really matters.

3

Jacob's Blessing

Gen. 26:34–27:40

story is told of a man walking down the street in a small town in Alabama when he saw a loose dog attack a little boy. Running up to help, he grabbed the dog by the throat and strangled it, rescuing the boy. A reporter from a local newspaper witnessed the event. As the man checked the child's wounds, called an ambulance, and located the boy's parents, the reporter ran up.

"That was amazing!" he said. "I can see the first line of this story already—'Local hero risks life to rescue child from vicious animal.'"

The rescuer replied, "Sorry, but I'm not from around here."

The reporter hesitated, then said, "OK, it will read, 'Alabama man saves boy from mean dog.'"

The rescuer then said, "Actually, I'm from New Jersey and just stopped for lunch on my way through town."

After taking down the man's name, the reporter circulated to interview the boy's parents, other witnesses, and the dog's owner. When the story appeared in the paper, the headline read, "Yankee Kills Family Pet."

A person's preconceptions or prejudices will influence how he remembers an event or tells a story. Like a biased reporter, when a Bible teacher or editor calls Genesis 27 "The Stolen Blessing," "he is pronouncing moral judgments of his own which are not at all founded on the actual Biblical statements concerning Jacob."[1] While Bible commentaries can influence the way a preacher interprets a passage, the chapter headings inserted by Bible editors have an even greater potential to influence the typical believer's understanding of the text.[2]

Let me emphasize that I am not suggesting that Jacob is without sin in this matter. I admit, though, to a presupposition of Jacob's general righteousness on the bases of a contextual reference in which God introduces Jacob as "perfect," or "without blemish," had the word been translated consistently, instead of "plain," as well as many other factors explained in the introduction. Therefore, I'm exercising the liberty of giving Jacob the benefit of the doubt. Other than the criticism of Isaac and Esau, which I believe to be self-serving and false, I find no place in the immediate text or elsewhere in Scripture that accuses Jacob of being greedy of material gain or of familial power or of spiritual influence. Further, I find no accusation from God that Jacob acquired the blessing or gained familial supremacy by deception—that he somehow wrested this blessing from God. The Bible uniformly treats Jacob's primacy as having been established by divine fiat, not Jacob's personal manipulation.

Granted, it would be possible for Jacob's personal greed and his grasping for something that was not rightfully his to coincide with God's plan to the point that God used Jacob's evil motive to accomplish God's will. That is how most writers interpret this event. However, had that been the case, I would have expected to find later evidence of specific admission of guilt and repentance of sin prompted by either a divine rebuke or an expression of overwhelming guilt in a crisis. I find no biblical evidence of either. God consistently blesses Jacob without any record of repentance. Those who write of Jacob's "change of heart" or "conversion" either at Bethel or at Peniel do so on the basis of their assumptions that he had been driven by personal greed up to that point but has begun to behave righteously and therefore he must have repented. Their assumptions have no more direct textual support than do mine, and I believe the weight of the indirect evidence of the uniform biblical testimony to Jacob's upright character supports a more favorable interpretation.

Jacob's deception of his father was clearly wrong. Still, the only words of criticism for Jacob's role in this event come from the lips of Isaac and Esau, men whose actions can be shown to have been even less admirable than Jacob's. The only words of criticism from the mouth of God concerning this event are reserved for Esau. Hebrews 12:16 calls Esau a "profane person," pointing out that he "for one morsel of meat sold his birthright," an action that Genesis 25:34 already told us was evidence that Esau "despised his birthright." To be a "profane" person was to be "completely concerned with temporal and material matters, with no thought for spiritual values," one "whose response to God was nonexistent."[3] Hebrews 12:17 goes on to describe the incident of the blessing: "For you know that even afterwards, when he desired to inherit the blessing, he was rejected, for he found no place for repentance, though he sought for it with tears" (NASB). After Esau sold his birthright, he changed his mind and decided that he wanted to inherit the blessing after all, but God rejected him. The repentance Esau sought was not for his salvation but to change the situation. He sought some way to get God to bless him instead of Jacob.

If the typical interpretation of this event were correct, we would anticipate the writer of Hebrews saying that it was Jacob, not Esau, who profanely pursued material gain over spiritual values by lying to his father to steal a blessing that was rightfully his brother's. We need to find a way to understand Genesis 27 as showing Esau, not Jacob, to have been unconcerned about honoring God. That is, we need to interpret this event in the light of God's inspired commentary, not Esau's angry outburst.

Furthermore, the only action on the part of Isaac that the Bible anywhere calls an act of faith is his blessing of Jacob and Esau (Heb. 11:20). Genesis 26 seems to depict Isaac's blessing of Jacob as unintentional. If so, Hebrews 11:20 probably refers to Isaac's reiteration of the blessing in Genesis 28:3–4, when he intentionally gives "the blessing of Abraham" to Jacob before sending him to Padan-aram to find a wife. However, Martin Sicker suggests that Hebrews 11:20 refers to the initial statement of the blessing made while Jacob was disguised as Esau. He puts forward the possibility that, at some point during Jacob's masquerade, Isaac discovers the truth and knows when he pronounces the blessing that he is giving it to Jacob. Citing thirteenth-century Jewish commentator Bahya ben Asher,[4] Sicker suggests that Isaac recognizes Jacob's voice and realizes the error he had almost committed in giving the blessing to Esau, so he proceeds to bless Jacob intentionally. When Esau comes in, Isaac's distress is over his own awkward position for having given away something he'd promised Esau. Isaac points the finger at Jacob for having deceived him, even though he "acknowledged to himself that Jacob did what was necessary to overcome his own misperception of Esau's ability to be a worthy successor to Abraham."[5] I think Sicker's view has merit, but it strikes me as an unnecessarily complicated interpretation. The more natural interpretation of the event seems to be that Jacob succeeded in fooling his father and that Isaac assumed he was blessing Esau when Jacob stood before him.

Regardless of Isaac's intent on the day Jacob deceived him, the writer of Hebrews treats this blessing as rightfully Jacob's, and Isaac's intentional pronouncement of the blessing upon Jacob as the most significant act of faith in God's promise that Isaac ever performed. Since that is God's infallible commentary on the event, it will be the underlying assumption upon which my own examination of this passage will be based.

Rebellion

Esau's Sin (Gen. 26:34–35)

Esau and Jacob are now forty years old. Isaac had been forty when he married Rebekah (Gen. 25:20). His marriage had been arranged by his father, Abraham, in order to assure a line of descent that was not commingled with the peoples from Canaan (Gen. 24:1–4). Isaac, however, has allowed his sons to reach the age of forty without making arrangements for their own marriages. Either he has been negligent in taking care of this vital matter, or he has been content to allow his sons to choose their own wives without sharing Abraham's concern for the integrity of the family line. Either possibility represents on Isaac's part a serious failure to safeguard God's promise.

Esau decides to take matters into his own hands and marries not one but two local beauties—Judith ("praiseworthy") and Bashemath ("fragrant"). Both are identified as Hittites. Since we are told that these marriages caused a "grief of mind" (Gen. 26:35, lit. "bitterness of spirit") for both Isaac and Rebekah, we can assume he married without his parents' consent or blessing.

Why is this information provided at this point in the narrative? It may suggest that Esau used his father's treaty with Abimelech, which God condoned, as an excuse for his own marital alliance with people native to Canaan, which God forbade. It may simply provide the necessary background so that Rebekah's later plea to send Jacob to Padan-aram will make sense.

More significantly, news of Esau's marriages reveals important facts about both Isaac and Jacob. We need to note that somewhere between the end of Genesis 26 and the beginning of Genesis 28 there is a significant chronological gap. To establish a timeline, we have to jump ahead several years. We will find that about fourteen years after Jacob leaves for Padan-aram, he will have a son named Joseph (Gen. 30:25; 31:41). We'll discover that when Joseph was 39 years old, 53 years after Jacob left home, Jacob was 130 (Gen. 41:46, 53; 45:11; 47:9). Subtracting 53 years from 130 shows that Jacob was about 77 years old when he left for Padan-aram to find a wife. While most commentators assume that Jacob left (fled?) shortly after Isaac blessed him unintentionally, the text does not say so. All we know for sure is that Jacob's deception of his father and Isaac's pronouncement of the blessing on Jacob instead of Esau happened sometime after Esau married at age 40 and before Jacob left at age 77.

The fact that when this scene opens Jacob is still unmarried and living at home reinforces what God has said about his sterling character. To honor God and his father, Jacob patiently allowed nearly forty years to pass after Esau's rebellious marriages, waiting for his father to arrange his own. Isaac, on the other hand, has neglected to arrange a proper marriage for Jacob, despite his distress over Esau's marriages, until Rebekah makes a pointed request that he do so (Gen. 27:46). It is possible that Isaac was intentionally using Jacob's submission to his father's prerogative to arrange a wedding as a means of preventing Jacob's becoming eligible for the blessing God had promised by denying him an opportunity to father a child. When Isaac finally relents, all he does is send Jacob away with instructions to find a wife, but with no help or support. Mentioning Esau's wives here points up Isaac's failure toward both sons, but it also reveals the radically different ways the two sons responded to their father's failure: Esau rebelled, Jacob patiently submitted.

Further, when Isaac thought he was pronouncing the blessing on Esau, we find hints within the Hebrew wording that may imply the influence of Canaanite idolatry. It is possible that the mention of Esau's Hittite wives is intended to provide a warning about the subtle influence of idolatry in Esau's life and its influence on Isaac. This would be consistent with the writer of Hebrews calling Esau "profane."

Isaac's Subtlety (Gen. 27:1–5a)

Apparently, several years have passed since Esau's marriages. Isaac has still done nothing to arrange a proper marriage for Jacob. Isaac is between 100 (his age when Esau married) and 137 (his age when Jacob leaves for Haran) years old, and his eyesight was dim. If this happens shortly before Jacob's departure, Isaac's fear of imminent death may have been aroused by the knowledge that he was the age at which Ishmael had died (Gen. 25:17). However, the account

is intentionally parallel to an incident that happened years earlier
between Esau and Jacob (Gen. 25:29–34). Having returned from
hunting exhausted, Esau claimed he was about to die and demanded
a bowl of lentil soup. Either in exchange for the soup or while eating
the soup, he agreed to sell his birthright to Jacob. After eating, he
went his way refreshed. He claimed he was about to die, but that was
an exaggeration in order to get something to eat. Here, when Isaac
tells Esau he is about to die and offers to confer on Esau "the blessing" if he will feed him his favorite meat, we find that after he eats he
lives at least another forty-three years (Gen. 35:28). The intentional
implication is that just like Esau, Isaac is more concerned with fulfilling his physical desires than with fulfilling God's purposes.

While it is not expressly stated until later, the blessing that Isaac
intended to confer upon Esau was a combination of the birthright
and God's promise to Abraham and his posterity. Sarna points out
that when Isaac called for Esau so that "my soul may bless thee" (Gen.
27:4), he meant that the blessing would come from "my innermost
being." Isaac was saying that "the source and sanction of the blessing
is not man but God."[6] Esau had already forfeited the birthright by his
character and had voluntarily sold it by choice, showing his disdain
for both the birthright and the promise. Even though God was clear
before the boys were born that His promise to Abraham would
be fulfilled in Jacob, not Esau, still, Isaac intends "to invoke God's
blessing upon [Esau]."[7] Since several decades have passed during
which Jacob has demonstrated his "integrity" (mistranslated "plain"
in Gen. 25:27; see chapter 1) and Esau his "profanity" (Heb. 12:16),
it is inconceivable that Isaac might not have known God's express
will. Hamilton suggests, "Perhaps Isaac is still unaware of the divine
oracle . . . , or he has misunderstood it, or he has forgotten it. Failing
eyesight and advanced years may be coupled with failing memory."[8] It
does not seem to have occurred to Dr. Hamilton that there is another,
more likely, explanation—Isaac simply chose to disregard God's will.
Leupold says, "With a stubbornness that does him little credit, Isaac
sought to circumvent this divine pronouncement."[9]

If we understand "stubbornness" as the equivalent of "iniquity
and idolatry" (1 Sam. 15:23), I can accept Leupold's characterization. Isaac not only planned to transfer God's promised blessing from
Jacob to Esau, he intended to do so in secret. The pronouncing of the
blessing would often have been accompanied by a feast and a celebration. The fact that Isaac attempted to do this without involving either
his wife or Esau's twin brother is evidence of the devious nature of

Isaac's plot. From the outset the narrator wants us to understand that Isaac's action was both a betrayal of his godly son Jacob and an act of rebellion against God. Isaac was trying to manipulate God into blessing a man he knew to be ungodly, and he hoped to do so successfully without Rebekah's, Jacob's, or God's interference.

Did Isaac think that God's purposes could be circumvented by man's manipulations? God insists that what He purposes, He will do (Pss. 115:3; 135:6; Isa. 14:27; 43:13; 46:9–10; Lam. 3:37; Dan. 4:35). Those who deliberately attempt to disrupt God's plans and defy God's will find themselves in grave danger of God's judgment (Ps. 2:1–5). I suspect Isaac knew that, too, which would explain why he reacts with terror rather than anger when he discovers he has actually blessed Jacob rather than Esau.

Intervention

Rebekah's Desperation (Gen. 27:5b–14)

When as a maiden Rebekah had been presented with the choice to stay in her father's household or to leave for a foreign country to marry a cousin she'd never met, she did not hesitate, but packed her things and left. Now, perhaps as much as ninety-seven years later, she overhears her husband scheming with Esau to confer upon him a blessing—and not just any blessing, but the Blessing promised to Abraham. Correctly surmising Isaac's intent, she is convinced that Isaac will try to transfer to Esau the blessing God intended to be Jacob's.

Sensing that her home was being threatened by her husband's plotting, Rebekah again acts without hesitation. She tells Jacob what she has heard and gives him specific orders to help her stop Isaac. Prefacing her instructions with two strong imperatives—"obey my voice" and do "that which I command thee" (Gen. 27:8)—Rebekah tells Jacob to bring two young goats that she will slaughter and prepare as the "savory meat" so loved by Isaac. She explains that Jacob will then take the meat to his father, implying that he would be impersonating Esau, so that Isaac will bless Jacob instead. The fact that she correctly assumes that Isaac will not be able to tell the difference between the goat meat she prepares and the venison Isaac requested indicates that there is something beyond appetite motivating Isaac to want to bless Esau.

Jacob does not want to do what his mother has told him to do. He objects, first, on the ground that it won't work. He might be able to convince his father that he is Esau if his father never touches him, but one contact with his skin will give him away since Esau was covered with hair and Jacob was not. Further, if Isaac were to touch him, Jacob's identity would be revealed, and Isaac would think he had come to mock him (not "deceive" as in the KJV, Gen. 27:12). If that happened, the whole plan would backfire—there would be a curse instead of a blessing. Jacob preferred to stay out of it.

Rebekah responds to Jacob's objection by insisting that she would bear any curse that might proceed from this action: "Upon me be thy curse, my son: only obey my voice" (Gen. 27:13). She means, "I am your mother; you do exactly as I say, and I will take full responsibility for the outcome." Since Jacob is over forty years old, and perhaps as old as seventy-seven, his mother's promise cannot absolve him of personal responsibility for his involvement in this deceptive plot. Nevertheless, ever the dutiful son, Jacob submits to his mother.

Rebekah and Jacob were certainly wrong to lie to Isaac, and commentators almost universally condemn them for it. One writer says, "Jacob is clearly less concerned with the rightness, the morality, of his mother's suggestion than he is with what happens to him if his disguise is discovered and his impersonation revealed."[10] Another goes so far as to describe this as "Jacob's successful plan to steal the blessing."[11] Does he really think it is possible for someone to successfully steal from God an eternal heritage? I don't believe God's program is so fragile that it is susceptible to being wrenched from its course and transferred to another by theft. Theodore Epp's evaluation is more on point: "Rebekah's sin was that she lacked faith in God's ability. She felt she had to help God accomplish His will. While the intended goal was legitimate, the means she used to accomplish the goal were not honoring to God."[12] As the story unfolds, we will see that everyone involved was wrong on some level. Alan Ross puts it this way: "God has always provided direction and enablement for His people to carry out their responsibilities in His covenantal program. Unfortunately, many simply persist in handling them in their own earthly way, often complicating matters greatly. Genesis 27 gives us a detailed look at an entire family living this way."[13]

The text of Genesis doesn't specifically address the motives of any of the people involved in this rather sordid tale of interconnecting deceptions, but nearly everyone makes his own assumptions depending on what he thinks of the character of the various participants.

Most believe that Isaac was a doting father who wanted to bless Esau, a man he admired as a rugged outdoorsman. Rebekah was a meddlesome wife with ambitions for Jacob, a man Isaac disdained as a "momma's boy." Jacob, afraid he'd get caught, has to be convinced to go along with his mother's plan to steal for himself an inheritance that rightfully belonged to Esau, who was the innocent victim of the whole charade.

Those who tell the story this way seem to consider it on a merely temporal, human level. They've misunderstood or overlooked what God has revealed and what later Scripture says about the character of Jacob, and they've ignored what the Bible has to say about Esau. They've set aside God's prophetic revelation about the destinies of these two men while they were still struggling in their mother's womb. They have failed to consider the implications of Isaac's desire for a secret meeting with Esau to confer on him the blessing God promised to Abraham. Expending all their sympathy on poor Esau, who ends up cut out of Isaac's will and God's blessing, they conclude that the real villain in the story is Jacob because he's the one who gets the blessing. They are in danger of diminishing God Himself by suggesting that Jacob successfully snatched God's blessing from its rightful recipient. I'm convinced that such an interpretation of this event overlooks indirect evidence in the text that, when properly considered, causes a significantly different picture to emerge.

We should not forget that Rebekah was more than just a woman of decisive action. She was also a woman of great faith. She trusted God enough to leave home to marry a cousin she'd never met. She trusted God to help her survive a difficult pregnancy that was itself an answer to prayer after twenty years of barrenness. She is the only one of the four matriarchs ever to hear from God directly and may be the only woman in history to receive a verbal message from God in response to her prayer. When she heard from God, she believed His promise concerning the destiny of the twins, even before they were born. It's difficult to imagine that she now thought all God's plans would come to naught because her husband wanted a private dinner with Esau during which he would speak words of blessing over him.

What did Rebekah think would happen if Isaac succeeded in pronouncing the blessing on Esau? The typical assumption is that she thought her favorite son, Jacob, would be left out and Esau would walk away with the blessing. That may have been what she thought, but once again in the absence of a biblical description of her motive, I'd rather give her the benefit of the doubt. I doubt if she thought

God's promises concerning His future plans for her family could be thwarted so easily. I think it more likely that she expected God Himself to intervene unless she could do something to stop Isaac. However, Rebekah's faith was limited. I suspect she feared that if God had to stop Isaac, it might cost her both a husband and a son. If Isaac succeeded in pronouncing the blessing upon Esau, God might kill Esau in order to transfer the blessing back to Jacob, and He might even kill Isaac for his rebellion. The biblical record shows that God has, in fact, taken the lives of individuals for crimes less significant than Isaac's intentional attempt to derail God's program of redemption through a particular line of descent. Rebekah probably assumed that God had providentially allowed her to overhear the scheme so she could intervene.

I don't want to defend a pragmatic philosophy here. The end does not justify the means. Rebekah and Jacob do, indeed, adopt an objectionable and inappropriate scheme to deceive Isaac. They had other options. Prayer certainly should have been part of their plan, and there is no indication that it was. If they felt the need to intervene, they should have tried direct confrontation. That is the biblical method prescribed in the New Testament for church discipline. Perhaps if she had confronted Isaac with her knowledge of what he was trying to do, he would have desisted. Of course, she may have feared that if Isaac canceled the meeting with Esau because of the confrontation, he might just reschedule it when she wasn't paying attention. Rebekah's memory of Isaac's attempt to pass her off as his sister to save his life may have left her less than confident that she'd be able to persuade him to do what was right. Nevertheless, Rebekah's and Jacob's taking matters into their own hands failed to factor God's wisdom, power, and grace into the picture. It would have been better for them to trust God to protect His own promises. Had they not interfered, it is likely that God would have so overwhelmed Isaac's intentions that the blessing he tried to pronounce upon Esau would have actually benefited Jacob. This would have resulted in better relationships afterward and greater glory to God in the eyes of all concerned.

Despite the sinfulness of their actions, it is not necessary to assume that Rebekah's and Jacob's motives were less than honorable since no motive is revealed. Instead of assuming that Jacob got everything and Esau got nothing, we should note that is not really what happened. The typical assumption is that Jacob's eventual departure and future ordeals come as the consequence of his sin, even though the Bible never says so. I don't think it's necessary to conclude that from what the text actually says. The real outcome is that God's program is not frustrated; it continues just as He planned. Jacob leaves because he needs a wife to continue the line of promise. While gone, God blesses him with twelve sons through whom He will establish His people as a nation. He will be deceived by his father-in-law, reflecting his deception of his father, but he will endure it with good grace. Rebekah and Jacob knew God's purpose was to bless the line of Abraham through the younger twin and that Isaac and Esau were well aware of God's plan and were intentionally trying to frustrate it. Jacob's holding Esau's heel at birth foreshadows not his usurpation of Esau's right as heir but his prevention of Esau's ungodliness being allowed to corrupt the line of God's future blessing. Hosea says, "He took his brother by the heel in the womb, and by his strength he had power with God" (12:3).

One writer says, "Rebekah's hare-brained scheme ran considerable risk of discovery."[14] Discovery was not just possible, it was inevitable. Esau would be back, and he would be back soon. They had neither hope nor intention of deceiving Isaac for more than a few hours. They would have to hope for the best. There is a sense in which Rebekah's plan was more than risky—it was sacrificial. No matter what happens between Jacob and Isaac, one immediate result would almost certainly be a permanent family rift.

I believe Rebekah and Jacob were both convinced that God's word would eventually be fulfilled and the blessing would fall to Jacob. So why do this? How do they benefit? Ultimately, the only people to benefit from this plan would be Isaac and Esau. Other than Isaac's and Esau's later accusation that Jacob took Esau's blessing by deception, there is no hint in Scripture that Jacob was ever in danger of losing God's blessing. It was not Esau's to receive, and it never would have been. The blessing was in danger of being "stolen" by Esau, but it was never "stolen" by Jacob. It was given by God and affirmed by Isaac. Paul emphatically says that God made His decree while Esau and Jacob were still in the womb (Rom. 9:10–12).

As far as the future of God's people is concerned, what happens in Isaac's tent in Genesis 27 is irrelevant to the future of Jacob but may have prolonged the lives of Isaac and Esau.

Rebekah and Jacob launched an action almost certain to bring upon them the wrath of Isaac and Esau. Commentators and readers who persist in assuming they did this for material gain seem to argue that God's decree was based on simple prescience—God knew Jacob would connive to take the blessing intended for Esau. Paul's statement flatly contradicts that notion. God was not merely predicting what would happen. He was guaranteeing that He would cause it to happen.

There are certainly times when God uses the ungodly intentions of men to accomplish His ultimate purpose. A dramatic example of that would occur in the lives of Jacob's sons, when most of them conspired to dispose of Joseph. However, in that case the text explicitly tells us of their evil motives and shows how they are restored to fellowship when they repent of their wickedness. In Jacob's case there is no attribution of evil motive, despite the deception. Further, we will find Jacob consistently blessed by God without any evidence—ever—of confession or repentance in regard to this incident. To persist in accusing Jacob of lust for wealth or power seems to reflect on God's righteousness, since He persists in blessing an unrepentant Jacob.[15] God calls Esau, not Jacob, "profane." It was Esau, not Jacob, who was party to a scheme to procure temporal blessing for personal satisfaction. Therefore, despite the fact that I am swimming against the current of interpretive opinion, I believe that the most consistent way to understand the text is to assume that Rebekah and Jacob deceived Isaac in order to rescue Isaac and Esau from the wrath of God, in whatever form that may have taken.

While many will accuse me of being overly generous to Jacob in this instance, it is not my intention to portray him as without sin. Rebekah and Jacob's concerted action to deceive Isaac was wrong. Why does God never accuse them of wrongdoing in this instance? I suspect it is because Isaac's and Esau's sin was far greater than Rebekah's and Jacob's, defying God to manipulate His blessing to their will; Rebekah and Jacob deceived Isaac to turn Isaac's blessing to God's will. Deceiving someone is wrong, but defying God is worse.[16]

Jacob's Deception (Gen. 27:15–29)

The plan is implemented. The meat is cooking. Jacob must be disguised, which is not as hard as we might expect. Bible picture books for children often portray Esau as a strapping outdoorsman and Jacob as a smaller, almost anemic counterpart. Elements of this story strongly imply that aside from Esau's hairy skin and Jacob's smooth skin, they were virtually identical. Since Esau's clothes fit Jacob, and Isaac embraced Jacob without noticing a difference in bulk or frame, they must have been the same size and height.

Rebekah takes Esau's best garments that were there in her tent. We have not been told otherwise, but it is unlikely that even after what may have been thirty or more years "Esau and his wives must be living with his parents."[17] Neither were these clothes that she had stored away long ago—Esau wore them often enough that they smelled like him. So why were his clothes there? This was still a patriarchal society. Since there was no independent priesthood, the patriarch of the clan acted as priest for sacrifices and holy days. This was one of the duties Esau had "despised" when he so glibly sold his birthright and one of the duties Isaac seems intent on conferring upon the profane Esau with the private transfer of the birthright and blessing. While we can't say for sure, it's possible that Esau was home on this occasion to participate in one such event, bringing the appropriate garments along and storing them in his parents' tent. If this was, in fact, a holy day or celebration, it makes Isaac's attempt to preempt the proceedings with a private feast with Esau that much more egregious.

Regardless of how the clothes came to be there, garments that were probably Esau's ceremonial garb are available to dress Jacob so he would smell like his brother. Fine-haired goatskins are also available from the slaughter of the kids for the meal, so Rebekah makes wrappings for Jacob's hands and neck to imitate Esau's hairiness. All of this was time consuming. The pressure must have been mounting to finish before Esau returned from hunting.

Finally, Jacob is ready. He takes the meat and goes to his father, saying, "Here I am" (Gen. 27:18). Perhaps he hopes he won't have to actually lie to his father. If so, that hope dissolves right away when Isaac asks, "Who are you, my son?" The fact that Isaac asks Jacob to identify himself before proceeding is usually interpreted to mean that he did not expect Esau to return so quickly. However, since Isaac's sense of smell seems to be fine, and the savory meat would have a distinct aroma, Isaac's question smacks more of secrecy and conspiracy than simple surprise. If Jacob is standing before him, Isaac doesn't want to say anything that implies he is expecting Esau for some special meeting. Still, the direct question traps Jacob in a lie: "I am Esau, thy firstborn"[18] (Gen. 27:19). He then explains that he has prepared the meat his father requested and invites him to eat so that he can proceed with the blessing.

For all Rebekah's attention to detail, one thing almost gives Jacob away. Isaac says it is his "voice" (Gen. 27:22). Usually this slip is attributed either to Rebekah's haste or Jacob's inability to mask his voice adequately. Hamilton says, "Here was an oversight in Rebekah's machinations. She made sure that Jacob felt and smelled like Esau.

But she had suggested nothing about voice imitation."[19] Similarly, C. F. Keil says, "[A]nd when he [Isaac] was satisfied with the reply, . . . he became suspicious about the voice, and bade him come nearer, that he might feel him."[20] Henry Morris says, "[T]he voice didn't seem quite normal."[21]

I suggest another alternative. Consider first that while the word *voice* in the Old Testament emphasizes an audible sound, it almost always refers to the words spoken, not the timbre of the speaker. Just a few verses earlier, Rebekah had ordered Jacob to "obey my voice" (Gen. 27:13), meaning "do what I say." When Saul said to Samuel, "I have obeyed the voice of the Lord" (1 Sam. 15:20), he did not mean that he had discerned God's voice from among other sounds but that he had fulfilled the words of the Lord. Second, consider what Jacob actually said to his father. He spoke briefly when he entered, "Here I am." When asked to identify himself, he spoke at length, saying, "I am Esau, thy firstborn; I have done according as thou badest me: arise, I pray thee, sit and eat of my venison, that thy soul may bless me" (Gen. 27:19). If Isaac's suspicions were not aroused after such a long speech, especially if Isaac were afraid that his own deception might be discovered, it seems obvious that Jacob's voice was virtually indistinguishable from Esau's.

Then why did Isaac say he heard the "voice" of Jacob? What Isaac heard that made him think he was talking with Jacob instead of Esau must not have had anything to do with how Jacob sounded but with what Jacob said. Benno Jacob concurs: "Jewish scholars (Rashi and others) think that the Hebrew word does not refer to the voice which might possibly have been similar in both or could be imitated by Jacob, but the manner of speech and the language . . . did not sound like Esau, but like Jacob."[22] Isaac does not become suspicious of the "voice" until he hears Jacob's answer concerning the preparation of the meat. Jacob says, "Because the Lord thy God brought it to me" (Gen. 27:20*b*).

Many writers are incensed at this, accusing Jacob of blasphemy for involving God in his lie. It is possible that they are correct, but I think there may be a better way to understand this. I believe that Jacob's slip is not his failure to mask his voice; it is his inability to disguise his heart. Esau would never have attributed his hunting success to God's provision. He would have boasted, "Hey, I'm good." It was Jacob who was concerned about God and His provision. When asked "How did you get the meat so quickly," his instinctive reply is to attribute success to God. It is his devotion to God that almost gives him away. That reply immediately makes Isaac suspicious, as he says, "The voice is Jacob's voice" (Gen. 27:22). Jacob is not a slick, sneaky conniver as he is usually described. He is such an awful liar that even when he tries to deceive he can't completely mask his characteristic righteousness, or "integrity" (Gen.25:27, where "plain" should be "blameless"; see chapter 1).

Perhaps Isaac attributes Esau's unexpected piety to his anticipation of the blessing. Maybe he even thinks this is a good sign—Isaac might not make God too angry by pronouncing the blessing on Esau if Esau is more willing than usual to honor God. Having felt Jacob's hands and smelled his clothing, Isaac is satisfied that he is dealing with Esau and can safely proceed. Having eaten the private feast, Isaac begins to pronounce his blessing on the son he thinks is Esau.

Isaac starts by promising that God will bless his son with temporal wealth in terms of agricultural bounty: he promises "plenty of corn [*dagan*] and wine [*tiros*]" (Gen. 27:28). Hamilton says, "That Dagan is a Canaanite (Philistine) deity is well known. Tirosh is also now recognized as the name of a Canaanite god, a kind of Bacchus from which the Hebrews obtained the term *tiros*, their poetic word for 'wine.' "[23] Referencing M. J. Dahood's analysis of similar Ugaritic texts, Hamilton cites the following translation of this blessing: "May God give you of the dew of Heaven and of the oil of Earth and of the spray of Dagan and Tirosh."[24] He explains, "That is, the God of Jacob will provide Jacob with all the ingredients of fertility that were thought to be given by the Canaanite gods Heaven, Earth, Dagan, and Tirosh."[25] If this analysis is correct, Isaac is guilty of invoking pagan deities/idols in pronouncing this blessing on the son he thought was Esau, possibly due to the influence of Esau's Hittite/Canaanite wives. It would not have mattered to Esau but would have been very troubling to Jacob.

Isaac then pronounces upon the son he thinks is Esau sociopolitical supremacy and possibly religious authority—peoples would serve and bow down to him. God had said the elder would serve the younger, but Isaac blasphemously invoked God's name in an attempt to reverse that, saying to the son he thinks is the elder, "Be lord over thy brethren, and let thy mother's sons bow down to thee" (Gen. 27:29).

The phrasing here raises an interesting question. Did Isaac and Rebekah have other sons? The reference to plural "sons" implies that they did. The Scriptures never explicitly say so, but there are two additional references to Jacob's "brethren" in Genesis 27:37 and 31:46. Either of these references could refer to other relatives, not necessarily blood brothers, but the expression "mother's sons" is specific. It would have to be taken as some kind of poetic expression if we are to assume it means anything other than natural brothers. Since there is nothing in the record to deny that Isaac and Rebekah had other sons, it is probably better to take these references at face value. Its main significance here is to indicate that Isaac is attempting to give Esau authority over the whole clan and to subjugate Jacob to Esau specifically and entirely, despite God's express intention to do otherwise.

The final clause of the blessing comes from the conclusion of God's blessing on Abraham. While Isaac has nowhere in this text invoked Abraham's name—for good reason, since he is trying to disrupt God's plan—he clearly intends to transfer to Esau all the provisions of the promise God made to Abraham, concluding with "cursed be every one that curseth thee, and blessed be he that blesseth thee" (Gen. 27:29*b*). There is a sense in which that provision seals the blessing, placing it beyond appeal. Anything Jacob might do to try to revoke the blessing pronounced on Esau (as Isaac assumed) would reflect as a curse upon him for not submitting to its terms.

Reaction

Isaac's Fear (Gen. 27:30–33)

Afterward, Jacob apparently leaves without speaking. He doesn't stay to gloat, as if he's snatched something away from his brother. Perhaps he is dumbfounded by the scope of his father's betrayal of God's plan. Whatever the reason, Jacob leaves just in time. No sooner has he gone than Esau returns from hunting with his meat ready to serve. Jacob has successfully forestalled his father's attempt to transfer God's promise to the ungodly son, but it will be only moments before his deception is discovered. Will his father banish him? Will his brother kill him? Despite the high drama and real tension, Jacob neither hides nor flees. We see him apparently going about his business as if nothing had changed, awaiting his father's instructions, and we have no way to know if those instructions come after a few days or after many years.

The scene in Isaac's tent is not so serene. When Esau presents Isaac with venison, Isaac asks the same question he had asked Jacob—"Who are you?" (Gen. 27:32). The first time, he was probably suspicious. This time he is confused and frightened. When Esau assures him that he is, in fact, his firstborn son, Isaac "trembled very exceedingly"

(Gen. 27:33). The Hebrew is quite graphic, reading literally that he "trembled with a great trembling greatly." Isaac's emotions were almost certainly complex. He may have been angry with Jacob for his deception. He may have been concerned for Esau, given the scope of the blessing he knew would go to Jacob. He may have resented having his plans thwarted. His "very great trembling" seems, however, to go beyond any normal experience of such emotions. It brings to mind the reaction of Belshazzar to the hand of God writing on the wall announcing his doom (Dan. 5). Henry Morris's comments on this are probably correct:

> [Isaac] quickly came to see that God Himself had spoken to him in judgment, and that he had incurred great peril to himself in so ignoring the will of God. He had betrayed the trust of his father Abraham and had practically destroyed his own home, all because of a carnal appetite and adulation of his son's physical exploits.[26]

Isaac's attempt to force God to bless the profane Esau has been discovered and thwarted. Giving Isaac the benefit of the doubt, it is likely that he realizes he has betrayed Abraham's trust, has tried to overthrow God's plan, and had it not been for Jacob's intervention would have brought God's wrath upon himself and Esau. That is why he told Esau that he knew absolutely that Jacob would indeed be blessed. That would also explain why he has no word of rebuke for Jacob and later intentionally affirms the blessing upon Jacob. It would also explain why his affirmation of the blessing upon Jacob, both at this time and later, is identified in Hebrews 11:20 as proof of Isaac's faith. It was not that he had faith that his initial blessing was binding but that he finally came to conform his own will to God's and act in concert with God's plan.

Esau's Fury (Gen. 27:34–40)

Esau's first reaction to the news of Jacob's blessing is dismay. "With a great and exceeding bitter cry," he begs his father to give him at least a secondary blessing (Gen. 27:34). Isaac says he has been so thorough in giving a blessing to the son he thought was Esau that he has effectively shut out any other son from any blessing he could imagine. He has given everything to Jacob and has nothing left to give Esau. What a confession and self-indictment! Isaac is forced to admit that he has done everything in his power to reverse God's plan for Jacob and shut him completely out of God's future provision. Still, wanting to justify himself before Esau, and unwilling to fully acknowledge God's hand in these events, Isaac blames Jacob—"Your brother came deceptively and took away your blessing" (Gen. 27:35). Now Isaac is being less than forthright with Esau. The blessing was never Esau's, except in the minds of Isaac and Esau. It was God's to bestow, and His will had been clear decades previously.

Latching onto Isaac's words, Esau then twists Jacob's name. As I explained in the first chapter, Jacob's name means "protected by God" but sounds like the word that means "heel-catcher." In his frustration, "Esau resorts to bitter sarcasm that expresses itself in word plays. He reinterprets the name Jacob (ya'akov) as deriving from the stem, '-k-v, meaning 'to supplant.'"[27] Esau dishonestly claims that Jacob has "supplanted" him twice—"he took away my birthright" and "he hath taken away my blessing" (Gen. 27:36). Neither charge is true. Esau sold the birthright, and God had announced that the blessing was Jacob's before the boys were born. Yet it is Esau's slanderous accusation that sticks in the minds of most readers, as if it had come from the mouth of God, leading many preachers to assume that Jacob's name means "supplanter."

While Esau begs for a secondary blessing, Isaac explains what he has done. Claiming personal power to bestow blessing, Isaac says, "I have made" Jacob Esau's master, "I have given all his brethren" to be his servants, and "I have sustained him with grain and wine" (Gen. 27:37). Then, since Esau weeps and asks for another blessing, Isaac speaks an oracle that is far less than a blessing and is almost a curse. The KJV, "Behold, thy dwelling shall be the fatness of the earth, and of the dew of heaven from above" (Gen. 27:39), "is apparently not quite correct at this point,"[28] since the meaning is that Esau would dwell "away from" the fatness of the earth and the "dew of heaven." That is, he would not enjoy the agricultural prosperity promised his brother. He would actually have to live as "a predator"[29]—existing by warfare and plundering. Even his sword would not enable him to subdue his brother. Still, there would be a time in the future in which Esau would "shake himself,"[30] or "become restless"[31] (Gen. 27:40, not "have the dominion" as in the KJV), and would at least temporarily "throw off the yoke" of Jacob. The Edomites—descendants of Esau—would attempt to achieve their independence first during the reign of Solomon (1 Kings 11:14–22) and from time to time after that. Their independence from the nation of Judah would not come until they successfully revolted against Jehoram (2 Kings 8:20–22; 2 Chron. 21:8–10).

Rebekah's and Jacob's method of intervention leaves much to be desired. While their means were clearly faulty, there is no reason to fault their motives. God used even their misguided plan to prevent

Isaac from doing something disastrous. It would not have been disastrous to God's program, for He was supervising the outcome all along, assuring that Jacob would be blessed while Esau would not (Rom. 9:9–16). Still, Isaac's plan could have brought calamity on himself and Esau, perhaps even costing them their lives.

Lessons

Writers often try to draw from this story lessons such as "Be sure your sin will find you out" (Num. 32:23). Theodore Epp says, "Jacob was found out! . . . Although in some cases a person's sin is not evident for a long time, in Jacob's case it took only a short time. He was suddenly found out as the schemer."[32] I'm not convinced this story is the best example of that truth. Even interpreting Jacob's actions in the worst possible light, his "scheme" worked. Yes, the deception was discovered, but Jacob got what he wanted—permanently—with no lasting harm to himself. From a thief's point of view, it could hardly have worked out better. It seems to me that if Jacob is truly the villain in this story, the lesson might be better stated, "Deception pays!" If, however, the motives and actions are a little more complicated than is usually assumed, there are other lessons that can be found here.

First, from Jacob and Rebekah we learn that fearing confrontation or having little confidence in God's ability to safeguard His own program can lead even the best of us to adopt sinful methods that do not honor God. How many churches have adopted worldly methods to attract a crowd because they are afraid to confront the world with their sin or lack the confidence that God can build His church by the simple expedient of preaching the Word?

Second, from Isaac we learn that trying to manipulate God and force Him to do what we want doesn't work. God will intervene through direct action or indirect circumstance, such as allowing somebody to discover our secret plans and disrupt them. God will accomplish His purposes despite our attempts to subvert them. Further, we see the rebellion against God to which our appetites can make us sink. We all know of men who had sterling reputations and great stature in the church who have allowed fleshly lusts of one kind or another to destroy their testimonies and damage God's reputation.

May God protect us from our appetites and give us such confidence in His sovereign control that we do not compromise the truth to accomplish His work.

4

Jacob's Worship

Gen. 27:41–28:22

n most situations what God wants us to do is very clear, since much of how we are to think and act is spelled out in Scripture. Many choices we make each day present us with well-defined distinctions between right and wrong. Others choices we could call "morally neutral." We don't need to agonize over the rightness or wrongness of which socks to wear or what kind of toothpaste to buy. However, we sometimes face decisions in which the choices we make will have a profound effect on our future.

I speak from personal experience when I say it is hard to be sure when it is time to leave a particular place of ministry and move to another. If there are problems or conflicts within your current ministry, you wonder, "Am I tempted to leave just to avoid dealing with these issues? Should I stay and resolve them? Won't there be similar issues to face elsewhere?" If there are no problems or conflicts, you wonder, "Why should I leave? What kind of problems might be lurking in the new ministry? How can I defend this decision to my family and congregation?" You don't want to leave when things are good, and you don't think you should leave when things are tough.

Decisions like this cause us to agonize in prayer for the Lord's direction. We pray for some kind of "sign"—a specific indication from Scripture, an unexpected word of encouragement, or a singular event that we can understand as evidence that one option is, in fact, God's plan for us. We know that making a choice motivated by anything less than a desire to honor God is potentially disastrous, so we cry out in the night, "Somebody tell me what to do!"

Jacob is faced with a similar decision. All his life he has known that God intended to perpetuate his promise to Abraham through him. He has desired to honor God and live in such a way that he would not be disqualified from participating in God's program. Having discovered that his father intends to make Esau the recipient of God's promise to Abraham, he has given in to his mother's pressure to impersonate Esau and deceive his father to secure the blessing to himself. His father is distressed over having been caught in his duplicity, and his brother is planning to murder him when Isaac dies, probably hoping to inherit the promise once Jacob is dead. Jacob was not the cause of all the conflict within Isaac's family, but his actions have contributed to the tension. Should he run away to escape his brother's anger? Or should he stay since he's just been acknowledged as the primary heir to the estate and the one through whom God will continue His program of redemption?

We don't know how long he waited, but Jacob finally gets the kind of clear-cut instructions that we wish we would get in similar circumstances. His mother urges him to leave, his father orders him to leave, and God confirms that he is headed in the direction God wants him to go.

The fact that Jacob leaves is usually interpreted through a negative filter, described as "Jacob's Flight from Beersheba"[1] or "Jacob Runs Away from Esau."[2] We tend to see Jacob's departure as merely an excuse to escape Esau. When he meets God along the way, we are prone to emphasize his fear and surprise rather than to give appropriate weight to what God has to say and how Jacob responds.

For one thing, the text doesn't say how much time may have passed between verses 40 and 41. It may have been only a few days since Jacob impersonated Esau. It is also possible that months or even years go by while Esau's anger turns into murderous bitterness at having been outwitted in his quest to secure the blessing of Abraham for himself. We have no way of knowing how long Jacob stayed at home on the job waiting for instructions. All we know for sure is that Isaac's attempt to thwart God's plan happened sometime after Esau's marriage at age forty and before Jacob's departure at age seventy-seven. Jacob may have spent years wondering "What next?" before Rebekah learns of Esau's desire for revenge and fearfully urges Jacob to "flee." He certainly doesn't leave immediately, or even after Rebekah urges him to go. He doesn't leave until his father orders him to go with Isaac's blessing to find a wife. His leaving is more deliberate than precipitous. The narrator does not say that Jacob fled the wrath of Esau but describes his departure as obeying his father and mother and going to Padan-aram (Gen. 28:7). Contrary to popular opinion, never in his life does Jacob run away from responsibility or conflict. Every time he goes somewhere, this time included, he is sent on a mission.

Further, Jacob's meeting with God on the way is not a confrontation, as if God were trying to get Jacob's attention to discover "what will he do with Yahweh?"[3] It is, rather, a confirmation by God that Jacob is the recipient of God's blessing. God is not warning Jacob of the dangers of straying from Him. He is encouraging Jacob to be confident that God is with him, guiding his steps and directing his circumstances.

Rebekah's Fear (Gen. 27:41–46)

It is not surprising to read that Esau hated Jacob, but it is disappointing. Even though Esau has made it clear that he thought Jacob "took away my birthright and . . . hath taken away my blessing" (Gen. 27:36), we should note that the narrator carefully avoids saying that his hatred was prompted by what Jacob had done to him. It simply says that he hated him "because of the blessing" (Gen. 27:41) given him by their father. Esau has become "a bitter, spiteful brother and son."[4] This is not a passionate rage that threatened immediate murder but a simmering resentment that plotted murder at some future date after their father died. Why wait? Once Isaac died, Esau probably expected he would inherit Jacob's blessing by right of being the elder brother. If he killed him while his father lived, Isaac would almost certainly see him as unfit and could transfer the blessing to one of their "brethren" mentioned in verses 29 and 37. It may be that this private vow of Esau had something to do with the fact that Isaac did not die right away—God kept him alive for forty-seven more years while Esau's anger abated.

How did Rebekah hear about Esau's murderous plan? The passive verb in verse 42, "these words . . . were told to Rebekah," indicates that this was something she could not have known without its being "revealed" to her (cf. Gen. 3:11; 41:24). But who told her? The text says only that Esau said this "in his heart," with no mention of his talking about it. That doesn't preclude the possibility that he did talk about it, and someone warned Rebekah, but it could also be that the Lord communicated Esau's plan to Rebekah. Whether God spoke directly to Rebekah, or someone else revealed it to her, the fact remains that for the third time Rebekah received special information from

God directly or from another source providentially that would impact Jacob's future.

For the third time in her life, Rebekah demonstrates that she is a woman of decisive action based on faith in God's promise. When she hears of Esau's plan to kill Jacob, she realizes that it is critical for Jacob to get away. Either fearing that Esau will move up the timetable and kill Jacob soon or fearing that Isaac is near death, she tells Jacob about the danger. Again demanding his obedience (cf. Gen. 27:8), she orders him to "flee . . . to Laban my brother in Haran" (Gen. 27:43). She tells Jacob to stay with him "a few days" until Esau's anger subsides. However, Rebekah forsook her earlier promise to Jacob that she would bear any curse that befell him for the action she had ordered to deceive Isaac. She blamed Jacob unfairly when she said he'd have to stay away until Esau "forget that which thou hast done to him" (Gen. 27:45). Her question, "Why should I be deprived also of you both in one day?" implies that she expected Esau to be executed if he killed Jacob—by Isaac or God.

It is unlikely that she really expected Jacob to be gone only a few days. Haran was over five hundred miles to the northeast. The round trip alone would take months. If he needed to be gone only a few days, he could have gone any number of places much closer to hand. Rebekah was actually sending Jacob away indefinitely, promising to send for him whenever it was safe to return. She would rather lose Jacob to distance and time, knowing he was safe with her family, moving forward in God's plan, than risk losing both Jacob and Esau to death. Although she and Jacob knew this would be a long separation, neither realized Rebekah would be dead by the time Jacob returned. Still, we will find later that the first seven years Jacob will spend with Laban working for the right to marry Rachel will "seem unto him but a few days" (Gen. 29:20).

Rebekah's real reason for sending Jacob all the way to Haran is to find a wife among her people. It was imperative for Jacob to marry and produce a son who would inherit after him lest Esau take the blessing by default. When she speaks to Isaac, she pleads on the ground that she so despised Esau's Canaanite wives that she wished she were dead (Gen. 27:46). Hamilton suggests that "here she plays on her husband's sense of disgust with Esau's earlier marriages,"[5] as if she were merely suggesting that they didn't want another Hittite daughter-in-law. While that is possible, judging by Isaac's response it seems more likely that she was appealing to whatever remnant of spiritual interest Isaac still possessed, provoking him to maintain his religious integrity. Either she assumed that Jacob would have to marry a woman from within their clan in order to stay within the plan of God or she wanted a wife for Jacob from her cultural background. The threat of Jacob's death had focused Rebekah's attention on his need to produce an appropriate heir. It was the possibility of another Canaanite marriage that finally got Isaac's attention.

Significantly, Jacob does not leave at Rebekah's urging. Having been identified by Isaac as the recipient of the birthright and the blessing, he apparently believes it would be inappropriate to depart without his father's instruction. We will find as we continue our study that Jacob never leaves one region for another without clear instructions. In this case, the orders came from his father. In every other case, the orders to move come from God.

Arranging a bride for Jacob is something Isaac should have taken care of years, even decades, before. Yet Jacob has patiently waited for his father to fulfill his responsibility. It is inexcusable that Isaac waited thirty-seven years beyond Esau's marriages, when Jacob is seventy-seven, and acts only upon Rebekah's urging.

Isaac's Faith (Gen. 28:1–5)

To his credit, when prompted by Rebekah, Isaac responds. This passage describes the only event in Isaac's life the Bible attributes to his faith (see Heb. 11:20). Recognizing Rebekah's wisdom, and remembering his own terror when he realized that he had tried to disrupt God's plan, he repents. While it is unclear if Esau ever changes his heart, Isaac does—to a degree. He calls Jacob to himself, blesses him, and forbids him to marry a Canaanite wife. Charging him to go to Rebekah's father's homeland, he orders him to marry a daughter of Rebekah's brother, Laban. He then explicitly reiterates the blessing he had unintentionally pronounced upon Jacob: material prosperity, multiplied progeny, and perpetual possession of "the land." The wording of the blessing this time is less detailed but more consistent with the wording of the blessing God had spoken to Isaac many years before (Gen. 26:3–5). This time there is no confusion about the identity of the recipient of the blessing. Isaac makes it clear that he knows this is "the blessing of Abraham . . . which God gave unto Abraham" (Gen. 28:4).

Instead of claiming that "I have made . . . I have given . . . I sustained" (Gen. 27:37), or even using the generic expression "God [elohim] give thee" (Gen. 27:28), Isaac indicated that the source of the blessing was "God Almighty [el-shaddai]" (Gen. 28:3). *Elohim* is plural and often applies to local false deities. Whether it is translated God or gods depends on context. Since there is reason to suspect Isaac included heathen gods in his initial blessing, it is possible that the reference in Genesis 27:28 should have been rendered gods. In this passage, though, Isaac leaves no question. He uses a name for God used previously only when God addressed Abram in Genesis 17:1—"I am the Almighty God; walk before me, and be thou perfect." Since our English versions insist on changing the word *perfect* to *plain* when referring to Jacob (see chapter 1), we miss the connection between this blessing, called "the blessing of Abraham," and the introductory comment on Jacob's character when he is described as perfect, not plain. What God commanded Abram to be, God said Jacob was.

Nevertheless, the scene here is far different from the one in which a bride was located for Isaac. A generation earlier, Abraham had decided it was time for Isaac to marry when Isaac was forty. He commissioned a servant to make the arrangements and sent him with ten camels loaded with rich goods to support himself and his attendants on the trip and from which he could provide a bride price (Gen. 24:10). In the ninety-seven years since then, Isaac has built upon the wealth he inherited from Abraham. There had been only one brief famine during that time, and Isaac had prospered through it. There is every reason to believe he was even wealthier than Abraham had been. He was prosperous enough that some forty years earlier his wealth is described as "very great" and his presence threatened both the economy and the security of the Philistines (Gen. 26:13–16).

Yet Isaac seems to have sent Jacob away empty-handed, which was not just inexcusable, it was reprehensible. It is as if Isaac were saying to Jacob, "All right, you've received the blessing of Abraham. It's up to God to provide for you—you'll get no help from me."

Apparently that was fine with Jacob. He left without requesting anything other than his father's blessing, counting on God to provide.

Esau's Folly (Gen. 28:6–9)

Opinions vary concerning Esau's reaction to what happens next— when Esau learned that Isaac had confirmed the blessing on Jacob and had sent him to Padan-aram to find a wife, he took another wife who was descended from Ishmael. Sailhamer says, "The final picture of Esau in this narrative is that of a bitter son seeking to spite his parents through deliberate disobedience."[6] On the other hand, Hamilton calls it "an attempt to redeem himself and please his parents."[7] Morris calls it "a belated attempt to partially correct this situation," adding that it is a "rather pathetic attempt."[8] I'm inclined to agree with Hamilton and Morris. It seems that after nearly forty years of marriage Esau realized how much his mother, and maybe his father, object to his Hittite wives. He sees that Isaac's attitude toward Jacob has been transformed, and Jacob now enjoys his father's full support. This may have been a turning point in Esau's attitude toward Jacob, even as Jacob was leaving.

Esau seems to have realized that his problems are not all Jacob's fault—he had disqualified himself from the promise. Esau finally decides to do something to please his parents other than hunt for meat. Discovering that they were sending Jacob to marry within the extended family, he tries to do the same by marrying a daughter of Ishmael, Isaac's half-brother.[9] This marriage doesn't seem to accomplish any improvement in Esau's relationship with his parents—there is no evidence that Isaac ever noticed.

Even in this action, Esau fails to understand God's program. Compounding his earlier error of intermarrying with the Canaanites, he is now entangled with the line of Abraham's son that is outside the covenant. While this links Abraham's firstborn son to Isaac's firstborn son by marriage, it confirms the sovereignty of God's will. God had determined to work through the second-born son of each—Isaac and Jacob—and the manipulations of men could not overthrow God's program.

Jacob's Future (Gen. 28:10–15)

An arduous journey, with minimal provisions and no companions, is summarized in the simple statement "Jacob went out from Beer-sheba and went toward Haran" (Gen. 28:10). Other than a brief stop to ask directions when he arrived in Haran, we are told of only one incident that occurred on the entire trip. It happened about fifty miles from home, after what would probably have been no more than two days' travel.

Apparently Jacob was traveling north without a clear itinerary. He wasn't looking for a particular place to stay and hadn't reached a habitation. The text indicates the randomness of his chosen campsite by saying that he "lighted upon a certain place" (Gen. 28:11) and referring to it as "that place" or "this place" five more times. Jacob was apparently unaware of the significance of this location to his grandfather Abraham. It was the first place Abraham camped after arriving in Canaan and being told by God that this was the land He had promised to give him. It was also the first place at which Abraham is said to have built an altar and "called upon the name of the Lord" (Gen. 12:8; 13:3–4).[10] This place he just happened to "light upon" indicates the truth expressed much later by the prophet Jeremiah: "O Lord, I know that the way of man is not in himself: it is not in man that walketh to direct his steps" (10:23). Jacob's journey to Haran was being directed by God, and Jacob is about to have that truth confirmed.

It was dark, and Jacob was tired. He found a place where he thought he could rest securely. Placing a stone under his "head place" ("pillow," KJV, Gen. 28:11), he fell asleep. The fact that he had to use a rock for a pillow confirms that Jacob was traveling unaccompanied and without more than meager provisions. While he is asleep, the Lord communicates with him in a dream. This would be the first of seven times the Lord would speak to Jacob in his lifetime.

In his dream, Jacob sees a "ladder," or better "a stairway," with the bottom sitting on the earth and the top reaching into heaven (Gen. 28:12). Upon this stairway angels, or "messengers," of God were ascending to heaven and descending to earth. Jacob also saw the Lord—Yahweh. The KJV says that the Lord "stood above it" (Gen. 28:13), implying that He was standing in heaven calling down to Jacob. It is more likely that He stood "beside" or "over" Jacob himself, not the stairway.[11] Using the same wording, Genesis 18:1–2 describes Abraham as seated while three messengers from the Lord "stood by" him, and 1 Samuel 19:20 says Samuel was "standing . . . over" the prophets.

This vision startles Jacob, and little wonder. One writer has tried to capture the verbal forms and changes in syntax by translating it as follows: "There, a ladder! Oh, angels! And look, the Lord himself!"[12]

This is easily the most vivid image of God's dealing with men thus far in the Old Testament. It provides for Jacob a glimpse of the "innumerable company of angels" (Heb. 12:22), who "do his commandments, hearkening unto the voice of his word" (Ps. 103:20) and serve as "ministering spirits, sent forth to minister for them who shall be heirs of salvation" (Heb. 1:14).

More specifically, it shows to Jacob God's interest in him. He has left home unaccompanied, ill prepared, and almost certainly afraid. He knows from his mother that God has promised to bless him and his offspring. He has been promised by his father that the blessing of Abraham was upon him. Surely he "longed for some kind of personal assurance that God was really there."[13] This dream is God's answer to Jacob's unexpressed (or unrecorded) prayer for guidance and assurance. Nearly two thousand years later the Lord Jesus calls Nathaniel to service. To satisfy his doubts, the Lord alludes to this dream, "Verily, verily, I say unto you, Hereafter ye shall see heaven open, and the angels of God ascending and descending upon the Son of man" (John 1:51). Jesus identifies Himself as the very stairway seen by Jacob. He is the means by which one can reach heaven. He is the One by Whose authority the angels minister.

No doubt, Jacob does not understand the full significance of this dream in its New Testament sense. He does know, however, that God has revealed to him something of the connection between heaven and earth, God's activity in both realms, and God's involvement in the affairs of men, particularly Jacob's.

Then the Lord speaks.

First, He identifies Himself as Yahweh, "the God of Abraham thy father, and the God of Isaac" (Gen. 28:13). By calling Himself the God of Isaac, He affirms Isaac's faith. By calling Abraham, not Isaac, Jacob's "father," He links Jacob more closely to Abraham than to Isaac. The Lord then promises Jacob that the land where he lay, as opposed to the land where he was going, would be given to Jacob and his seed. He also promises that Jacob's seed will spread out in every direction and that "all the families of the earth" will be blessed (Gen. 28:14). By this, God confirms that the Abrahamic covenant is rightfully Jacob's by God's design and that Jacob is next in line of the promised Messiah. More immediately, it implies the success of Jacob's journey to find a wife—she would be necessary if he were to have any seed at all. The Lord finishes by promising His constant companionship wherever Jacob goes and that He will bring Jacob safely back to this land (Gen. 28:15).

When God made a similar affirmation to Isaac, He qualified it "for my servant Abraham's sake." God makes these promises to Jacob without that qualification. Further, the promise of His presence with Jacob is much more explicit, detailed and forceful. To Isaac He said,

"I am with thee" (Gen. 26:24). To Jacob he said, "And, behold, I am with thee, and will keep thee in all places whither thou goest, and will bring thee again into this land; for I will not leave thee, until I have done that which I have spoken to thee of" (Gen. 28:15). Don't misunderstand the "until" clause. It does not mean that after God brought Jacob back to the land He would then forsake him. It is an affirmation of the absolute nature of God's promise—He will keep it in every detail without fail.

Further, this was a blessing that could only be bestowed, not obtained. That is, it was manifestly not Jacob's because he managed to take it. Neither he, Esau, Isaac, nor anyone else could have forced God to bestow it upon anyone other than the one He intended to have it. Far from being a rebuke for bad behavior or mistrust, or even a veiled question of Jacob's desire to serve God, this was God's affirmation of His relationship with Jacob. As soon as Jacob got away from Isaac and Esau, and started looking for a proper wife, God has directed him to this place for this meeting. This was not a confrontation but a convocation. It comes at this point in Jacob's life so that he will realize that everything that will happen to him in the years to come in Haran will be under God's divine guidance and will not threaten God's program. Within the narrative, it serves as a signal to the reader to watch for the ways God will work to fulfill His promises.

Jacob's Faith (Gen. 28:16–22)

When the Lord has finished speaking, Jacob wakes up. He now realizes that "the Lord is in this place," and he is appalled that he had not realized it before (Gen. 28:16). He is frightened and amazed, possibly by his own ignorance, and certainly by his proximity to God. Some suggest that Jacob's fear is evidence of weak or nonexistent faith, saying that Abraham and Isaac never expressed such fear.[14] It is true that on more than one occasion God "appeared" to Abraham without Abraham being terror-stricken, but such theophanies were usually, and perhaps always, in human form (Gen. 18:1ff.). There is no evidence that Abraham or Isaac ever had any encounter with God that so vividly revealed His heavenly majesty, His power over angels, and His involvement in earthly affairs as did this revelation to Jacob. If Jacob hadn't been frightened, we could rightly assume that he hadn't understood.

Other biblical figures who had similarly vivid visions of God's glory include Isaiah (Isa. 6:5) and John (Rev. 1:17). Both were terrified, and John collapsed as one dead. Daniel had a similar reaction to his vision of the angel Gabriel (Dan. 8:18, 27). No one doubts the piety of Isaiah, John, or Daniel on the basis of their fear. On the contrary, it seems that the greater one's reverence for God, the greater his fear in God's presence. We should have been astounded if Jacob were not terrified.

Jacob readily admits his fear and awe of God. He does not flee. He does not ask God to depart. Instead, he proclaims, "This is none other but the house of God and . . . the gate of heaven" (Gen. 28:17). He immediately erects a pillar, using the stone on which his head had lain when he had the vision of God. Later developments associated such pillars with Canaanite idolatry, so God ordered their destruction (Exod. 23:24; 34:13; Deut. 7:5; 12:3; 16:22). Later yet, such pillars would be associated with the worship practiced by the descendents of Jacob—Israel and Judah—when they lapsed into idolatry (1 Kings 14:23; 2 Kings 17:10). At times, God will link these pillars to forbidden "graven images" (Lev. 26:1; Deut. 7:5; 12:3; Mic. 5:13). However, in the days of the patriarchs, Moses, and the judges, the use of an upright stone or pillar was acceptable and legitimate as a memorial of a meeting with God (Gen. 28:18, 22; 31:13; 35:14; Exod. 24:4), to mark a boundary or signify a treaty (Gen. 31:45), or to identify a loved one's burial place (Gen. 35:20; cf. 2 Sam. 18:18). No stigma should attach to Jacob's erection of a pillar here.

Having set up the pillar, Jacob takes oil from his meager supplies and pours out an offering as he worships God. There is no justification for interpreting this as an act of repentance or an offering for sin since no animal sacrifice is involved. It's equivalent to what will later be called a thank offering, an expression of gratitude for God's blessings. The pillar thus serves as both a focal point for Jacob's worship and a memorial of God's appearance to him there. This is not evidence of insensitivity toward God, nor of a broken and repentant spirit as if he'd been grievously wrong in "stealing" a blessing. It is, instead, evidence of great reverence for God and acknowledgement of dependence upon Him.

Also as part of his worship, Jacob gives the place a new name: Bethel, meaning "the house of God" (Gen. 28:19). The narrator tells us that the name of the nearby city had formerly been Luz, meaning "nut, almond, hazelnut," or "nut tree." It may originally have been pronounced Loz or Lauz, which would mean "place of refuge."[15] If the former is correct, Jacob is saying that he has found his provision (a "nut tree") at "the house of God." If the latter is preferred, Jacob's new name for the place signifies that he had found his refuge in "the house of God." Either is a profound profession of faith. Getz even calls this Jacob's "born again experience."[16]

Jacob closed his worship with a statement of personal commitment to the Lord, which he expressed as a solemn vow (Gen. 28:20–22). Since Jacob begins his vow by saying "If God will . . ." some interpret this as an attempt to strike a bargain with God. This view says that Jacob is placing conditions on his "faith," as if he means that the Lord would be his God if, and only if, the Lord first "will be with me, and will keep me in this way that I go, and will give me bread to eat, and raiment to put on, so that I come again to my father's house in peace." Jacob will worship God only after God does all these things for him.[17]

For such an interpretation to be correct, it would require believing that Jacob still doesn't really know God and is thinking of God only in terms of how He can benefit Jacob. This interpretation presupposes that Jacob is interested only in material prosperity and cares nothing for spiritual submission to God. It ignores the significance of Jacob's thank offering, conflicts with God's introductory characterization of Jacob as "perfect" or "upright," and fails to consider the evidence of God's own words to Jacob.

If we give proper weight to the prior evidence, another perspective on Jacob's vow emerges. It is not necessary to interpret the "if" as a condition. It is more likely that Jacob is making a formal restatement of what God has promised, with more detail focused on Jacob's immediate needs. His sustenance, which God has promised, will depend upon God's supply of bread to eat and clothes to wear, since Isaac had sent him away with nothing. Jacob is not asking for wealth; he's explaining that all he expects of God in the fulfillment of His promise is basic subsistence. Essentially, Jacob says, "Since God will [not if God will] do all these things for me, He will surely be my God." Or, changing the form to direct address, Jacob means, "God, if You are going to do all this for me, how could I not acknowledge You alone as my God?" The apostle Paul says much the same thing using a similar construction: "If God be for us, who can be against us?" (Rom. 8:31*b*). One Jewish commentator explains it this way:

> This vow, the first in the Bible, has been misunderstood as if Jacob set a number of conditions before acknowledging the Lord as his God. Yet all he wishes is to be protected on the way, abroad, and

to survive. The "conditions" only mean, if I stay alive. This does not imply that he would otherwise not be willing, but rather not be capable of doing it. Jacob's words are a model vow; they imply the confession that the fulfillment depends upon God alone. He wishes to stay alive to be able to serve God. It is . . . the self-dedication of the whole man.[18]

Jacob goes beyond acknowledging Yahweh as "my God" (Gen. 28:21). Saying that he would always think of Bethel as God's house, Jacob vows that when God brings him back to the land, he will come to this place and give to God a tithe ("tenth") "of all that thou shalt give me" (Gen. 28:22). Since nothing is said about to whom such tithes could be paid, and no priestly mechanism existed for the receipt of tithes and offerings, presumably Jacob either intended simply to offer a great sacrifice to God when he returned—a tenth of any property God gives him while he is away—or to use those resources to benefit others (which might explain the generosity of his gift to Esau upon his return). The law requiring tithing would not be established for nearly five hundred years. Jacob is promising a substantial sacrifice for God's glory, and it was in no way required of him.

The only person prior to Jacob said to have tithed was Abraham (Gen. 14:20), when he gave tithes to Melchizedek. In that context, it is questionable whether Abraham tithed on his own property. He had just returned from rescuing the people and property of the cities of Sodom and Gomorrah from the marauding forces of Mesopotamia under the command of Chedorlaomer (Gen. 14:1ff.). Before returning the recovered property to the cities' respective kings, Abraham paid tithes "of all," giving the rest back without keeping anything for himself. Jacob promises more than Abraham had given. On the basis of his confidence that God would sustain him, Jacob vows to give a tenth of it all back to God.

We are not told the specifics of when Jacob fulfills this vow. We will find that immediately upon his return after his lengthy sojourn in Padan-aram, Jacob will send to Esau a lavish gift of animals from all his flocks. It may be that he is honoring his vow in that way, trying to benefit the elder brother who had not been chosen to receive the blessing of God. Sometime after that, Jacob will return to Bethel. He will build an altar and worship there, again identifying it as Bethel, the house of God (Gen. 35:1–15). While the tithe is not specifically mentioned, it may be presumed by the worship, the altar, and the reiteration of God's promise to bless Jacob. "At either end of the Jacob narratives, then, the writer has placed the reminder that God was with Jacob in all that he did and that God was faithful to his promises."[19]

Whether or not this event marks Jacob's conversion is uncertain. Based on God's own testimony, and what I believe to be the best way to understand events in Jacob's life up to this point, I think it's likely that he was already a believer who had not yet had a personal encounter with God. It's possible, however, that his expression of faith at Bethel and his worship of God there indicate that this was the place where Jacob was converted. I realize that it is popular to interpret Jacob's later experience at Peniel (Gen. 32:22–32) as his conversion experience. Still, given all that God and Jacob say here, and what we will see as the clear evidence of God's direction and Jacob's faith in the years to come, it is difficult to imagine that Jacob left Bethel in unbelief.

Lessons

In this chapter we find both positive and negative examples of the importance of marrying within the will of God—"Be ye not unequally yoked together with unbelievers: for what fellowship hath righteousness with unrighteousness? and what communion hath light with darkness? and what concord hath Christ with Belial? or what part hath he that believeth with an infidel?" (2 Cor. 6:14–15). Jacob had done well by preferring to remain single rather than taking a wife who was not a believer or marrying without his parents' blessing.

On the other hand, Esau's marriage to pagan wives had disqualified him from continuing the line of God's promised Redeemer and had been the cause of much grief for his parents. When he realized something of the magnitude of his error, he tried to fix it by marrying another wife who was closer to the line of promise but still outside it. In the New Testament church of Corinth there were apparently many in the first generation of believers who had trusted Christ whose spouse had not. Finding themselves "unequally yoked" to an unbeliever, many of these believers, it seems, had tried to fix the problem by divorcing. What should you do if you are in that situation, a believer married to an unbeliever? Ask God to help you make the best of the situation while you also ask God to save your spouse. Paul writes to correct the error in Corinth,

> If any brother hath a wife that believeth not, and she be pleased to dwell with him, let him not put her away. And the woman which

hath a husband that believeth not, and if he be pleased to dwell with her, let her not leave him. . . . But as God hath distributed to every man, as the Lord hath called every one, so let him walk. (1 Cor. 7:12–13, 17a)

This chapter also deals with the concept of tithing. The Bible repeatedly teaches that all we have comes from God. In fact, it all still belongs to Him, and we are just managers of His property. We are to return part of our income to Him as evidence of our gratitude and confidence in His promise to provide for our needs.

The most important lesson to emerge from this text is that we can trust God to direct our steps in His will. When faced with difficult decisions, the Lord will help us know what to do. Having given us the Bible as His complete Word, He no longer communicates with us verbally. Still, He will use Scripture, people, or events to guide us in the way He wants us to go. If we will do what He clearly tells us to do in His Word, even when we "light upon a certain place" (Gen. 28:11) seemingly by chance, we will find that we are where God intended us to be. "Trust in the Lord with all thine heart, and lean not unto thine own understanding. In all thy ways acknowledge him, and he shall direct thy paths" (Prov. 3:5–6). We don't need to hear Him say audibly, "I am with thee and will keep thee in all places whither thou goest" (Gen. 28:15). To us "he hath said, I will never leave thee nor forsake thee. So that we may boldly say, The Lord is my helper, and I will not fear what man shall do unto me" (Heb. 13:5b–6).

5

Jacob's Wives

Gen. 29:1–30

 few years ago, I took my family to an air show that featured the Air Force Thunderbirds. Watching the precision flight of the F-16 fighter jets was truly amazing. After the show, I took my son to meet the pilots, and he was deeply impressed by the officers who flew the jets: one captain, four majors, and one colonel. To many, the idea of flying fighter jets seems glamorous and exciting. I have news for you: if that is your career goal, you have your work cut out for you.

Since all air force pilots are officers, the first step is to qualify as an officer. There are three ways one can do this. Some choose to attend the Air Force Academy, qualify for admission, and stick with it through graduation. Others enlist in the air force and then apply for Officer Training School (OTS). Most prefer to train through a college Reserve Officer Training Corps (ROTC) program, which is the route our son chose to take. Besides the academic and leadership training, the ROTC cadets must also complete a four-week field training program during the summer after their second year in college. The officers' field training is in several ways more demanding than "boot camp" for enlisted airmen. To become a pilot, a cadet must distinguish himself as a leader among his peers, achieving high marks in several different disciplines, both physical and mental. Those who manage to become one of the few selected for pilot training must then pass a four-day flight physical. Having cleared that hurdle, they have really just started. Many of the pilots-in-training will be assigned to fly the unmanned Predator "drones." Others will be assigned to one of the "heavies"—the large, multi-engine aircraft used for radar surveillance, transport, or refueling missions. Only a few will be selected to fly the F-15 Eagle or the F-16 Falcon, and fewer still the new F-22 Raptor or the F-35 Lightning.

Among the most difficult tasks in the program is SERE (Survival-Evasion-Resistance-Escape) training. This program is similar to that employed by the army to train the Rangers, with the added difficulty that the air force pilots do much of their training alone rather than as part of a team. While the Rangers are infantry and work as a group, the air force assumes that a downed pilot will have to survive harsh environments, evade enemies, resist under torture if captured, and escape—all without help. While we may be tempted to think of swaggering fighter pilots as overgrown kids with an expensive and exciting toy, it would be unjust to overlook the extraordinary discipline and effort it took for them to win and maintain that assignment.

We tend to idealize various professions without thinking much about the often rigorous discipline involved in both preparation and performance. Much of the discipline is painful enough that it can feel like punishment. Similarly, God's program for training His children often involves trials that are far from comfortable. The account of Jacob's life emphasizes some of the difficulties he faced in the trying of his faith as God prepares him to become the father of the nation that will be His people.

At Bethel, God had revealed His presence to Jacob in a manner more startling and profound than He ever had for Isaac or Abraham. Jacob left Bethel with a much better appreciation for the presence and power of God.

Jacob doesn't know it yet, but he will spend twenty years in Padan-aram, specifically in the house of Laban in Haran. Many writers interpret the events of those years as God's punishment for Jacob's treatment of his brother, Esau. It's true that Jacob will experience the same kind of deception he played on his father and will learn an important lesson about God's ability to accomplish His will with or without the devious intervention of others. There is also evidence of at least tension, and perhaps strife, within Jacob's own family. However, these are mostly happy years filled with God's blessing Jacob with great prosperity, despite his having to endure mistreatment by his father-in-law, Laban. While we won't get to it in this chapter, we'll see that by the end of Jacob's sojourn in Laban's house it's Laban, not Jacob, who is the loser.

Jacob's Arrival (Gen. 29:1–8)

Bethel was about 50 miles from his parents' home. That left him with another 450 miles to Haran. The rest of Jacob's trip to Padan-aram is summarized in a single verse. The phrase "went on his journey" (Gen. 29:1) translates a Hebrew phrase that means "lifted up his feet." That probably implies that Jacob left Bethel with a lighter heart and quicker step, thanks to God's message of blessing.[1] More significantly, the wording serves to remind us that Jacob was on foot. Isaac had not only failed to send along gifts as a bride-price, he had not even outfitted him for travel. As difficult as this journey of 450 miles on foot must have been, it is passed over without comment. We are simply told that Jacob arrives among the "people of the east" in Mesopotamia. He had not traveled eastward across the Arabian Desert but north-northeast along the trade route to the east through the region known today as the Fertile Crescent, arriving in the land along the northern Euphrates River.

As Jacob gets close to his destination, he comes upon a well. There are a few similarities between this event and one a generation earlier when Abraham's servant had come to this same land in search of a bride for Isaac, but this was not the same well. The earlier well is described as being "without the city" of Haran (Gen. 24:11) and as serving the women of the city who came out to draw water in the evening. The well Jacob sees is "in the field" (Gen. 29:2) at a sufficient distance from the city of Haran so that Jacob isn't sure the people he meets are from that city. It's also a well that is blocked by a large stone, which typically required the joint effort of several shepherds to remove it for the watering of their flocks.

Coming to the well, Jacob sees three flocks of sheep lying around waiting to be given access to the water. Approaching the shepherds, he asks a series of questions. Interestingly, they seem to have been able to communicate without a translator. Jacob's family probably spoke Hebrew, but the people of Haran would have spoken Aramaic. Evidence of this language difference is found in Genesis 31:47, when Laban names a monument in Aramaic and Jacob calls it by its Hebrew equivalent. As a prosperous businessman from the southwest, Jacob was undoubtedly able to converse in at least two, and probably three, languages (including Egyptian/Coptic). When he speaks to these shepherds, he presumably addresses them in their own language.

Wanting to know if he has arrived at his destination, he first asks from what city they had come (Gen. 29:4). He knew he was at the right place when they told him they were from Haran. Jacob then asks about his mother's brother. Do they know Laban, the son of Nahor? When they say that they do, he asks, "Is he well?" (Gen. 29:6, lit., "Is peace to him?") Answering that Laban is well, they volunteer the information that Laban's daughter Rachel would soon be bringing his sheep to this very well for water.

I imagine that this conversation was exciting to Jacob because it confirmed that God has kept His promise in three regards so far: 1) Jacob has arrived safely in his mother's homeland, 2) Jacob has discovered that her brother's household was doing well, and 3) Jacob has learned that Laban has at least one unmarried daughter (a married daughter would not be tending her father's sheep). As perhaps an unexpected blessing, Jacob also discovers that Laban and his daughter are involved in animal husbandry, the same occupation to which Jacob has given his life and at which he is an expert.

Jacob demonstrates his interest in caring for sheep by raising an issue that has probably puzzled him since he arrived. It was still "high day" (Gen. 29:7), too early for bedding down the sheep for the night. This was the time of day that sheep should be grazing. The shepherds should water them and get them back to the pastures. Jacob's comments imply that he is amazed that these shepherds would waste so much time bedding down the flocks in the middle of the day—they seemed to be neglecting their responsibilities. The shepherds explain that they can't water the sheep yet. They have to wait until all the flocks have gathered to remove the stone from the mouth of the well.

Jacob's Welcome (Gen. 29:9–14*a*)

While Jacob is talking with the shepherds by the well, Rachel arrives with Laban's sheep. Her arrival on this day was not unusual. The phrase translated "she kept them" means literally that "she was a shepherdess" (Gen. 29:9). Laban had sons (Gen. 31:1) and an older daughter (Gen. 29:16). For Laban's younger daughter to be responsible for the sheep is unusual unless the sons are younger still or Laban's flocks and herds are great enough that his sons are occupied elsewhere. Regardless, Rachel's care for the sheep indicates her strength, industry, and trustworthiness—all characteristics a man like Jacob would prize.

When Jacob sees Rachel and realizes she is "the daughter of Laban his mother's brother," Jacob performs the first of two recorded feats of superhuman strength (cf. Gen. 32:22–29)—he removes the stone from the well by himself (Gen. 29:10). Many writers read into this story a modern romanticism, assuming that his action is prompted by his being smitten with Rachel—"love at first sight."[2] His unusual strength has been attributed to his "joy at finding his beautiful cousin."[3] Even great joy, though, is unlikely to endow a man with superhuman strength, and the narrator does not mention Rachel's beauty until verse 17, after at least a month passes (cf. Gen. 29:14). It is more consistent with Scripture to attribute Jacob's sudden strength to the fact that the Lord is with him (Gen. 28:15).[4]

Furthermore, a plain reading of the text indicates that Jacob's immediate concern is not for his uncle's daughter, but for his uncle's sheep. He is exasperated with the other shepherds, and probably with Rachel, too, for showing up early to get in line for water later in the day. They should be working harder and taking better care of the sheep. Jacob wants to provide water "for the sheep of Laban his mother's brother," so he removes the stone and waters "the flock of Laban his mother's brother" (Gen. 29:10). This will provide the animals with water at midday and allow Rachel time to take them back to graze before they bed down for the night.

The use of the phrase "Laban his mother's brother" three times in the same verse seems tediously redundant to our ear today. The narrator's purpose in using this device is to emphasize the family connection between Jacob and Laban. More than simply indicating Jacob's motive in helping Rachel, it also underscores that Jacob has done exactly as his parents commanded (cf. Gen. 28:1–2). From the moment of his arrival in the region near Haran, Jacob is honoring his father and mother. The emphasis on this relationship lays the groundwork for Jacob's request for permission to marry Laban's daughter as another step in completely fulfilling his parents' orders. At the same time, it makes Laban's bad treatment of his sister's son especially shameful.

Only after seeing to the needs of the animals does Jacob turn his attention to his cousin Rachel. This is one of the rare times that the Old Testament narrative mentions a man kissing a woman. There are only three other instances: in Genesis 31:55 Laban kisses his sons and daughters (cf. Gen. 31:28); in 1 Kings 19:20 Elisha kisses his father and mother; and in Song of Solomon 1:2 the loved one expresses a desire to be kissed by her beloved. Far from being a flirtatious sign of Jacob's love for Rachel, his greeting her with a kiss was evidence of the close family relationship the narrator has made so clear.

Anything else would have been a gross violation of social conventions. Of course, since Rachel did not know Jacob, his kissing her had to be startling, and maybe frightening. To make matters even more confusing, he "lifted up his voice and wept" (Gen. 29:11).

When he was able, Jacob explained to the confused young woman that he was "her father's brother"—a euphemism for a close relative—Rebekah's son (Gen. 29:12). Rebekah's story was probably legendary within the family. Nearly one hundred years ago a stranger had appeared at a well and spoke to Rebekah, claiming to have come from a country far to the southwest to represent a man who was a cousin of Laban's father, Bethuel (Gen. 24:15). Bringing with him a caravan of ten heavily laden camels, he offered rich goods as a bride-price to take Rebekah back to marry his master's son. Rachel's aunt Rebekah had not hesitated but had agreed to marry the rich heir to Abraham's fortune in that faraway land. While both Bethuel and Abraham, and later Laban and Isaac, lived near a heavily traveled trade route, there has been no biblical record of communication between the families. Jacob's presence represents the first known contact between these families in nearly a century.

No wonder there is so much kissing and weeping and running going on! Rachel runs home to tell her father of Jacob's arrival (Gen. 29:12). Laban runs to meet Jacob "his sister's son." He is even more demonstrative than Jacob as he both embraces him and kisses him. When the text says that Laban "brought him to his house," it means that Laban welcomed Jacob as a member of his family (Gen. 29:13). The fact that Rachel is not mentioned again until much later implies that Laban and Jacob went to the house while Rachel returned to tending the sheep.

At the house, Jacob tells Laban "all these things" (Gen. 29:13). It's possible to think that Jacob's tale was restricted to recounting merely the events of the last few hours (Gen. 29:2–12),[5] but it probably included at least some information concerning how Jacob had come to be there. Jacob surely told Laban that he was sent by his parents to visit. He probably told him how the Lord had appeared to him at Bethel and had promised to be with him on his journeys and make him prosperous. Having come with nothing to offer as a bride-price, he may have omitted the part about coming for the express purpose of marrying one of Laban's daughters. Whether Jacob mentioned the blessing of Abraham and the conflict with Esau is open to conjecture. Laban would want to know why Jacob arrived virtually empty-handed. If Jacob were to have any hope of marrying one of Laban's daughters,

Laban would need to know how he expected to support her. However broad or narrow Jacob's account may have been, Laban's only reply was to identify Jacob as close family—"my bone and my flesh" (Gen. 29:14; cf. Gen. 2:23; Judg. 9:2; 2 Sam. 5:1; 19:13; 1 Chron. 11:1).

Jacob's Labors (Gen. 29:14*b*–20)

Jacob has been working with Laban for a month before Laban brings up the subject of compensation. Laban's words to Jacob may be a pair of questions: "Are you my relative?" and "Why should you serve for nothing?"[6] If so, Laban is now denying family ties and privileges and is reversing his earlier assertions of relationship in order to subordinate Jacob to an employee. On the other hand, if the text is understood as a statement of family relationship—"you are my relative"—followed by a question about compensation—"why should you serve for nothing?" (Gen. 29:15), the result is the same. Laban does not offer Jacob any kind of partnership or profit-sharing in the business. Rather, Laban is saying that although Jacob is technically a relative, he ought to be treated like an employee and hired for wages.

This proposal was a thinly veiled maneuver to give Laban the advantage over Jacob. In a move designed to look more generous than it is, Laban offers to let Jacob name his own wages. His compensation will still be "wages" and Jacob will answer to Laban as his employer. Jacob is independently wealthy but "cash poor," being in a foreign land without any personal resources. He doesn't need to build a fortune; he just needs enough to live on. He knows he has come to marry Laban's daughter, so he's careful not to offend Laban. Whatever Jacob names, it is likely to be much less than he is worth, especially if you calculate into the equation the blessing that God had promised to Jacob.

Probably to ratchet up the tension of the story, the narrator interrupts to tell us that Laban has two daughters (Gen. 29:16–17). Leah, the elder, is described as "tender eyed." Most modern translations describe her as having "weak" eyes, which could imply that she was less attractive than her sister because she squinted, had some problem with her eyes, or had eyes that were merely dull and not as bright and fiery as her sister's. The word could also be taken to mean "timid" (cf. Deut. 20:8—"faint"). It is, however, more likely to mean "gentle," "soft," "delicate," "young," or "tender" as in "young and choice" (cf. Gen. 18:7). Hamilton points out that Gen. Rabbah 70:16

"chose to translate *rak* as 'lovely' (*y'yn*)" and adds that "Leah's eyes were 'weak' on account of her weeping over the possibility that, as the elder sister, she would have to marry Esau, the older brother."[7] He concludes, "Leah may be older, but her eyes are the beautiful eyes of a person who looks much younger."[8] If Hamilton is correct, the text is not describing Leah as unattractive and Rachel as gorgeous. Leah has especially lovely, compassionate eyes, but there is something about Rachel that makes her more generally beautiful.

This brings us back to the salary negotiation. Jacob, of course, knows he has no real need of wages. He will inherit as much as two-thirds of Isaac's vast wealth, which will almost certainly make him much better off than Laban. He is content with room and board. He hadn't come all this way for a job. Still, Jacob is in no hurry to get home to face Esau's threats. Knowing that he has come without the means to offer a proper bride-price, Jacob proposes that he work seven years for the right to marry Laban's younger daughter, Rachel. Whatever the specific differences in the two young women's appearances, it was Rachel whom "Jacob loved" (Gen. 29:18).

It may be appropriate to fault Jacob for not having consulted God in this matter as had Abraham's servant when he came here to find a bride for Isaac. On that occasion, Abraham's servant had proposed a specific test, asking God to lead him to the right bride for Isaac (Gen. 24:12–14). Perhaps had Jacob asked God, the Lord would have directed him to Leah rather than Rachel. We will find in Leah indications of greater faith in Yahweh, Jacob's God, than we will find in Rachel.

However, we should not go so far as to suggest that Jacob was attracted to Rachel solely because of her beauty.[9] Yes, her beauty is mentioned just before his love for her is indicated, but the word translated "love" indicates an act of the will more than an impulse of attraction. It is associated with a covenant choice—Rachel is the one whom Jacob had chosen to be his bride. We must not forget that Rachel is introduced as a shepherdess caring for her father's sheep, which is important to Jacob. Further, she is the first woman of the region Jacob meets, which is significant to Jacob because it coincides with what happened when Rebekah was recruited to be Isaac's bride. Abraham's servant had come with only Abraham's instructions and no direct promise of guidance from God. Jacob had left with his parent's instructions and had received the absolute promise of God's direction on his journey. Rather than accusing Jacob of acting on impulse, we should see that he acts in faith that Yahweh had in fact led him immediately to the young woman whom he should marry.

Laban's response to Jacob's proposal may be intentionally am-biguous, since his reply does not include Rachel's name. He may already have in mind the deception he will play on Jacob. Perhaps he is already scheming to marry his elder daughter to Jacob in hopes of staking a greater personal claim to Jacob's inheritance. Surely a man of Laban's wealth should have been able to arrange a suitable mar-riage for Leah in the course of seven more years, but he does not do so. Whatever his initial intentions may have been, Laban agrees to Jacob's proposal because it was so obviously to his benefit. He should have been thrilled to have his daughter marry into Jacob's family any-way. To get seven years of free labor from such a skilled and energetic worker was considerably more than he had any right to demand or expect as a bride-price. For Jacob, the next seven years pass as if they were "but a few days" (Gen. 29:20; cf. 27:44) because of his love for Rachel.

Laban's Treachery (Gen. 29:21–30)

Jacob has gladly endured what may be the longest betrothal in the biblical record. For seven years he has waited for the consummation of his marriage to Rachel. While the years passed as if they were but days, Jacob has not lost track of the time. Laban, however, seems to be paying no attention to the completion date of Jacob's contract. Laban's negligence is worse than inexcusable. It's downright insult-ing. It's bad enough that Jacob-the-employee has to demand the wages he has earned. It is much worse that Jacob-the-son-in-law has to remind his bride's father that it's time for the wedding (Gen. 29:21).

Marriage customs may not have been formalized by this time. There is no evidence of elaborate preparations or ceremonies at-tached to any marriages in the record thus far. When Rebekah was brought to Isaac, she was presented as his wife and he took her to bed to consummate the marriage (Gen. 24:67). Jacob apparently antici-pated the same sort of transaction. Jacob's words to Laban here are phrased as a demand—"Give me," he says. Rachel is not referred to by name but by position. Because his contractual obligation has been fulfilled, she is no longer "your daughter" but is now "my wife." Jacob expects to be given his wife now and to "go in unto her," that is, to take her directly to his bed as an act of marriage.

Laban does not reply. Instead, he gathers the men of the area together for a feast (Gen. 29:22). Since it was a feast for the men, it seems that his daughters were not invited. Then, when it was dark, he brought to Jacob Leah, not Rachel, apparently cloaked in such a way as to be unrecognizable. Jacob took Leah to bed, thinking she was Rachel, and had sexual intercourse with her to consummate the marriage. To Jacob's shock, "in the morning, behold, it was Leah!" (Gen. 29:25).

All sorts of questions occur to the reader of this passage. How could Jacob not know that the woman with whom he was having sexual relations was Leah and not Rachel? Hamilton, following Josephus, suggests that he might have overindulged in wine at the feast.[10] However, the text makes no such suggestion. The fault is entirely Laban's, with Leah's cooperation. The dark, Jacob's long-restrained anticipation of the event, and his trusting nature could have been enough to blind him to the truth if Leah and Rachel were alike enough in face and figure. If the only significant difference in their features was the cast of their eyes, such a deception would not be that difficult.

The masquerade would, of course, require Leah's active participation. To what degree was she complicit in this deception? She certainly had to convince Jacob that she was Rachel as he slept with her that night. Was this something she wanted, or was she simply following her father's orders? Did she care what Rachel would think about her for having taken away her husband? And speaking of Rachel, where was she while all this was going on? Was she out with the flocks, unaware of her father's treachery, or had she come dressed as Leah to assist in the charade? Was she, perhaps, aware of the customary practice that the younger could not marry until the older sister wed? If so, had her father assured her that the only way she could be given to Jacob was if Jacob married Leah first? Is it possible that Laban had never arranged a marriage for Leah because he planned all along to manipulate this situation so that both of his daughters, or at least the elder, would marry into Abraham's/Isaac's clan? These are questions we cannot answer with any confidence.

Jacob's discovery that he had spent the night with Leah, not Rachel, is interesting. He confronts Laban, "What have you done to me?" He reminds Laban of his contractual agreement to serve seven years for Rachel and asks, "Why have you deceived me?" (Gen. 29:25). Jacob expresses no anger toward Leah. While his questions to Laban could be interpreted as outrage, they might just as well have expressed injury and confusion. The text makes no direct reference to anger.

Laban's self-justification may have been merely "a rehearsed answer,"[11] stating that the customary practice of their land was for the older daughter to marry before the younger. However, the forcefulness of his statement gives it some credibility: "It must not be so done" (Gen. 29:26). This is an expression that "refers to serious violations of custom that threaten the fabric of society and is tantamount to rebuke."[12] It is the same expression used by Abimelech after discovering that Abraham had deceived him (Gen. 20:9). It is the expression used by the sons of Jacob after they hear that their sister Dinah has been raped (Gen. 34:7). It is also the expression used by David's daughter Tamar when she tried to convince her half-brother Amnon not to rape her (2 Sam. 13:12).

Whether or not Laban's explanation was true, it may be that what silenced Jacob was the wording of what must not be done: "to give the younger before the firstborn." Those words must have smitten Jacob's conscience as he realized how closely this event paralleled the deception Rebekah and he had worked on Isaac over seven years before. Many writers consider Jacob's actions toward Isaac parallel to Laban's toward Jacob. The parallel is more obvious if seen between two pairs of people: Rebekah compares to her brother Laban, and Jacob compares to Leah. In the earlier event, Laban's sister Rebekah had sent her younger son, Jacob, to impersonate her elder son, Esau, to prevent Isaac's giving a blessing to the elder son. In this event, Laban had sent his elder daughter, Leah, to impersonate her younger sister, Rachel, to prevent Jacob's marriage to the younger daughter.

Jacob is not angry with Leah because he sees in her actions a reflection of his own—she did what her father ordered her to do. Jacob does not express anger with Laban because he sees in Laban's actions a reflection of his mother's. He is not justifying any of them, but he surely realizes that what has happened to him is no more than he deserved. "Jacob's past had caught up with him, and he could do no more than accept the results."[13] He is learning a vital lesson about God's sovereign ability to accomplish His will—God accomplishes His will and preserves His program without or despite human scheming and deception.

Laban, continuing to manipulate the situation, tells Jacob he need wait only another week. If he will fulfill Leah's marriage week, live with her for seven days, Laban will keep his original agreement and give Jacob his younger daughter also (Gen. 29:27). There was one

significant stipulation: Jacob would have to work for him without pay
for another seven years. Obviously less than thrilled with the outcome
of the day's events, Jacob accepts the proposal. He fulfills Leah's
week, then takes Rachel also as his wife (Gen. 29:28). As evidence of
their father's blessing, each daughter is presented with a maid as a
wedding gift. Leah is given Zilpah (Gen. 29:24), and Rachel is given
Bilhah (Gen. 29:29). This will be important in the years to come.

One difficulty for the Christian mind is that Laban's scheming
results in Jacob's becoming a bigamist. In our own culture polygamy
is illegal—at least for now—for good reason. However, frequent and
easy divorce and remarriage has allowed for the common practice of
a kind of "serial" polygamy. In the culture of Jacob's day, polygamy
was not unknown and may have been common. Abraham had taken
both Sarah and Hagar as wives, but you'd think Jacob might have
learned something from the less-than-ideal outcome of that situation.
Jacob's brother had two wives when he left, and we know he took a
third shortly after that. Of course, patterning one's actions after Esau
would not be wise. Nevertheless, God used the situation to provide
the sons through whom He would build His nation. Much later, a
significant descendent of Jacob named David would have at least
eight wives yet still be described as "a man after God's own heart." We
have to note that while there are many examples of polygamy in the
Bible, there is not a single example of a happy and peaceful polyga-
mous household. All were plagued with problems stemming directly
from the fact that a man had taken more than one wife. The "serial"
polygamy practiced today normally involves much heartache and
serious family problems too. Nevertheless, God often uses and blesses
people within such situations. The fact that God may use an event to
His glory does not justify the use of inappropriate means to that end.
God established marriage to be between one man and one woman—
"For this cause shall a man leave father and mother, and shall cleave
to his wife: and they twain shall be one flesh" (Matt. 19:5).

We should not be surprised to read in verse 30 that Jacob loved
Rachel more than Leah. She had been the object of his adoration
for seven years and the reward toward which he had labored so long.
Leah had deceived him and forever altered his future. However, a
lesser man than Jacob might have behaved quite differently. Some
might have divorced or even murdered Leah rather than live with
her. That is what Esau plotted to do to Jacob for his deception. Some
might have simply eloped with Rachel as his rightful reward for the
years of labor, abandoning Leah. Not Jacob. Despite the deception,

he kept Leah as his wife. Having slept with her, he seems never to have considered an annulment or divorce. While he never loved her as he did Rachel, he was apparently unwilling to reject her. At the end of his life, it is Leah with whom he will be buried (Gen. 49:31).

Despite the fact that Laban virtually forced bigamy upon him, Jacob maintained a profitable working relationship with his father-in-law. He even honored his agreement to work an additional seven years for the right to marry Rachel—he didn't take his wives and run out on his contract. Laban obviously considered Jacob a man of integrity. He trusted him to keep his word, work hard, and care for Laban's daughters. While this story reveals much that is bad about Laban's character, it says much that is good about Jacob's.

Centuries after this event, Jacob's multiplied offspring will leave Egypt as a nation called "the children of Israel." "Israel" is a name that God will give Jacob later (Gen. 32:28). God will lead them almost directly to Mount Sinai, where He will communicate to them His Law that will govern how they are to live. This gathered nation, divided into tribes named after the sons of Jacob, will not be able to escape the significance of one stipulation in the law of marriage: that no man is to marry his wife's sister while his wife still lives (Lev. 18:18). While we must not judge Jacob by a law not yet stated, the Law does reveal the unchanging character of God. Although Jacob would not have known it, this provision implies that once Jacob had officially married Leah, God apparently intended to work through her, not Rachel.

Lessons

This section and the next actually serve to illustrate the truth of Hebrews 12:5*b*–7—"My son, despise not thou the chastening of the Lord, nor faint when thou art rebuked of him: for whom the Lord loveth he chasteneth, and scourgeth every son whom he receiveth. If ye endure chastening, God dealeth with you as with sons; for what son is he whom the father chasteneth not?" God sometimes uses painful situations to remind us of our own failures. He may do this for one or more of three reasons: to bring us to repentance, to teach us to trust God, and to remind us that we don't deserve God's favor.

God works "all things after the counsel of his own will" (Eph. 1:11*b*). Laban has mistreated his nephew Jacob and his own daughters. However, despite his devious methods and motives, his actions served to further God's purposes. For all the apparent misfortune of Jacob's having to perform fourteen years of slave labor for Laban and live in a bizarre and difficult domestic situation, Jacob was able to be happy in Laban's household. How did he avoid bitterness and hatred? He believed God was fulfilling His promise to be with him in Haran.

We, too, have the promise of God's continual presence to give us confidence in the face of mistreatment: "[F]or he hath said, I will never leave thee, nor forsake thee. So that we may boldly say, The Lord is my helper, and I will not fear what man shall do unto me" (Heb. 13:5b–6). God may well put us through distressing, even potentially destructive circumstances. His purpose may be chastening for our own sins or disciplinary training for future challenges. Like Jacob, we can find happiness and contentment in difficult situations, learning to trust God when life is hard because "we know that all things work together for good to them that love God, to them who are the called according to his purpose" (Rom. 8:28).

6

Jacob's Prosperity

Gen. 29:31–30:43

eople are naturally competitive. That competitive spirit is a good thing when tempered with wisdom, spurring a person on to achieve excellence. An unchecked competitive spirit, however, can become nothing more than a harmful drive for personal preeminence.

The things over which people will compete vary somewhat from culture to culture, but almost anything can be turned into a contest. A new genre of television programming has been spawned by people's apparently insatiable appetite for contests—and I'm not talking about traditional sporting events or game shows. Besides occasional broadcasts of silly competitions like hot-dog-eating contests, there are television series that feature survival contests, cooking contests, home decorating contests, even weight loss contests.

Competition often generates a lot of emotion, and that is not always a good thing. Many of us remember the story out of Texas several years ago about a mother of a teenage girl who plotted the murder of another girl who had beaten her daughter out of a spot on the high school cheerleading team. It has not been long since figure skating superstar Tonya Harding hired a thug to break the legs of her top competitor, Nancy Kerrigan. Recent news has been full of reactions to a report identifying dozens of Major League baseball players who have violated the law, if not the rules, by using performance-enhancing drugs such as steroids and human growth hormones to help them gain an advantage over their opponents.

In the passage we'll study in this chapter, we find two sisters married to the same man engaging in a child-bearing competition. One bears a child every year or so, while the other is unable to conceive. The rivalry becomes bitter and their behavior strange. While neither resorts to murder, both adopt tactics of dubious morality to gain some measure of status.

Jacob has passed seven years in the land of Haran, joyfully serving Laban for the right to marry Rachel. Some such arrangement would have been necessary because Isaac had failed to provide a bride-price for his son to present to Laban. Still, Laban has taken full advantage of Jacob's unnecessarily generous offer. To Jacob, the seven years of servitude to Laban have seemed to him but the "few days" his mother Rebekah had said he would need to stay until Esau's anger had cooled.

The fact that Jacob had to go to Laban at the end of his service contract and demand his wife set an ominous tone for the events that followed with Leah and Rachel. At best, his home life will be complicated, plagued by strained relations with his father-in-law and tension between his wives.

For a man whom Bible teachers usually described as a lying, sneaking, conniving, thieving rascal, Jacob demonstrates remarkable integrity—actually consistent with how God describes him. In this passage, he faithfully fulfills his seven-year contract with Laban, working hard for his father-in-law's benefit, all the while struggling to keep peace within his family. At the end of his second seven-year contract, not having received any indication from the Lord that he should go home, Jacob will agree to continue to work for Laban at wages set to Laban's distinct advantage. He will work hard without complaint, despite repeated wage changes due to Laban's attempts to keep him from becoming too prosperous. Do you think that maybe God was right, after all, when He introduced Jacob as *tam*—"perfect"?

Jacob's Family (Gen. 29:31–30:24)

Jacob's sons represent the first generation in which God's promises to Abraham will be conferred upon more than one individual. In this, the third generation, all Jacob's sons will be included in the promise. It is in Jacob that God makes the transition from a chosen man to a chosen people. Therefore, the text provides a detailed account of the birth of the first eleven of Jacob's sons (the account of the twelfth will come later in Genesis 35:16–21) and mentions the birth of one daughter, who would be important in later events. It provides insights into the brothers' relationships to one another and to their father that will shed some light on later events. Despite its detail, it remains a relatively spare account of at least seven years of Jacob's life, with hints of the tensions, conflicts, and jealousies through which he had to navigate to maintain a reasonably happy and peaceful home.

Picking up right after Jacob's marriages to Leah and then Rachel, the Lord (Yahweh) is mentioned for the first time since Jacob left Bethel (Gen. 29:31). God has not forsaken the man He promised to guide and bless. He did not stay behind at the stairway in Bethel but has come with Jacob as He said He would. Because He is mentioned here, we are assured that He has been working through events thus far and that He is particularly involved in establishing Jacob's family.

The cause of the tension in the family is due to Jacob's having two wives. The fact that he does not treat them with equal affection doesn't help. Jacob favors Rachel to the point that Leah seems to be "hated." Jacob doesn't despise Leah, for he is obviously spending time in her bed; but his heart is not bound to her as it is to Rachel. This should surprise no one. Rachel was the wife for whom he asked, for whom he contracted, and for whom he labored diligently for seven years. Leah was the wife he was given by deceit, for whom he had never asked, and because of whom he was trapped by Laban into another seven years' servitude for the wife he wanted all along. It is the previous verse that tells us how to understand "hated" in this context—"[Jacob] loved also Rachel more than Leah." He never abuses Leah. He does not treat her as a servant. He does not send her away in disgrace. He loves Leah insofar as he cares for her, provides for her, and spends some time with her. Still, he chose Rachel, and his preference for her is so obvious and profound as to make Leah appear to be hated by comparison.

Not only did Jacob treat his wives unequally but the Lord treated them unequally as well. The difference is that the Lord favored Leah, not Rachel. Sailhamer is probably correct in contending, "Jacob had planned to take Rachel as his wife, but God intended him to have Leah."[1] The fact that Jacob produces children by Leah is evidence that he assumed the Lord was in control of the circumstances that made her his wife. The fact that he consistently prefers Rachel implies that he was not entirely satisfied with the wife God gave him.

In rapid succession, Leah gives birth to four sons. She recognized this as evidence of God's blessing on her life and proves this either in the names she gives them or the comments she makes upon their births. The text never explains why Jacob seems to have left to Leah and Rachel the naming of all his children, with the exception of Benjamin in Genesis 35:18.

Leah names her first son Reuben, an expression of joy at his birth that means "See, a son!" (Gen. 29:32). Some see a subtle wordplay in her two statements about his birth, finding the consonants that make up Reuben's name within each clause.[2] Mainly, they express the pathos of her situation—"Surely the Lord hath looked upon my affliction" and "therefore my husband will love me." The name is an expression of joy and heartache—joy in Leah's confidence of the Lord's having acted to address her affliction and heartache in her longing for her husband's undiluted love. Rather than naming him "my distress," Leah has chosen a neutral name that expresses both her distress in her circumstances and her confidence in the Lord.

Leah names her second son Simeon, meaning "hearing" or "has heard" (Gen. 29:33). In this name, Leah intentionally focuses on the blessing of the Lord, not the anguish of her experience. Rather than naming her son "unloved one," she chooses a name that points to the Lord's having heard that she is unloved. She leaves room for Jacob to have a change of heart. Her son's name does not necessarily connote anything negative.

Her third son's name points more to her circumstances, not in bitterness but in hope. She names him Levi, meaning "attachment," hoping that since she has borne her husband three sons he would now attach his affection upon her (Gen. 29:34).

With the birth of her fourth son, Leah seems to resign herself to motherhood with an indifferent or unloving husband. Focusing only on the Lord's blessing, she names him Judah, meaning "praise" or in expanded form Jehudael, "may God be praised."[3] Explaining the name, she says, "I will praise Yahweh" (Gen. 29:35).

These last two sons will become especially significant. Two of Levi's most important descendents will be Moses and Aaron, through whom will come the spiritual leaders of Israel. Two of Judah's most important descendents will be David, through whom will come the national leaders of Israel, and Jesus the Messiah, the ultimate King and Savior of God's people. It cannot be accidental that the priesthood and the kingship will arise by divine direction from sons born to Leah, the wife given to Jacob through circumstances he couldn't control.

The concluding clause of verse 35—"[she] left bearing"—is usually taken to mean that God stopped her from conceiving for a while.

However, the text says that the Lord "opened her womb" and never says that He closed it. When the Lord later hears Leah so that she conceives (Gen. 30:16–17), it is in the context of her having to make a deal with Rachel to force Jacob to spend the night with her. It may be better to understand Leah's having "left bearing" as indicating that Jacob stopped having sexual relations with her. The first verse of chapter 30 may explain why.

Rachel, fed up with Leah's constant childbearing while she has no children, irrationally, blames Jacob. Motivated by envy, she demands, "Give me children, or else I die"[4] (Gen. 30:1). Rachel seems to think that if he'd spend more time in her bed she too might conceive. It is not that Jacob has not been lying with her. He has not withheld seed, but the Lord has withheld "fruit." He's probably just as frustrated as Rachel. We know he would prefer to have children by Rachel, but thus far God has not given her a child.

At her accusation, Jacob snaps back with a hint that there is something in her life that has kept the Lord from giving her children. Jacob's question "Am I in God's stead?" (Gen. 30:2) indicates that he is still trusting God to build his family as God sees fit. Still, for the first time in the record of his life, Jacob is described as angry. His anger may indicate that he, too, is frustrated with the way God has been building his family. However, since the anger is directed at Rachel, not God, it's more likely that Jacob is angry with Rachel's discontentment and impatience. His own mother had waited twenty years for children before God blessed her with sons. Rachel has taken no more than four years to lose patience out of jealousy. Her indignant selfishness stands in stark contrast to the anguished faith of Leah, and Jacob is angered by it.

In desperation, unwittingly taking a page from Jacob's grandmother Sarah's book, Rachel resorts to a human means to have children by a surrogate. When Abraham and Sarah employed this method, the results were not happy (Gen. 16). Rather than praying, as had Rebekah and apparently Leah, Rachel orders Jacob to take her handmaid Bilhah as a secondary wife and "go in unto her"—a euphemism for having sexual relations with her (Gen. 30:3). Any children Bilhah would bear to Jacob would be considered Rachel's by a sort of adoption. In this, Jacob emulates his grandfather and falls short of his father. Rather than entreating God on behalf of Rachel, as Isaac had done for Rebekah (Gen. 25:21), Jacob does what Abraham had done and goes along with Rachel's plan.

As expected, Bilhah conceives. Rachel claims the son she bears and names him Dan, which is the first part of the word that means "has vindicated me" (30:6). As Rachel explains, she intends the name to signify that God had seen her hopeless, helpless condition and granted her justice by giving her this son. Since Rachel is still barren, Jacob continues to have relations with Bilhah, who is now his third wife. She bears a second son. This one is also adopted by Rachel, who names him Naphtali. The name itself means "my conflict,"[5] but it is connected with her statement "With great wrestlings I have wrestled," or "I have been entangled in a desperate contest"[6] (Gen. 30:8). It may be significant that while Rachel acknowledges God's involvement, so far she refers to Him only as Elohim, a generic name for God, not Yahweh (Jehovah), His covenant name. While Leah regarded her children as gifts from God that might cause her husband to love her, Rachel considered these sons of Bilhah as trophies in a contest with her sister.

Possibly because she had become infertile, but more likely due to Jacob's having neglected her bed, Leah resorts to the same method used by Rachel to have additional children. She has apparently been provoked by Rachel into treating the bearing of children as a contest between the two of them. Not content with her four sons, she convinces Jacob to take her maid Zilpah as a fourth wife so she can adopt any sons born to Zilpah as her own. Like Bilhah, Zilpah produces for Jacob two sons in quick succession. Leah names the first Gad, meaning "fortunate," a name "associated with a pagan god of luck"[7] (Gen. 30:11). The KJV reading of her comment, "a troop cometh," is more accurately rendered "Good fortune has come!"[8] Leah named the second of Zilpah's sons Asher, meaning "the happy one," or "the bringer of happiness" (Gen. 30:13). At his birth, she proclaimed her own happiness and her expectation that other women would recognize that she had been made happy.

Do you find yourself marveling at the machinations of these two sisters married to the same man? Caught up in a jealous contest over who could produce children, they display a mind-boggling lack of jealousy over physical intimacy with Jacob. They even show a kind of "vicarious satisfaction when their husband would have sexual relations with their respective maids."[9] This may be Jacob's greatest failure—his allowing himself to get caught up in his wives' jealous manipulations, going from bed to bed in an attempt to keep peace and avoid being charged with favoritism. Yes, God will use this activity to produce a large number of sons of nearly the same age to provide the foundation for the nation of Israel, but Jacob's multiplying of wives and the competition it engendered will set a negative tone for later events in his life and the lives of his sons.

In the midst of all the rush for children, Rachel is still barren and Leah has not had relations with Jacob for a while. A day comes in which Reuben, possibly only four years old,[10] finds some mandrakes out in the field. Mandrakes are a small, aromatic fruit that grow close to the ground. They look something like a cherry tomato but are slightly smaller, being about the size of a crab apple and yellow to orange in color. Ancient cultures prized mandrakes as an aphrodisiac and a fertility inducer. Even today they are often called "love-apples." A four-year-old Reuben would not have had to know what they were and would have needed no help in bringing a bunch of them home to his mother.

When Rachel discovers that Reuben has brought Leah some mandrakes, she immediately asks Leah for some of them. Leah replies, "Is it a small matter that thou hast taken my husband? And wouldest thou take away my son's mandrakes also?" (Gen. 30:15). Since Rachel has convinced Jacob to spend his time in her bed, to Leah's neglect, how could she dare ask for an aphrodisiac as well? Rachel proposes a trade. If Leah will give Rachel the mandrakes, Rachel will send Jacob to Leah's bed that night. Notice that Leah refers to Jacob as "my husband," yet when Rachel responds, she promises that tonight Jacob will "lie with you." When the phrase "to lie with" is used in Genesis "with a sexual nuance, [it] never connotes a relationship of marital love but is invariably used in unsavory circumstances."[11] Rachel is intentionally insulting Leah by implying that her relationship with Jacob is illicit.

When Jacob comes in that evening from working with the animals, Leah meets him with the news that she has arranged for him to sleep with her (Gen. 30:16). For Leah to have to hire him for the night would have been humiliating for Leah, especially in the light of Rachel's slur, but it is also a reminder to Jacob of how he has neglected Leah.

Leah has apparently been praying for more time with Jacob. Although she was still caught up in this contest for children, her real longing has always been for Jacob's love. Through this one night with Jacob, God gives Leah a fifth son. Her prayer was probably just that Jacob would spend intimate time with her. Having another son was a bonus. She names this son Issachar, meaning "man of reward,"[12] and credits God with having given her what she paid for (Gen. 30:17–18). Unaccountably, though, she seems to think this vindicates her having given Zilpah to Jacob as a wife. Nevertheless, Jacob has returned to her bed. After bearing Issachar, she quickly conceives again and bears a sixth son, whom she names Zebulun (Gen. 30:19–20). This name is more difficult to define but probably means "exalted abode" or "elevated dwelling."[13] Her comment, "God hath endued me with a good dowry; now will my husband dwell with me," should be understood to mean "God has endowed me with a good endowment. Now my husband will honor me" (ESV).

Before closing the discussion of Leah's children, the text adds that later she would bear him a daughter, Dinah (Gen. 30:21). No clue is provided for the meaning of this name, but Morris suggests that it means "judgment,"[14] apparently assuming it comes from the same root as Dan. Jacob would have other daughters (Gen. 37:35; 46:7, 15) whose names are unrecorded. There are two likely reasons for Dinah's inclusion in this account: her birth brings the number of children born to Leah to a full seven, and the reader is alerted to her presence in anticipation of the events of Genesis 34.

Rachel's mandrakes apparently don't work—or even work in reverse, since the wife who doesn't have them conceives and the one who does remains barren. God wants Rachel, and you and me, to understand that such attempts at manipulation are unsuccessful without His involvement and are unnecessary with it. When Rachel conceives, it is not due to scheming, aphrodisiacs, or fertility drugs but because "God remembered" her and "hearkened unto her." It seems that once the mandrakes fail, Rachel finally turns to God, and He hears her cry and "opened her womb" (Gen. 30:22). Yes, this could have happened shortly after the affair of the mandrakes, but apparently enough time has passed that not even Rachel attributes her conception to their aid.

Rachel names her son Joseph. She uses a play on words, a sort of pun, in explaining the name, saying first, "God [Elohim] hath taken away ['asaph] my reproach," adding, "the Lord [Yahweh] shall add [yoseph] to me another son." In so doing, Rachel combines the ideas of God's having removed her shame in being childless and her hope for the future. This is also the first time Rachel has attributed the circumstances of her life to the work of Yahweh, the covenant name for God.

While all these events reveal glimpses into the problems of a home with multiple wives, they really show us a lot more about how the hand of God can work. God has demonstrated that He is capable of giving Jacob the promised offspring through Leah—the wife God gave him. God is also able to prevent Jacob from having any children through Rachel—the wife Jacob wanted. Still, God is gracious and merciful and will answer our prayers. While the consequences of Jacob's folly in taking multiple wives will endure, they will not disrupt God's program. Through God's mercy and grace, all the sons born to these four women will participate in the blessing of the promise God made to Abraham, Isaac, and Jacob. They would establish a nation to be known as God's people.

Jacob's Flocks (Gen. 30:25–43)

This section begins with the end of Jacob's fourteen-year commitment to serve Laban. According to Genesis 31:38, Jacob was with Laban for twenty years. The first seven of those years were spent working for Laban in lieu of a bride-price, followed by his marriage to Leah and Rachel. That allows only thirteen years for the birth of his eleven sons (and Dinah) and for all the livestock birthing cycles necessary for Jacob's management of Laban's flocks and herds that resulted in the growth of Jacob's wealth.

If we understand the previous section as a strictly chronological sequence describing the birth order of Jacob's eleven sons, it seems impossible to fit all the births into the seven-year span between his marriage to Leah and Rachel and the fulfillment of his contract. It is possible that Jacob's contract had expired two or three years earlier, but he has waited to leave until Rachel has delivered a child. If so, he's been working for those years for nothing at all—no bride-price debt to work off and no wages for his labor.

The difficulty of time is best resolved by seeing the previous section as an expanded chronology emphasizing the relationship of Jacob's sons to their birth mothers rather than giving us a strictly chronological birth order. Leah's first four sons could have been born in rapid succession in less than four years. Rachel's dismay at being childless surely surfaced before the birth of Judah, Leah's fourth son. Bilhah could have born Dan and even conceived Naphtali before Judah's birth. If Leah stopped having children due to Joseph's neglect rather than to a lengthy period of barrenness, not much time needed to pass before she induced Jacob to have relations with Zilpah. Gad could have been born within a year or so of Judah, with Asher following the next year. If the incident with the mandrakes occurred before the birth of Asher, Leah could have conceived Issachar while Zilpah was still expecting Asher. If Zebulun were then conceived shortly after Issachar's birth, and if Rachel conceived Joseph before Zebulun's birth, it is possible for all eleven sons to have been born during the first seven years of the sisters' marriage to Jacob. The text's note that Dinah was born "afterwards" means that she need not have been born during that span at all. She was probably born during the years of Jacob's labor for wages but is included here to identify her with her mother. If this compression of events is correct, Jacob could have approached Laban at the completion of his fourteen-year commitment, allowing ample time for Jacob's livestock management through many birthing seasons during the six remaining years of his twenty-year sojourn in Haran.

Finally, Jacob has finished the task for which he had come to Haran—he has married and worked off the bride-price. He has no flocks or herds of his own, but he has a large family. It's time to start thinking about providing for his sons. He expects to inherit property from his father, so he assumes he should get back to work in the family estate. Since he has not had any word from home that Esau's anger had abated, he has to assume that Esau is still planning to kill him. Therefore, it is probably with mixed feelings that Jacob approaches Laban to tell him that he needs to return to Canaan.

In another example of his godly character, Jacob does not just pack up his family and leave. He had stayed with Laban and faithfully worked Laban's flocks and herds for the entire period upon which they had agreed. Jacob does not simply announce that he is leaving, but neither does he "ask Laban for permission."[15] Jacob's words to Laban are closer to a command than a request—"Send me away. . . . Give me my wives and my children. . . . Let me go" (Gen. 30:25–26)—anticipating the words of Moses to Pharaoh (Exod. 5:1). What Jacob really wants is Laban's official acknowledgment that his obligation has been fulfilled. Like a person who has made the final payment on a car and wants to have the title issued, Jacob wants Laban to sign off on the completion of his contract.

In contrast to Jacob's integrity, Laban evades the issue. Without ever admitting that Jacob has completed his contract, Laban asks Jacob to stay. Translators disagree on how best to express Laban's words rendered in the KJV as "I have learned by experience" (Gen. 30:27). This wording implies that Laban has watched his flocks grow under Jacob's care and deduced that his increasing wealth has been God's blessing on Jacob. However, the word translated "experience" is usually rendered "enchantments/enchanter" (Lev. 19:26; Deut. 18:10;

2 Kings 17:17; 21:6; 2 Chron. 33:6). This may suggest that Laban has sought for an explanation for Jacob's amazing success by using divination or sorcery.[16] However, some suggest that the Hebrew word used here derives from an Akkadian word meaning "to flourish, prosper."[17] If that is correct, the phrase "I have learned by experience/divination" becomes "I have become rich." The basis of Laban's observation remains uncertain—either experience, enchantments, or the simple fact of his increased wealth. His conclusion remains unaffected—he knows that his vastly increased wealth was due to Yahweh's blessing him on Jacob's behalf.

Once before, Laban had taken advantage of Jacob's humble integrity by asking Jacob to set his own terms for wages. Now, begging Jacob to continue working for him, Laban again offers to let Jacob name his own wages (Gen. 30:28).

Jacob does not immediately agree to stay. First, he restates what Laban has said was the basis of his desire to have Jacob tend his animals. He reminds Laban that he has been personally responsible for the care of Laban's livestock. Furthermore, when Jacob arrived at Laban's home, Laban's property was meager. It was under Jacob's careful management that his property became abundant. The one factor that had changed in propelling Laban from "rags to riches" was Jacob's involvement. Nevertheless, Jacob acknowledges that all this blessing had come from the Lord. Jacob then says that he has to provide for his own household, with the implied reminder of his initial demand that Laban admit he was finished and let him leave (Gen. 30:30).

A salesman who doesn't want a potential buyer to think about alternatives will try to close the sale with lines like "What will you give me?" or "Make me an offer." Similarly, Laban still fails to acknowledge Jacob's right to leave. He tries to close the deal, asking, "What shall I give thee?"

Jacob could have named wages so high that Laban would have changed his mind and let him leave. Perhaps if he had heard from home that it was safe to return, he would have done so. However, Jacob's parents had ordered him to stay until someone called for him. If Laban is willing to pay him for his labor, Jacob would name reasonable wages.

Demonstrating a persistent bias against Jacob, some accuse Jacob of naming wages that would allow him to manipulate the system and take advantage of Laban for personal gain.[18] We must not forget that Laban continues to treat Abraham's grandson and his own son-in-law as a common hired servant. The honorable action would have been to make Jacob a partner and give him a substantial portion of the property Laban had acquired under Jacob's management. Laban had gained far more than any bride-price he might have legitimately expected for his daughters. Abraham had shown much greater generosity toward his nephew Lot than Laban ever extended to his nephew and son-in-law Jacob.

Jacob actually names wages that are amazingly generous to Laban. To Laban's question, "What shall I give thee?" Jacob replied, "Thou shalt not give me anything" (Gen. 30:31). Reminiscent of Abraham's words to the king of Sodom (Gen. 14:21–23), Jacob trusts God to provide for him through his management of Laban's flocks and herds. He will take nothing from Laban's existing stock. Jacob then names the only wages he wants for his labor—he would keep any cattle, sheep, or goats that were unusually marked. Any new speckled or spotted calves, brown lambs, or spotted or speckled kids would be Jacob's. Furthermore, to assure Laban that Jacob is not intentionally breeding such stock, Jacob will first cull the flocks and herds of all such animals and keep them from interbreeding with the other animals. In fact, those animals would be under Laban's care, and their offspring would not be included in the deal. That is, Jacob would remove "today" (Gen. 30:32) all such animals, and his wages would be only those similarly marked animals born to the flocks and herds "in time to come," literally "tomorrow" (Gen. 30:33). Jacob says that his "righteousness," or his "integrity," would be evident in that his animals would be identifiable by their markings whenever Laban wanted to inspect the flocks and herds (Gen. 30:33). Jacob and Laban both know that herds of cattle and flocks of goats made up exclusively of solid colored animals will produce predominantly solid colored calves and kids and that a flock of solid white sheep will only rarely produce a brown one.

Jacob has named wages that "at most . . . would amount to twenty percent of the flocks"[19]—far from an equal partnership even in "profit sharing," and barely a decent wage. Little wonder that Laban immediately accepted Jacob's offer. Laban's natural bent to deceive and manipulate does not allow him to trust Jacob to properly cull the animals and keep them separate. In a move that is highly insulting, Laban insists on culling the flocks and herds himself. He places the animals in his sons' care and has them pastured a three-day's journey from the pastures used by Jacob, presumably to make sure they couldn't possibly interbreed. Without further comment, Jacob sets to work tending "the rest of Laban's flocks" (Gen. 30:36).

The next few verses give a rather enigmatic description of Jacob's flock management techniques. It tells us what he does but not why he does it. First, he takes branches from three kinds of trees, peeling strips of bark from them so the white wood was exposed in stripes, and places the rods in the animals' watering troughs when they came to drink (Gen. 30:37–38). He did this especially when the females were "in heat," rendered "conceived" in the KJV (Gen. 30:41). The animals that mate when the rods are in the water produce a disproportionate number of striped or spotted or discolored offspring, increasing Jacob's own flocks. Jacob also put the rods in the water when "the stronger cattle" were in heat, not "when the cattle were feeble" (Gen. 30:41–42). This may mean that he concentrates on breeding the stronger animals before the rods and not the weaker, or it may refer to the summer and fall breeding seasons. The animals could bear twice a year. Many cultures considered animals conceived in the summer and born in the fall stronger than those conceived in the fall and born in the spring.[20] The result of Jacob's actions is that the stronger animals produce striped, spotted, or discolored offspring for Jacob and the weaker produce solid colored offspring for Laban. With each birthing cycle, Jacob separates those animals that are his from the rest of the animals.

Diverging interpretations of this section are based on differing assumptions concerning Jacob's rationale and understandings of verse 40, which says, "And Jacob did separate the lambs, and set the faces of the flocks toward the ringstraked, and all the brown in the flock of Laban; and he put his own flocks by themselves, and put them not unto Laban's cattle."

Most commentators contend that Jacob was using striped rods to try to influence the animals in some way to produce striped offspring. The same commentators usually interpret verse 40 to mean that Jacob kept the monochrome flocks and herds facing the other animals so they would have a visual example of what kind of offspring they should have. Most of these interpreters attribute Jacob's actions to some kind of prescientific superstition or "sympathetic magic."[21] Keil actually claims some kind of scientific basis: "This artifice was founded upon a fact frequently noticed, particularly in the case of sheep, that whatever fixes their attention in copulation is marked upon the young."[22] If either suggestion is correct, the vision the Lord sends Jacob later is intended to correct his misunderstanding—to prove that he becomes rich by God's design, not through his own manipulation.

I think there is a better way to understand what is going on, although I admit I don't know any more than anyone else does about what Jacob is doing with the rods. I seriously doubt that after decades of highly successful management of many varieties of flocks and herds Jacob believes that he can induce them to have striped, spotted, or discolored offspring by having them look at striped wooden rods in their water or having them facing variegated flocks and herds as they graze. Such a notion strikes me as superstitious nonsense. Further, verse 40 does not say Jacob kept the variegated flocks in sight. It says that he kept the monochromatic animals facing Laban's flocks, which were three days away, and separated his own animals from Laban's. If anything, Jacob wanted the monochromatic flock to be "reminded" whose they were, while keeping all the striped, spotted, and discolored animals out of their sight.

Additionally, an important point is almost always missed. We find later that over the course of several breeding seasons Laban changes Jacob's wages repeatedly (Gen. 31:7). As Laban observes the growth of Jacob's flocks, he tries to limit Jacob's success by allowing him to claim only the spotted or only the striped. Yet nowhere is there any indication that Jacob ever changed his method of livestock management. That fact alone seems to disprove the theory that Jacob was trying to manipulate the animals into bearing offspring that looked like striped poles. There is no evidence that putting striped poles in their water could have any affect on the genetic combinations that would determine coloration of the animals' coats.

The best suggestion I've found comes from Jewish commentator Nahum Sarna: "The three plants placed in the watering troughs, each known to contain toxic substances and used in the ancient world for medicinal purposes, could have had the effect of hastening the onset of the estrous cycle in the animals and so heightened their readiness to copulate."[23] That certainly seems consistent with the text, since that is precisely what happened when the rods were in the water. The fact that Jacob used this technique with the stronger animals and not the weaker proves only that he was doing his best to make sure the flocks and herds were as strong as possible. Jacob expected his methods to result in the greatest benefit to Laban, since he might normally expect about 80 percent of the young to belong to him.

For that matter, there is no evidence that this is a new technique. It may simply be the narrator's explanation of the practical means Jacob had been employing for years to build Laban's meager property into great wealth, the difference being that now God is seeing to it that the strongest and best of the animals would be Jacob's. If so, his later vision is God's way of explaining to Jacob how He had turned all Jacob's honest and well-intentioned efforts to Jacob's benefit.

Once again, a bias against Jacob has led to misunderstanding. Jacob is neither a trickster nor a thief. Those are merely the jealous accusations of dishonest men—Esau (Gen. 27:35–36) and Laban (Gen. 31:26). Unfortunately, most commentators have taken their word for it. However, one Jewish writer responds to such accusations by saying, "It has been claimed that Jacob used a trick which might be called a fraud in order to influence the births in his favor. . . . [But] nothing is more exclusively in God's power than life, breeding, and giving birth. . . . Even the old cattle breeder, Laban, never thinks of blaming Jacob for this. The story is an example of Jacob's trust in the promised divine aid and transforms a folkloristic superstition through higher religion."[24] Another simply says, "The entire action is thus attributed to divine intervention, not to Jacob's ingenuity."[25]

In truth, Jacob serves Laban honorably and well. For the first fourteen years, God makes Laban rich. Then, during the next six years, He makes Jacob rich without reducing Laban at all. The wording of the final verse is significant—"And the man increased exceedingly, and had much cattle, and maidservants, and menservants, and camels and asses." That should sound familiar. God said almost exactly the same thing about Abraham—"and he had sheep, and oxen, and he asses, and menservants, and maidservants, and she asses, and camels" (Gen. 12:16). He described His blessing of Isaac in very similar terms—"For he had possession of flocks, and possession of herds, and great store of servants" (Gen. 26:14).

> The summary recalls quite clearly God's blessing of both Abraham and Isaac and thus puts the events of this chapter within the larger context of the themes developed throughout the book, namely, God's promise of blessing and his faithfulness to that promise. Jacob's wise dealings with Laban then are an example of the way God caused him to prosper during this sojourn.[26]

Lessons

One of the lessons to be drawn from this chapter is to see the danger of a competitive spirit that escalates into bitter rivalry. Even otherwise fine people have been known to employ underhanded manipulation and ungodly methods to gain an advantage. Such a spirit is especially destructive within a family or within a church. Siblings turn against each other. Spouses bicker. Friends become rivals or even enemies. And the Lord's name is tarnished.

I've known many churches to use different kinds of contests in an attempt to boost attendance. "Bring a visitor to church" contests are bad enough, but "soul winning" contests border on blasphemy. Don't misunderstand—I'm all for bringing visitors to church and leading the lost to Christ. But when we turn bringing friends or neighbors to church into a contest, we move the focus from others to ourselves. We ought to invite them to church because God told us to, not because we want to win some sort of recognition or prize. Even worse, making "soul winning" a competitive sport or game is a travesty on several levels. For one thing, it trivializes the miracle of conversion by reducing the newborn believer to a statistical point earned toward a prize. More importantly, it presumes that you and I are capable of bringing a person to faith without the involvement of the Holy Spirit. If we award a prize for the one who "wins the most souls," or a penalty for the one who "wins the fewest," we must believe that "soul winning" is all about technique. The witness, called the "soul winner," is responsible for opening blind eyes and reviving dead spirits, and the glory that is God's alone is credited to men. The deliverance of a soul from condemnation to glory is no more due to our technique than Rachel's conception of Joseph was due to her mandrakes. Without God's involvement, manipulation will be unsuccessful. With God's involvement, manipulation is unnecessary.

Another important lesson from this chapter is that each of us must learn to be content with God's work in us and God's provision for us. It is often discontentedness that fuels covetous competition. Rachel and Leah both wanted what the other one had. Leah had children, but not her husband's love. Rachel had her husband's love, but no children. We have no right to demand from God what He has given to someone else. He has promised to work all things to our good (Rom. 8:28). We need to trust Him and learn to be content in whatever condition we find ourselves (Phil. 4:11).

One final lesson comes from Jacob's flock management. I believe that we should see this as an example of a man who applies himself diligently to his work for the good of his employer and trusts God to provide adequately for his own needs. That is how God explains the situation in the next chapter (Gen. 31:12). Jacob worked hard and with integrity, and God blessed him for it. May we, like Jacob, faithfully do our best while remaining content with the blessings God bestows.

7

Heading for Home

Gen. 31:1–55

think my brother-in-law was at least half serious when he told me that if he ever had to move again he'd rather just set fire to his house—it would be easier to replace everything than to pack it up and move it. I understand. I hate packing up my household and moving to a new home. I haven't had to do it in years and would be happy to never do it again. Whether moving across town or across the country, it's a daunting task. The prospect of packing everything in boxes, loading a truck, delivering it all to the right address, unloading the truck, unpacking the boxes, and reorganizing, reassembling, and repairing everything can be downright depressing. I've been told that the older you get the harder it is to move because you've accumulated more stuff. That's probably true, but moving when you are younger and have young children is no picnic. I don't even want to think about how hard it would be if I were old and settled and had young children.

In this chapter, Jacob will move and do it quickly. He's been living in one location for twenty years—about twice as long as I've lived at my current address. True, people in his day didn't have to deal with moving large, heavy appliances or pianos, but neither did they have trucks in which to haul their belongings. Everything had to be packed and loaded onto donkeys or camels. To complicate matters, Jacob has accumulated vast flocks of sheep and goats and herds of cattle, all of which will have to be driven along as they travel on foot to their destination, a mere five hundred miles southwest. Furthermore, he has four wives, which might be helpful if they work well as a team in organizing and packing but could be a real problem if they all have different opinions on how things should be packed and loaded. Oh, and when this chapter opens Jacob is ninety-seven years old and has at least twelve children, the oldest of whom is only twelve. Doesn't this sound like fun?

It has been twenty years since Jacob left his parents—and an angry brother—in Beer-sheba and journeyed to Haran. He had fulfilled his fourteen-year contract to Laban, and Laban had asked him to stay on, which he did for six more years. During those six years Jacob has seen his own flocks grow from nothing to great wealth, while Laban's flocks have grown at a slower pace and with generally weaker animals. The conversations recorded in Genesis 31 give us a little more information about events during those years, but the action of the chapter is driven by two things Jacob hears almost simultaneously after twenty years in Haran. First, he hears the jealous complaint of Laban's sons. Then he hears the encouraging words of the Lord.

Once again, we must not succumb to the temptation to interpret the situation through the eyes of the disgruntled ones dispossessed by God. Laban and his sons will charge Jacob with all sorts of misconduct. None of the accusations are true. The real culprit in this chapter is Laban, not Jacob.

Jacob's Escape (Gen. 31:1–21)

The God-ordained time for Jacob to leave Haran has come, and God lets Jacob know. He uses three means to communicate to Jacob and confirm for him that it is, indeed, time to go back to Canaan. First, a change in circumstances makes staying in Padan-aram difficult. Second, an unambiguous message from the Lord makes the solution clear. Third, the support of his family confirms Jacob's commitment to obey the Lord.

Laban and his sons have prospered during the fourteen years Jacob worked for wives and no wages. Paying him to stay on was the obvious course for Laban's continued prosperity, especially at the wages Jacob named. However, after six years, things were not going as expected. Jacob's flocks have multiplied while Laban's have not, and Laban's sons are jealous. Jacob overhears his brothers-in-law complaining that he has become rich by stealing their father's livestock (Gen. 31:1). Jacob's father-in-law is not as happy with him as he had been in the past (Gen. 31:2).

Despite the tense situation with his family/employers, Jacob continues to do his job. He knows Laban and his sons are unhappy with his prosperity, but there isn't much he can do about that. Jacob hesitates to break off his agreement with Laban, even though there was no time stipulation in the contract. Then the Lord speaks to Jacob directly. The message from God states succinctly, "Go back to the land of your fathers and your relatives, and I will be with you" (Gen. 31:3).

Jacob has known all along that his stay in Padan-aram was temporary—he has actually been there a lot longer than he had expected to stay. The place of real and perpetual blessing from God would be the land of Canaan, which God had promised to Abraham, to Isaac, and now to Jacob. Nevertheless, just as he had not left his family estate near Hebron until his father sent him away, Jacob has been unwilling to leave Laban's home without Laban's approval. That changed only because God gave him a direct order to go. We must not miss the point that "it is not fright or intuition that drives Jacob back to Canaan, but a directive from Yahweh."[1]

Organizing four wives and at least twelve children[2] ages twelve and younger would not be a move to be undertaken lightly. Preparing his many servants to organize his sheep, goats, cattle, donkeys, and camels (Gen. 30:43) would be a huge undertaking. To top it off, it has to be done quickly and in secret. This move will be impossible without everyone's cooperation. As a good husband, Jacob communicates first with Rachel and Leah. He calls for his wives to meet him in the field with the livestock (Gen. 31:4). This keeps the conversation private for two reasons. First, it prevents anyone from eavesdropping who might get word to Laban prematurely of Jacob's plan to leave. Second, it gives his wives liberty to react candidly—if there is an argument, Jacob won't have to worry about the children or the servants overhearing.

Jacob starts by contrasting the fickleness of their father and the faithfulness of God. Laban has turned from Jacob, but God has continued to be with him as He had been from the start (Gen. 31:5). God's "relationship with Jacob has neither changed nor deteriorated."[3] God had said, "I will be with you," and He has kept His word. Jacob then contrasts his own consistent work with Laban's inconsistent wages. Jacob has worked "with all my power" for Laban (Gen. 31:6), but Laban has "deceived me and changed my wages ten times" (Gen. 31:7). Despite that, Jacob has become wealthy only because God has not permitted Laban's cheating to hurt Jacob. Jacob had worked hard, but his prosperity was God's doing. Jacob even explains how Laban had changed his wages. The original contract called for all the spotted, striped, or discolored animals to be Jacob's. When Laban saw the animals producing a disproportionate number of such offspring, he cut Jacob's pay to only the spotted ones. When they started bearing spotted offspring, Laban paid Jacob only the striped. Then the animals produced only striped young (Gen. 31:8). The only possible explanation is that God was taking away animals that one might have expected to be Laban's and was giving them to Jacob by somehow causing them to produce young that fit into Jacob's wage category at any given time (Gen. 31:9).

Commentators and other readers accuse Jacob of hiding the truth from his wives by not telling them of his use of striped rods in the animals' watering troughs (Gen. 30:37–42). Apparently thinking him some kind of sorcerer inexplicably blessed by God,[4] they ignore that there is no implication in the text that Jacob changed his methods when his wages changed. Jacob is thought to have influenced the livestock to sometimes bear spotted young, other times striped ones, and still other times discolored ones on demand by placing in their water sticks from which he had peeled strips of bark. The notion is ludicrous, and the text never says that is what happened. The Bible actually says Jacob put those sticks in the water so the animals would mate (Gen. 30:38) and never makes a connection between the striped sticks and the markings of the young animals. The fact that the animals always seemed to bear offspring that fit whatever description Laban happened to be paying him at the time puzzled Jacob as much as it does us. Jacob has merely practiced good flock management. He sees no relationship between his methods and the markings of the animals' young.

Jacob then tells his wives about a dream in which the Lord revealed His involvement in the animals reproducing according to Jacob's wages (Gen. 31:10). Some suggest that Jacob is making this up or giving a spiritualized interpretation to a natural dream "wrought up by an excited imagination" to "place his dealings with Laban in the most favourable light for himself."[5] Such a negatively biased interpretation does real damage to the text, not to mention Jacob's reputation. It is much better to see this as a fuller explanation of the Lord's communication, summarized in verse 3 and given in more detail in verses 11–13. This is God's word to Jacob explaining how he had acquired so many animals.

God revealed through this dream that the male animals breeding with the females were striped, spotted, or discolored. How could this be so? There were no such animals in the flock Jacob tended. Only through the modern study of genetics have we learned something of the mechanics of how an unblemished animal could occasionally produce marked offspring. God alone could see the genetic code of the animals as they mated, and He manipulated the situation to produce animals marked according to the wages Laban happened to be paying Jacob each season.

This has profound implications for God's sovereign ability to control details of life. Over four hundred years later, Moses will complain to God that he is "slow of speech, and of a slow tongue" (Exod. 4:10*b*). God replies with a series of questions: "Who hath made man's mouth? Or who maketh the dumb, or deaf, or the seeing, or the blind? Have not I the Lord?" (Exod. 4:11). God does not flinch from taking full responsibility for children born with handicaps—He engineered our genetics and can manipulate the combinations as He sees fit and for His own purposes.

God not only explained how the flock had produced so many animals for Jacob but why. God did this as recompense for the way Laban had mistreated Jacob (Gen. 31:12) and affirms Himself that Jacob did not cheat Laban. Jacob served Laban faithfully even though Laban did his best to cheat Jacob. God then reminds Jacob that He had met Jacob at Bethel (Gen. 31:13). Jacob had worshiped Him there and made a vow before Him. God had also told Jacob not to make Haran his permanent home but to return to Canaan when God directed. The Lord had promised to be with him on his journey and to bring him safely back. The time has come for Jacob to return.

Jacob may have been worried about how his wives would respond. Would they be willing to leave their father's household and their homeland? Would they be willing to admit their father's duplicity? As far as we can tell, this is the first time Jacob has commented on Laban's constant manipulation of his wages. He couldn't be sure they would not be angry with him for criticizing their father. He also says, "Your father hath deceived me" (Gen. 31:7), which they could have understood as a reminder that his marriage to Leah was not by choice. Nevertheless, he never brings that up directly, and he never suggests that Leah stay behind. She is his wife too. He has made a point of consulting both Rachel and Leah together concerning God's instructions to depart.

The sisters were so unified that their response is recorded as a single speech. Their father has denied them a dowry and an inheritance. He has treated them as foreigners and servants, providing nothing for them while living off wealth earned by their husband, at least part of which should have been theirs. They consider anything God has given Jacob as their due, and their children's due—God has exacted from their father what their father should have provided without compulsion (Gen. 31:14–17). With that said, they announce that they are prepared to support Jacob in anything God has told him to do.

Jacob needn't have worried. Rachel's and Leah's frustration with their father had apparently been simmering for years. Still, such enthusiastic support for a move was a demonstration of their faith. It takes a lot of confidence in God for anybody to leave steady employment and move a long distance away, and maybe even more for a wife to trust that the Lord has led her husband to make such a move. The last time a daughter of their clan had moved south, they had never seen her again, and may not have heard from her in nearly a hundred years. This move would represent a permanent departure from home and family.

With God's instructions and his wives' encouragement, Jacob doesn't bother going back to Laban to tell him he's leaving. There was no contract term to finish. There were not even any flocks to tend other than his own since Laban had collected his animals to have them sheared (Gen. 31:19). God had told Jacob it was time to leave at what may have been the only time of year during which he could do so without neglecting his obligations to Laban. The confluence of God's communication and of Jacob's circumstances was divinely directed. Jacob's relationship with Laban had disintegrated, through no fault of Jacob's. Jacob's job responsibilities had been suspended. Jacob's family was supportive. We should note that Jacob's reason for leaving is more spiritually motivated than his wives'. Rachel and Leah are concerned with material things, while Jacob wants to obey the unmistakable and nonnegotiable instructions from God.

The description of Jacob's departure is carefully worded to emphasize his integrity. None of his possessions have been swindled from Laban. Everything had been "gotten," literally "acquired" or "earned" (Gen. 31:18). When he leaves, he takes nothing that belongs to Laban. He takes his children, his wives, his livestock, his goods— all that is his (Gen. 31:18). This will be important a few days later when Laban accuses Jacob of taking things that belonged to him, giving the lie to his claim that these are my daughters, my children, and my livestock (Gen. 31:43). Twice using the word *fled*, and saying that Jacob "drove away" (Gen. 31:18, "carried away," KJV) all his livestock, the narrator emphasizes Jacob's haste in escaping before Laban can do something to prevent it. Jacob takes his family, his animals, and his goods across "the river" (presumably the Euphrates) and starts for the mountains of Gilead, about three hundred miles to the southwest (Gen. 31:20–21).

Unfortunately, Rachel is not as scrupulous as Jacob. She steals something that belongs to Laban—his household images (Gen. 31:19*b*). Apparently striking their tents, packing their goods, and organizing the family and animals for the trek to Canaan takes long enough that Rachel is able to get to her father's house in Haran and make off with his images while he is busy sheering his sheep. The narrator doesn't tell us why Rachel stole Laban's images. It's possible that Rachel was given to idolatry and wanted their protection on the journey to Canaan or while living in a distant land.[6] However, that seems unlikely for three reasons.

First, the narrator uses two different words to describe what Rachel took: *teraphim* and *elohim*. The first, translated "images" (Gen. 31:19, 34), emphasizes their form—they were statuettes. This is the word used when the narrator is describing what Rachel takes and what she hides. The second, translated "gods" (Gen. 31:30), emphasizes their superstitious significance and is used by Laban to describe what he is missing. By using the terms this way, the narrator seems to imply that Rachel takes them for some reason other than religion. Related to this is the fact that she hid them in the cloth padding of her saddle, upon which she sat during her menstrual period (Gen. 31:35). Since idolaters would have considered that a defilement of their gods, it is difficult to imagine Rachel's doing such a thing to an object of worship so important to her that she would steal it from her father. To Rachel, they are images; but to Laban, they are gods.

Second, such gods were usually thought by their worshipers to have power that was restricted geographically. Generally, ancient polytheistic cultures did not believe that a god of one territory or region could exercise power or authority in another. In fact, they often believed that transporting an image to a foreign region subjected it to the gods of that region. For instance, the Philistines of Eli's day took the captured ark of the covenant to the temple of Dagon, believing they were forcing Israel's god into subjection to theirs (1 Sam. 5:2). If there was any latent superstition involved in Rachel's taking Laban's images, it was probably to prevent their assisting him in pursuit of Jacob's family. She would have believed she was rendering them powerless to intervene, which might also explain the hiding place she chose.

My final objection to the idea that Rachel took the images as objects of worship is that she has shown no indication to date that she is involved in idolatry. There is no hint of her having invoked false gods during her years of barrenness, and when she finally conceived, she credited Yahweh for Joseph's birth (Gen. 30:23–24). She also joins Leah in attributing Jacob's wealth to his God and in encouraging Jacob to act on God's instructions.

But if she isn't worshiping them, why would Rachel steal Laban's images? She may have taken them in an attempt to subject them to the authority of Jacob's God so that Laban couldn't use them against Jacob if he pursued them. She may have taken them simply out of greed or spite. She may have taken them out of nostalgia, wanting mementos from home. It is even possible that she took them as title to an inheritance after Laban died since there is some historical evidence that the possessor of the household gods was the presumptive heir.[7]

While there is no evidence that Rachel worshiped idols, she still shouldn't have taken Laban's images. By stealing them she put Jacob's whole family at risk of God's judgment and Laban's wrath.

Laban's Pursuit (Gen. 31:22–42)

Six years previously Laban had removed all the spotted, striped, and discolored livestock from the flocks tended by Jacob. To prevent any possibility of Jacob's cheating him by intentionally breeding similar offspring, he had insulted Jacob's integrity further by placing them in his sons' care and pasturing them three days' journey from where Jacob tended Laban's main flocks and herds. "A day's journey" was about thirty miles for a traveler, while livestock would usually be driven or led no more than ten or fifteen miles in a day. Since it took three days for a messenger to reach Laban with word of Jacob's departure, it seems that Laban is still keeping the flocks at least ninety miles apart, and possibly much farther since a messenger could be expected to make much better time than a typical traveler. After hearing that Jacob had fled, Laban organized "his brethren"—a broad term for kinsmen or even countrymen—and pursued him. It took him seven days to catch up (Gen. 31:22–23).

Either Jacob had pushed his animals to have reached the mountains of Gilead in ten days, or there was a time lag not mentioned by the narrator between Laban's receiving word of Jacob's departure and his setting out to catch him. It could easily have taken a couple of days or more to finish the sheep sheering, to arrange for the care of his livestock, and to organize his "posse." Regardless, Laban traveled quickly, covering the three hundred miles or so to the mountains of Gilead in only seven days. By mentioning the time and the location of Laban's confrontation of Jacob, the narrator indicates the urgency with which Jacob "fled" and Laban "pursued."

I suspect that for seven days Laban mentally rehearsed what he would say and/or do to Jacob when he caught him. Why, then, is his speech so anemic and even incoherent when he finally talks? The night before Laban overtook Jacob, God spoke to Laban in a dream (Gen. 31:24). Unlike His messages to Jacob, this was not a promise of blessing or protection. It was a warning similar to the dream He sent to Abimelech, the Philistine king who had taken Sarah from Abraham. The primary difference between the two messages is that in Abimelech's case God said that He knew Abimelech had taken Sarah "in the integrity of thy heart" (Gen. 20:6) before telling him that if he didn't return her unharmed he and all his would die (Gen. 20:7). God warned Laban not to speak to Jacob anything "from good to bad" (Gen. 31:24b, Hebrew). That does not mean that Laban was forbidden to speak to Jacob at all but that he must not say anything "good" that might entice him to return to Padan-aram or anything "bad" as a reproach for leaving. Whatever Laban had planned to say, he improvised an impromptu, hypocritical, contradictory, and pompous oration for the sake of his relatives who are his audience.

Laban accuses Jacob of leaving suddenly and unannounced so he could take away "my daughters, as captives taken with the sword" (Gen. 31:26). He is accusing Jacob of "fraud, breach of trust, and kidnapping."[8] Laban neglects to mention that he had effectively sold Rachel and Leah to Jacob in exchange for fourteen years of free labor. Next, he says that by leaving in secret Jacob has denied Laban the joy of a festive send-off and the privilege of kissing his "sons[9] and daughters" good-bye (Gen. 31:27–28). In verse 26, Laban presents himself as a vengeful father out to rescue his children from their captor. In verses 27–28 he claims to be an aggrieved but kind father who wanted to throw a party for his children before they have to leave. In verse 29 Laban reverts to the vengeful man, claiming that it was only the protection of Jacob's God that kept him from exercising his ability and authority to "do you hurt." The rendering in the KJV obscures Laban's use of the plural here. Rather than threatening Jacob alone, Laban is now threatening to "harm every one of you" (NIV).

If Jacob had really taken Laban's daughters as prisoners, why would Laban want to celebrate? If he wanted to celebrate, why would he have pursued with an armed band? If he really wanted to give them a loving send-off, why would he now threaten great harm to all of them for having left? Laban is babbling incoherently, stringing contradictory accusations together that must have left his audience completely baffled.

At this point, Laban changes the subject. He suggests first that Jacob left because he had been longing to return to his father's house (Gen. 31:30). Jacob has been with Laban for twenty years, and as far as we know, he has mentioned a desire to go home only once—six years previously. At that time, Laban prevailed upon him to stay. Jacob has for years had ample reason to leave, but he stayed on the job until God told him to go.

Laban then accuses Jacob of stealing "my gods" (Gen. 31:30b). Epp suggests that Laban knew they were missing because he had gone "to inquire of them immediately on learning that Jacob had fled."[10] Laban has finally brought up his only legitimate complaint, since his "gods" were the only things missing that were really his. Laban's problem is that he misidentifies the culprit. Jacob had no interest in Laban's gods, had no reason to take them, and knew nothing of the theft.

Jacob gives a reasonable response to Laban's nonsensical tirade. He explains that he left the way he did because he was afraid that Laban would try to "take by force thy daughters from me" (Gen. 31:32). The validity of that fear would have been patently obvious to everyone present since Laban's posturing and accusations indicate that he had that in mind. Jacob goes on to pronounce the penalty of death upon anyone in his company found with Laban's "gods"[11] (Gen. 31:32). Even more significantly, Jacob tells Laban to lay claim to anything he finds that belongs to him. Jacob calls upon all present to witness Laban's search and any property he claims. Emphasizing his own familial relationship to Laban, he refers to the witnesses collectively as "our brethren."

Probably fuming and furious at having been upstaged, Laban starts the search in Jacob's tent. Whether or not he thought that the most likely place to look, it was certainly the place he wanted to find his "gods" so he could make Jacob look bad and maybe even take his life. Finding nothing that belonged to him, Laban proceeds to Leah's tent, to the tents of Bilhah and Zilpah, and finally to Rachel's. At this point the narrator tells us that Rachel has hidden the images she has taken in her camel's "furniture," or saddle (Gen. 31:34). Probably in an effort to placate her father with her deference, she speaks respectfully and asks his forgiveness for not getting up, explaining that she is having her menstrual cycle (Gen. 31:35). Some commentators suggest that she lied, others that we cannot know whether she lied; but I suspect she was telling the truth and used it as a cover. Jacob would probably have known if it were not true and would have become immediately suspicious had he heard her excuse.

Other than Rachel's saddle, Laban searches everywhere and can't find the images. There is a subtle humor employed in this account. "The ancient reader would not miss the sarcasm in this story, for here is a new crime—'godnapping'!"[12] Who can read this without asking, "Can someone steal gods?" What kind of power can be wielded by a god who can be abducted, imprisoned in cloths, and hidden in a saddle? What help can be provided by a god who must be rescued from the hands of a burgling woman? What allegiance is owed to a god who can't be found by someone diligently seeking for it and who can be hidden from the seeker by someone's sitting on the god? Contrast Laban's impotent, helpless "gods" with what the Lord God says about Himself in Deuteronomy 4:29—"But if from thence thou shalt seek the Lord thy God, thou shalt find him, if thou seek him with all thy heart and with all thy soul."

Jacob is justifiably furious with Laban. Remember that he is still speaking as if in court before witnesses. He gives what could be thought of as his summation speech. Jacob's plea before them is similar to that of David before Jonathan as he wonders why Saul wants to kill him (1 Sam. 20:1). Jacob asks, "What is my crime? What is my offense that has caused you to pursue me so relentlessly?" (Gen. 31:36). Jacob then challenges Laban to present before these witnesses anything of Laban's that he found among "all my stuff" (Gen. 31:37). Jacob still wants a verdict—he knows he will be vindicated.

Earlier, Jacob had called on all present as impartial witnesses, referring to them as "our brethren." Now Jacob acknowledges a widening rift between his household and Laban's, and refers to the witnesses as two separate groups: "my brethren" and "thy brethren" (Gen. 31:37). His reference here and again in verse 46 to Jacob's "brethren" may be a figurative way of speaking of his sons and servants. However, his firstborn son, Reuben, is no more than twelve or thirteen years old, and he calls on "his brethren" to erect a stone monument, something his sons might not have been able to do.

Either he has been joined at Mount Gilead by other sons of Isaac and Rebekah (cf. Gen. 27:29, 37), or some of the relatives who had come with Laban have already indicated that they were taking Jacob's side in this dispute.

Jacob continues his summation by telling everyone present about his twenty years' service to Laban. In describing his care for Laban's sheep, he uses the word *ewes* for the first time (Gen. 31:38). This word is the plural form of a word that shows up often in this narrative in the singular, transliterated rather than translated, as Rachel. He had "indeed cared for Laban's 'Rachels,' all his 'rachels' and his one 'Rachel.'"[13] Jacob's care for Laban's flock has been so attentive that Laban's female animals never miscarried. Also, unlike most shepherds, Jacob has not lived off Laban's flocks. As protector of Laban's flocks, Jacob has guarded them from wild beasts (Gen. 31:39). No shepherd could guarantee that no predator would ever attack the flock and kill an occasional animal. Generally, an alert shepherd was expected to kill or chase away the wild beast and recover the carcass of the animal from his flock. If he then presented the carcass to the flock's owner as evidence of his having kept the beast from eating it, he had done all that was expected of him. Jacob had gone well beyond the call of duty by making good any loss from Laban's flock, never presenting him with torn carcasses. He had either replaced or paid for any animal killed while under his care. Further, he had sacrificed personal comfort by caring for Laban's animals in all weather and conditions, day and night (Gen. 31:40). He had expended fourteen years of such labor in exchange for Laban's two daughters and six for the livestock. During those six years, Laban had changed Jacob's wages ten times (Gen. 31:41).

Jacob concludes by acknowledging his faith in his God, not Laban's "gods." Leaving no question about his religious loyalties, Jacob proclaims that had it not been for the intervention of "the God of my father, the God of Abraham, and the fear of Isaac," Laban would surely have sent Jacob away with nothing (Gen. 31:42). God's rebuke of Laban the night before had been to recompense Jacob for his affliction and his labor. The fact that this summation is made before witnesses, many of whom were hostile, and that Laban has no rebuttal for the charges puts to rest any doubts as to the truth of Jacob's case.

A Covenant of Separation (Gen. 31:43–55)

Laban just won't quit posturing for his companions. In a pathetic attempt to save face, he makes a statement that is transparently false. Laban claims that he didn't have to find anything in particular among Jacob's stuff that belonged to him—everything was his (Gen. 31:43). Unwilling to admit he was wrong, Laban tries to appear gracious. Claiming that he is really concerned only for his daughters' and grandchildren's welfare, and making it appear that he doesn't trust Jacob to take care of them without supervision, Laban demands that Jacob enter into a covenantal oath with him (Gen. 31:44). Everyone who was there knew that Laban had trusted Jacob with both daughters as wives, trusted him to work out a seven-year contract after the weddings, acknowledged that God's blessing of Jacob had made Laban rich, trusted Jacob to name his own wages and tend his flocks for another six years, and is now willing to turn over everything in Jacob's possession that Laban claims is his if Jacob will give his word. The irony of Laban's saying that he did not trust Jacob seems to have been lost on Laban.

Without a word to Laban, Jacob starts building a monument to solemnize the oath he would make with Laban. Instructing "his brethren" to gather stones, Jacob completes the monument and apparently offers a sacrifice on it (Gen. 31:45–46). Typically, "cutting a covenant" involved animal sacrifice followed by a meal in which the meat from the sacrifice is eaten by the participants in the covenant. While no sacrifice is mentioned, the fact that they ate upon the monument after its erection assumes that a sacrifice had been offered. In the first textual indication of a language difference between Laban and Jacob, Laban names the monument "The Heap of Witness" in Aramaic/Syriac—*Jegar-sahadutha*—while Jacob translates the same name into Hebrew—*Galeed* (Gen. 31:47).

Laban then makes a grandiose speech that finally reveals why he wanted this covenant. In a tacit admission that Jacob had no interest in Laban's gods, Laban invokes the name of Jacob's God, Yahweh, to serve as witness between himself and Jacob. Laban says that Jacob's God will be watching how Jacob treats "my daughters" (Gen. 31:48–50). Laban still can't bring himself to call them "your wives" even though they've been married for thirteen years. He says he is concerned that Jacob might "afflict my daughters" or "take other wives beside my daughters." What an absurd suggestion! The only person in this narrative to have afflicted Laban's daughters was Laban himself. The only reason Jacob had any wives other than Rachel had begun with the manipulation of Laban. Jacob had lived for over seventy years in Canaan without taking a wife from among the Canaanites. He had traveled five hundred miles to Padan-aram to marry Laban's daughter (singular) for religious reasons and had worked for many years for the privilege. There was no reason to suggest Jacob might get back to Canaan at nearly one hundred years of age and decide that he should marry another wife. Not even Laban could have believed this nonsense. Of course, it was an oath Jacob could make easily because he had no intention of behaving the way Laban feared he might.

Laban then refers to the monument and pillar, "which I have cast between me and thee" (Gen. 31:51), as if Jacob had not been the one to build them. He says he wants them to stand as monuments to their separation. Laban would not pass beyond the monument to the southwest for the purpose of harming Jacob, and Jacob would not pass beyond it to the northeast for the purpose of harming Laban. Laban's words are often quoted as a covenant of fellowship when believers are separated for a time: "The Lord watch between me and thee, when we are absent one from another" (Gen. 31:49). Such a use of Laban's oath gives his words an application far different from what Laban intended. The monument was not to be a point of union but a barricade of separation, and God was to be the guardian making sure neither of them crossed the line to contact the other.

Proving that he really does not know Jacob's God, Laban finishes his ridiculous speech by invoking "the God of Abraham, and the God of Nahor, the God of their father" to "judge between us" (Gen. 31:53). Laban's use of the word Elohim here for "God" could just as well have been translated "gods." Abraham and Nahor were sons of Terah (Gen. 11:26), and Laban knows they did not all serve the same God/gods. Jacob is a descendent of Abraham, and Laban is a descendent of Nahor. Abraham left the region where Laban lived because he was following the instructions of the Lord God. Nahor probably believed in the same God, which would explain why Abraham and Isaac were concerned that their sons marry wives from Nahor's descendents. It is possible, though, that Nahor's gods were the same as Laban's, or at least that Laban thinks they are. Regardless, Joshua 24:2 specifically tells us that Abraham's father, Terah, "served other gods." At best, Laban's view is syncretistic. He either sees all "gods" as essentially the same, or he wants all the gods honored within his family heritage to be invoked as witnesses.

Jacob is not willing to merely second Laban's oath. He needs more clarity in his identification of the God in Whose name he swears, so he vows "by the fear of his father Isaac" (Gen. 31:53b). There is no way Laban could have misunderstood. Jacob has refused to acknowledge Laban's "gods" as divine. Laban might think that Abraham had merely added a new god to his pantheon when he moved to Canaan and still honored the "old gods" that their fathers had served. Isaac, however, had never been exposed to the false gods of Terah and Laban. By swearing in the name of the only God ever revered by Isaac, Jacob avoids any possible confusion and affirms his faith in God, and God alone.[14]

After the oaths are pronounced, Jacob offers sacrifices and calls for his brethren to join him in a meal (Gen. 31:54). This may be the same meal mentioned in verse 46, or it may have been another at the end of the day. After eating, they sleep. In the morning, before departing, Laban makes one final pompous gesture: kissing his sons and daughters, he "blessed them" (Gen. 31:55). He then leaves for home and is never again mentioned in Scripture.

Lessons

Laban provides a good example of the nominal believer that can be found in many churches today. Henry Morris provides an excellent summation of Laban's life and character:

> Laban is an unfortunate example of a worldly, covetous man, one who knows about the true God and to whom a thorough witness has been given. He had seen the reality of God in the life of Jacob, along with the power of God in His blessing and protection of Jacob. He himself had even enjoyed many of the blessings of God through his relationship to Jacob. Nevertheless, he continued in idolatry and covetousness, seeking material gain for himself to the exclusion of all other considerations. Rather than seeking to follow the truth of God's plan as witnessed by Jacob, he merely resented and coveted the blessing of God on Jacob. He finally ended up with neither. His life constitutes a sober warning to a great host of semireligious but fundamentally self-worshiping and self-seeking men and women today.[15]

Laban was superficially religious but essentially self-centered and materialistic. We would do well to heed the implied warning of the text.

Jacob, on the other hand, provides an example of humble patience, waiting on God's timing for the fulfillment of His promise. God had promised to be with Jacob while he was away from home and to bring him back to the land He had promised Abraham, Isaac, and Jacob. Living and working for Laban under the conditions in which Jacob served would have been virtually unbearable, but Jacob never complains. He remains quietly contented until God finally tells him to leave.

Jacob also demonstrates faithful obedience when God tells him to move. His mother had told him to stay in Padan-aram until she sent for him. Not having heard from her, Jacob still has reason to fear a confrontation with Esau. Yet for Jacob God's command overrules all other considerations. He wastes no time organizing his family and setting out. When confronted by Laban, he doesn't back down. Even when given the opportunity to resolve the conflict diplomatically by agreeing with Laban's proposed pledge in the name of several gods, Jacob makes a courageous affirmation of his faith in the one true God. He did not want a fight with his father-in-law, but he was unwilling to compromise his faith.

Like Jacob, we need to learn to trust God to guide us through the circumstances of life. Sometimes He wants us to stay put in a difficult situation longer than we want to stay. Other times He wants us to pack up and move. Both have their challenges, and both their blessings. May each of us be willing to "trust in the Lord with all thine heart, and lean not unto thine own understanding. In all thy ways acknowledge him, and he shall direct thy paths" (Prov. 3:5–6).

8

Wrestling with God

Gen. 32:1–32

fter spending several years as a music teacher and part-time minister of music, the Lord led me to take a full-time position at another church as minister of music and assistant pastor. I had been there for less than two years when I had an unexpected visitor one evening. He had evidence that the pastor had been immoral, and he asked me what to do. He had no idea the difficulty of the position in which he had put me by involving me in the matter. I would have preferred to know nothing about the situation and to have stayed completely separate from its resolution; but if the allegation were true, it would need to be addressed. I told him that I did not want to know the details but that he should go to the deacon chairman with his information. If the chairman thought the allegation seemed genuine, he would have to confront the pastor with the charge and give him an opportunity to defend himself. The man who had brought the charge against the pastor should be prepared to participate in the confrontation because the deacons owed it to the pastor to face his accuser.

Two days later, the board met with the pastor and four accusers, who testified to the pastor's sins. Initially, the pastor confessed and resigned in writing. Just four days later, he changed his mind. Hand-delivering letters to each member of the board, he rescinded his confession and demanded a hearing before the whole church. That hearing was scheduled for Sunday evening two weeks later, as stipulated by the church constitution. All witnesses, including the pastor, were notified by registered letter that they were expected to attend. The witnesses would be expected to testify, and the pastor would be expected to present his rebuttal and defense. Any witnesses who failed to attend would be presumed to have withdrawn their charges. If the pastor failed to attend, it would be presumed that he had no defense to offer. Because of the seriousness of the charges, the pastor's leadership role was officially suspended pending resolution of the matter, and I was appointed to stand in as temporary preacher/leader.

As you might imagine, the closer we drew to the date of the hearing, the more intensely I felt the need to pray. The Saturday night before the meeting I was so distressed that I couldn't rest. Shortly before midnight, I went to the church, going to the platform in the auditorium to pray, but I couldn't sit still. I moved up and down the aisles, pausing at the end of each pew. As I visualized the people who typically sat in each row, I prayed for them by name, asking the Lord to give each one discernment to determine the truth, wisdom to know what to do, and the courage to do whatever was necessary. As I reached the last row, I suddenly felt a sense of peace. I received no verbal message from the Lord but was impressed with a sense that the Lord was in control of the situation. I knew that the next day would be difficult, and the aftermath could be even harder, but I had been reminded that the Lord was still on His throne and that He still loved us. I was able to go home and get a few hours of sleep.

The next day was tough. The hearing began as scheduled, with all the witnesses present, but the pastor didn't show up. He'd actually left the country and didn't return until the next week. The hearing proceeded in his absence. After three hours examining the witnesses, the congregation unanimously found the pastor guilty and dismissed him. If anything, the following months were even harder than the weeks leading up to it as the church dealt with the aftermath of the scandal. I still look back on those months as one of the worst experiences of my life.

Ironically, though, that period was also one of the best experiences of my life. While it wasn't nearly as dramatic or important as what happens to Jacob in this chapter, I learned something about what it means to "wrestle with God" in prayer when anticipating a difficult confrontation. It was also a significant transition in my life as the Lord used the incident to propel me into pastoral ministry. A few months after the dust settled, the church voted to call me as their pastor—a ministry I fulfilled for nearly seven years before the Lord led my family to my current pastorate.

Jacob's two main adversaries have been his twin brother, Esau, and Laban, his uncle and father-in-law. Jacob has just survived Laban's confrontation. He is probably relieved to consecrate the event with a sacrifice to seal a covenant of separation between Laban and himself. One antagonist has been removed from the scene. His other nemesis, Esau, remains to be faced.

Encounter with Angels (Gen. 32:1–2)

For the second time in his life, Jacob sees angels (Gen. 32:1). The first had been at Bethel when he was leaving Canaan to go to Laban. Now he encounters them upon his return to Canaan. While the word *angels* means "messengers," on neither occasion did the angels speak to Jacob. In the first instance, Jacob was asleep and dreamed of angels who were ascending and descending a ladder that reached from heaven to earth. That night, the Lord spoke to him. Jacob learned that the angels are servants of God and that they are actively involved in the affairs of men. This occasion is different. Jacob is awake, in the light of day, and sees the angels as a military encampment. This time, there is no verbal message.

What could this mean? Jacob is not terrified of the angels, so he doesn't see them as a threat. They are there to protect him, not to harm him. They are revealed to encourage him. When he sees them, Jacob cries out, "This is God's army!" He names the place Mahanaim, which means "two camps, hosts, or armies" (Gen. 32:2). In so naming the location, Jacob declares his confidence that his protection does not depend upon his own small "host." He is also being guarded by "God's infinitely more numerous and powerful host."[1]

The angelic host appears at this time so that Jacob will understand that in all his negotiations with Laban the angels had been present but not visible. Jacob had been protected from Laban both by the word of the Lord and by the presence of "God's army." Their presence confirms that God will keep Jacob safe in his inevitable encounter with Esau. Jacob's own servants will be ill-equipped to defend Jacob's family and property if Esau brings a force of any size against him. The presence of the angels proves that the host of God has "joined his host as a safeguard" signaling "the help of God for the approaching conflict with Esau . . . and a fresh pledge of the promise, 'I will bring thee back to the land.'"[2] Very few people in Scripture were ever given such visible evidence of God's protection.

Jacob's fear of Esau is reasonable, but his confidence in the Lord is greater. He continues on his way, making sure that this confrontation with Esau will happen quickly. He does not run away, hide, or in any way try to avoid Esau, but neither does he want to provoke him.

Emissaries to Esau (Gen. 32:3–8)

Jacob was so encouraged by his meeting with God's hosts of *angels* that he sends his own *messengers* to Esau. The narrator uses the same Hebrew word in both cases to tie the events together (Gen. 32:1, 3). In the two decades of Jacob's absence, Esau has moved southward from his parents' encampment at Beer-sheba to the land of Seir, the country of Edom. Both of those place names remind us of the early stories about Esau. Seir is associated with his description as a hairy man (*se'ar* in Genesis 25:25 and *se'ir* in 27:11) and Edom is associated with his being identified with the color red, referring to his hair or complexion (*adomi* in Genesis 25:25) and to the red lentil soup for which he sold his birthright (*'adom* in Genesis 25:30).[3]

The text doesn't say whether Jacob knew Esau was living in Seir in Edom or if he simply sent his servants to Esau and that is where they found him. Regular trade between Egypt and Syria would have provided a news grapevine that may have kept Jacob informed of the general condition of his family's affairs.

The narrator also doesn't tell us why Esau has moved away from home. We know that before Jacob's departure Esau had a lifelong pattern of disinterest in his family's business and worship. When Jacob left, Esau married another wife from the line of Ishmael, who lived to the south, which may explain his move in that direction. It seems evident that even though Jacob was gone, Esau still demonstrated no interest in his family's estate. True, he would not inherit the birthright, but as much as a third would still be his.[4] Building the estate would have been in his best interest. Nevertheless, Esau seems to have struck out on his own. After Isaac's potentially disastrous attempt to hijack God's program and transfer it to Esau, Isaac apparently never again tried to give the property or blessing to Esau. Isaac's foolish decision to bless Esau, which had driven Rebekah and Jacob to deceive him and widened the rift between the brothers, may well have broken the tenuous link between Isaac and Esau maintained by Isaac's love for Esau's venison.[5]

Unlike the angels that Jacob saw, Jacob's messengers have something to say. The wording of Jacob's message to Esau is significant. He tells them to address Esau as "my lord" and to describe Jacob as "your servant" (Gen. 32:4). In part, this demonstration of humility is intended to pacify Esau's anger. It is also an acknowledgment of Esau's sociopolitical superiority. Esau is still the elder brother. Even though Jacob had been promised sovereignty over his brethren, he wants Esau to know that he is not moving into the region to enforce his will. He hopes Esau will view his return as a reunion, not an invasion.

Jacob also tells his servants to mention Jacob's prosperity in brief, general terms (Gen. 32:5). Without making too much of his wealth, he is telling Esau that his return will in no way diminish Esau's property or expectation of inheritance. Jacob has sufficient to support himself. However, Jacob's words couch a subtle reminder of the distinction between Jacob and Esau regarding the promised blessing. Unlike Esau, Jacob has obeyed his parents and stayed with his uncle Laban since he left, and during those years God has prospered him (Gen. 32:4*b*). To leave that out would have been less than forthright. To emphasize it might have been provocative. Jacob is not hiding the fact of his obedience and God's blessing, but neither is he beating Esau over the head with it.

The message from Jacob closes with the purpose of this communication. Again addressing Esau as "my lord," Jacob says that he hopes he will "find grace in thy sight" (Gen. 32:5). Jacob wants reconciliation with Esau, not conflict, and he is approaching him as a supplicant to a superior.

Most commentators seem to think that this was a coward's last ditch attempt at reconciliation. Again, that is an unnecessarily negative assumption. Rather, it was at worst "a diplomatic initiative aimed at softening Esau's anticipated hostility [by offering him] a munificent gift."[6] It might help if we consider the situation from Esau's perspective. Jacob could not approach in secret. Esau probably knows already that he is coming and that he has vast flocks and herds, a large family, and many servants with him. Esau well knows that he and Jacob were estranged when Jacob left. Esau has almost as much reason to believe that Jacob resents him and wishes to be rid of him so that he can inherit his blessing as Jacob has reason to fear Esau. Jacob never threatened Esau, but neither did Esau threaten to murder Jacob verbally. It was something he said "in his heart" (Gen. 27:41), and he may not have believed anyone else knew his thoughts. Jacob's emissaries announcing with humble words that he is coming in peace and that he hopes for reconciliation may well be designed as much to set Esau's mind at ease as it is to benefit Jacob.

The outlook for Jacob turns much worse when his servants return from meeting Esau with no message other than that he "cometh to meet thee, and four hundred men with him" (Gen. 32:6). It's probably significant that the messengers identified Esau as "thy brother" rather than "thy lord," but Jacob has no way to know why Esau has assembled 400 men to accompany him to meet them. Four hundred men could be a significant fighting force. Abraham had once mustered a force of 318 of his own servants and rescued the inhabitants of Sodom and Gomorrah taken captive by raiding bands under the command of five kings from Mesopotamia (Gen. 14:14). Esau's 400 men comprise a "host" far superior to any force Jacob might muster to meet it.

Jacob immediately assumes the worst, or at least prepares for it. It looks as if Esau is coming to attack him. He has no idea how much time he has before Esau arrives, but Esau and his 400 men could not be far behind Jacob's returning messengers. Jacob immediately adopts a survival strategy to minimize his losses if possible. Using a tactic common for caravan travelers facing marauders, he divides his animals and people into two companies and puts some distance between them (Gen. 32:7–8). He hopes that if Esau comes upon one company and destroys it, he will think he has wiped out Jacob's band and leave without finding the other group.

Some chide Jacob for not trusting the Lord. Various questions can be raised. Why is he worried after seeing the host of angels? Remember that there has been no communication from those angels. While he has now seen angels on two occasions, those events were separated by twenty years. He has never seen angels do anything that proves they would defend him from Esau's attack. He assumes they can and will but has no proof or promise of their aid. Isn't he demonstrating a lack of faith in the promise if he now thinks that Esau can kill him? It would be possible for God to fulfill His promise if only one of Jacob's sons survives an attack. The danger to Jacob and his family is real. The fact that Jacob immediately goes to prayer and invokes the promise indicates faith, not distrust. Why doesn't he pray first and wait for God to tell him what to do? Jacob has had no indication from the Lord that God would give him instructions in his day-to-day business. The danger is imminent. He is responsible for the safety of his people and property. He takes immediate, wise precautions, "after which he could pray in good faith, knowing that he had done all he could and the Lord would have to take over the rest of the way."[7]

Jacob's tactics are designed to protect his animals, his servants, and especially his family. Often overlooked is the fact that although he is terrified, Jacob does not organize an armed defense or launch any kind of preemptive strike. He has no intention of doing anything that would harm Esau. He casts himself on God's protection and Esau's mercy.

Entreaty for Deliverance (Gen. 32:9–12)

Having done all he can, Jacob turns to God. Both the similarities and contrasts between God's instructions to Abraham in Genesis 12:1–3 and of Jacob's prayer here are striking and intentional. In the former case, God told Abraham to leave his country and kindred. In this situation, God tells Jacob to return to his country and kindred. In the former, God promised to bless Abraham and make him a blessing. In this situation, God promises to "deal well" with Jacob. In both cases, the men obeyed without hesitation. When Abraham arrived in the land and found it difficult because of famine, he kept going and ended up selling his wife to Pharaoh to protect his life. When Jacob gets to the land and finds it difficult because of possible attack, he stays and prays. Whose actions provide the greater example of obedient faith? Not Abraham's.

As Jacob prays, he focuses on God as the God of his family, worshiped by Abraham and Isaac. He then points out that he is doing exactly what God told him to do—he left Haran to go back to his parent's home (Gen. 32:9). Rather than railing at God for leading him into danger, Jacob humbly admits that he is unworthy of "the least of all thy mercies, and of all the truth" that God had showed to "thy servant" (Gen. 32:10). The word rendered "unworthy" means "little" and describes "a person who is totally dependent on another for his welfare."[8] Jacob admits that he had nothing but his staff when he left that land to go to Haran, but now, having divided his flocks and herds, he has become "two bands."

Jacob then cries out for deliverance (Gen. 32:11–12). He confesses that he fears Esau may "smite" or "kill" him and his family.[9] If Esau were to do so, he would effectively invalidate God's promise. Jacob bases his plea for deliverance, then, on God's fidelity to His promise to multiply his descendents and cause him to prosper.

This is not the self-serving, petulant prayer of a sneaky manipulator. His prayer is based on God's word, and he asks for nothing God has not already promised. He humbly claims those promises on the basis of God's mercy, not his own merit, and expects God to do whatever is necessary to fulfill them. His prayer "is a fine pattern of prayer for believers under similar circumstances, when after doing all they know how to do, and trying as well as they know how to follow the Lord's guidance, they are still confronted with what seem to be insurmountable problems. Jacob 'reminded' God of His promises, thanked Him for His previous blessings and leading, acknowledged his own unworthiness, and then thrust himself on God for deliverance."[10]

Endowment for Esau (Gen. 32:13–21*a*)

It's easy to forget that all the events of this chapter happen during a single night, from the servants' return with word of Esau's approach to the dawn departure of Jacob's wrestling partner (which we will consider shortly). Having done what he can to protect his property and family and having made his plea before the Lord, Jacob decides that there is more that he can do to deflect or defuse Esau's wrath. He quickly assembles for Esau an extravagant gift of 580 animals, separates them into five groups by kind, and sends them toward Esau in waves. Having no time to select specific animals for this gift, he pulls out "that which came to his hand" (Gen. 32:13). The herdsmen are instructed to stagger their delivery times and with each delivery to tell Esau that the animals come as a gift from "thy servant Jacob" to "my lord Esau" (Gen. 32:18). They are also to say that Jacob is coming behind them. Jacob hopes that Esau's anger will be worn away by the time Jacob gets there. He has no intention of fleeing but neither does he want to fight.

I am mystified that so many commentators insist on treating even this part of Jacob's story negatively. Victor P. Hamilton describes Jacob as a coward: "Jacob hardly emerges in this event as the epitome of bravery. Always he is in the rear, behind something or somebody. . . . Jacob . . . would rather die than face his brother."[11] What would he have Jacob do? Pick up a sword and face him man to man? Consistent with his negative interpretation of almost everything concerning Jacob, John H. Sailhamer says, "A very familiar picture of Jacob emerges in this narrative. It is Jacob the planner and the schemer. As he had taken Esau's birthright and blessing, as he had taken the best of Laban's herds, so now he had a plan to pacify Esau."[12]

I've already explained what I believe to be the fallacies in the assumptions of wrongdoing here, but even if we were to stipulate that Sailhamer could be right about Jacob's character, just how is a plan to pacify Esau an example of scheming parallel to taking birthrights, blessings, and herds that did not belong to him?

Theodore H. Epp says, "Instead of trusting God alone, Jacob plotted how he could appease Esau by giving of his possessions. . . . Jacob lacked confidence in God to the extent that he actually distrusted God."[13] I wonder if Epp thinks Jacob should have just stood there and let God stop Esau. I simply don't understand how seeking to make peace in a case like this, without any instructions to do otherwise, is evidence of distrusting God.

Other possible explanations for Jacob's actions better fit what the text actually says. Even if his critics are correct in assuming that Jacob had been guilty of stealing Esau's birthright and blessing and taking Laban's flocks and herds, isn't it possible that Jacob has had a change of heart and in this case wants to make amends? Many centuries later the Lord Jesus would say,

> Therefore if thou bring thy gift to the altar, and there rememberest that thy brother hath aught against thee; leave there thy gift before the altar, and go thy way; first be reconciled to thy brother, and then come and offer thy gift. Agree with thine adversary quickly, whiles thou art in the way with him; lest at any time the adversary deliver thee to the judge, and the judge deliver thee to the officer, and thou be cast into prison. (Matt. 5:23–25)

Every word of Jacob's speech and every step he takes are consistent with a man who is remorseful for previous offenses and wants to make them right. Jacob's actions could be considered a perfect illustration of how one should act according to Jesus' later instructions.

It's also possible that I'm right in contending that Jacob has taken nothing that God hadn't expressly given to him, which I believe is the view most consistent with what God has to say about Jacob. It is supported here by the fact that for all his desire for reconciliation, Jacob offers no apology, admits no wrongdoing, and asks no forgiveness. Both the birthright and the blessing were rightfully Jacob's by God's decree before his birth and later confirmation. Further, Esau had despised the birthright and sold it to Jacob, and he had forfeited the blessing—his inappropriate and unapproved marriages and his "profane" lifestyle disqualified him from carrying on the line of the promised seed. The flocks and herds were Jacob's, despite being less than his contractually agreed salary due to Laban's manipulation of his wages, and were large by the express design of God.

Nevertheless, since Jacob has not heard from his mother that it was safe to come home, he has reason to fear that Esau still believes he has a legitimate grievance against Jacob. It's entirely possible that Jacob hoped to rescue Esau from great danger by appeasing his anger so that God would not have to call on His angels to defend Jacob in combat. Jacob's actions are those of the "poor in spirit" (Matt. 5:3) and of the "meek" (Matt. 5:5), and, above all, of the "peacemaker" (Matt. 5:9). Jacob is afraid because he refuses to defend himself, but he will do whatever he can to win his brother's heart.

The gift of flocks and herds was neither a bribe nor a diversion so that Jacob could escape. It was at least a demonstration of good will and a desire for reconciliation. For that matter, since there is no evidence of any established pattern or system for tithing by this time in history, this lavish gift may have been Jacob's way of offering a tenth of all God had given him while in Haran (cf. Gen. 28:22). Jacob should be applauded, not condemned, for presenting what was probably a peace offering to Esau and a thank offering to God.

Encounter with God (Gen. 32:21*b*–32)

This section is obviously one of the most important in the Jacob narratives. Still, it is aptly described as "enigmatic,"[14] full of "unanswered questions,"[15] and "one of the most difficult to understand in the Bible."[16] Several details are left unclear or unexplained. The movement of Jacob and his family, the purpose of Jacob's solitude, the identity of the wrestler, the point of the wrestling match, the nature of Jacob's injury, the meaning of the name change, and even the result of the encounter are all open to significant differences of interpretation.

Some question the reality of the event, thinking it only a metaphor for the inner turmoil of Jacob's spirit. That seems the least likely of the suggested interpretations. The concrete details involving gathering his family, crossing the Jabbok, and grappling with someone, along with the resultant injury leaving Jacob with a permanent limp, all argue for a literal understanding of whatever happened that night.

While commentators who treat this as a real event present views that vary in nuance, the majority are basically agreed in the overall outline of events. Jacob is trying to get away, to avoid a confrontation with Esau, when he is apprehended, wrestled to a stop, brought by injury into submission to God's will for him, and given a new name to signify the end of his life of fleshliness and the beginning of his life of spirituality.[17]

Among those who hold this outline of events there are variations in the explanation of the details. Some believe that by moving his family across the river without going himself, Jacob placed them between himself and Esau because he was willing to sacrifice them to Esau to save his own life. Others believe he was moving them to a place of safety for their protection. While the text says Jacob wrestled with "a man," some believe that the wrestler was an angel, based on Hosea 12:2–4. Others believe the wrestler was God, based on Genesis 32:30. Most believe that Jacob's injury involved the wrestler's having thrown his hip out of joint based on the reference to the "shrinking" of the "sinew" and Jacob's resultant lifelong limp. "Venerable Jewish tradition identifies this unique and cryptic term . . . with the sciatic nerve."[18] A less common view is that the injury was to his groin or testicles, since that it is more consistent with the description of "the hollow of his thigh" and that while there is no part of an animal's thigh or hip considered inedible by the Jews, eating the male genitals is forbidden. These details are interesting, and are not unimportant, but they cannot be allowed to distract us from the central questions raised by the event: Why is Jacob wrestling, and what is the result?

I believe the generally accepted interpretation of this event to be fatally flawed for three reasons. First, it assumes that Jacob is resisting the will of God despite the evidence that he has done exactly what God has told him to do every time he has heard from God. Second, it requires us to believe that at least on some level Jacob lost the wrestling match, that "when he contended with God, he utterly failed,"[19] despite the fact that God says Jacob "prevailed" (Gen. 32:28). Third, it gives a uniquely spiritual significance to Jacob's new name, despite the fact that in the future both names will be used interchangeably, with his birth name often being used in reference to his positive relationship with God (unlike what happened when Abram's name was changed to Abraham).

Here is what I think happened that night.

Having separated his livestock into two major encampments, Jacob pours out his heart to God in prayer (Gen. 32:9–12). Immediately after doing so, perhaps prompted by the Lord through his prayer, Jacob decides to offer a conciliatory gift to Esau (Gen. 32:13–20).

After organizing the animals and sending them on their way, he tries to get some rest—he "lodged that night in the company" (Gen. 32:21)—but he is so troubled by what he expects to be imminent conflict with Esau that he cannot sleep (Gen. 32:22*a*). Perhaps fearing that Esau may attack during the night or at dawn, Jacob decides he needs to make his wives and children more secure, so he gets his family out of bed and takes them from the camp. When he locates a secure hiding place on the other side of the Jabbok, he sends them across the river (Gen. 32:22–23). The Jabbok is fifty miles long and winds through steep canyons on its descent from its source at 1900 feet above sea level to where it issues into the Jordan at an elevation of about 115 feet below sea level.[20] One could cross the river several times while traveling in a more or less straight line. Putting his family in one of the canyons would not have been an effective way to use them as a shield behind which to hide but would have been very effective for their protection.

Having seen to his family's safety, Jacob "was left alone" (Gen. 32:24). What was he doing when he suddenly found himself wrestling with a man for the rest of the night? I'm reasonably certain he was not fleeing to escape Esau. That would mean the man was trying to keep Jacob from getting away, but the text says that the reverse is true. Jacob is trying to win the match and keep the person with whom he is wrestling from getting away (Gen. 32:24–26). I'm also pretty sure Jacob is not tormented over his sins against his brother. First, as I've already explained, that assumes he had committed grievous sins against his brother, which I do not believe. Further, in neither this text nor any other does the Lord rebuke Jacob or suggest that he repent. There is no evidence in the text that the wrestling match changed Jacob's heart, and Jacob never asks forgiveness.

We cannot know for sure what Jacob was doing or thinking just before the wrestling began, but given what the text does say, two or three possibilities exist. He may have been fretting over what else he could do to make his family safe. He may have been trying to think of anything he might have left undone that could stave off destruction at the hands of Esau without having to take up arms against him. Or he may have been praying. While the first two were probably on his mind, I am inclined to think Jacob was praying.

Jacob does not know at first that the "man" with whom he wrestled was actually God in human form.[21] Perhaps Jacob thinks the man is there to harm his family. For whatever reason, they wrestled the rest of the night and Jacob is unable to "prevail." When it is nearly dawn, the Lord injures Jacob, either by throwing his hip out of joint or by striking him in the groin. Even with his injury, Jacob grapples with the Lord and will not let Him go. As dawn breaks, Jacob realizes he is wrestling with the Lord. When the Lord asks Jacob to release Him, Jacob refuses "except thou bless me." Only in times of great crisis are we likely to pray so persistently that we will not "let God go" until we sense His "blessing." What is the blessing Jacob sought? Assurance that he and his family would survive to see God's promises fulfilled. It was that for which he prays in verses 9–12, and it is that for which he praises in verse 30.

Contrary to what many commentators say, God does not wound Jacob so he will stop relying on the flesh and surrender but so he will persevere through his pain without relenting. Jacob's whole life has been about obeying and seeking God's blessing despite obstacles, difficulties, and pain. This is another example to force Jacob to focus on God's will despite being outmatched and nearly overcome. The permanent limp will remind him of both his weakness and his victory in weakness.

How does Jacob draw that confidence from how the Lord actually responds to his request for a blessing? The Lord asks him, "What is your name?" When he replies that his name is Jacob, the Lord tells him he will not be called Jacob anymore but will be called Israel, "for as a prince hast thou power with God and with men, and hast prevailed" (Gen. 32:28).

Most commentators assume that God asked Jacob to say his name to force him to confess "the appropriateness of his name. Only now would Jacob agree with Esau that Jacob is the perfect name for him (27:36)."[22] Even more explicitly damning, Epp says, "Jacob's name had haunted him everywhere he had gone. His name presented him as a fraud, a sham, a cheat, a supplanter, a contender and a deceiver. When Jacob answered that his name was 'Jacob,' he actually confessed to being all the things his name stood for."[23] But is that really the point? Does the name "Jacob" really stand for the old, fleshly, lost self and the name "Israel" for the new, spiritual, regenerated man?

Consider the similarities and differences between God's changing Jacob's name to Israel and His changing Abram's name to Abraham. After introducing the name "Abraham," the birth name "Abram" is never again used. However, after Jacob's name is changed to Israel, he continues to be called by both names interchangeably. Even in the account of his deathbed prophecies for his sons, he is called both Jacob and Israel in Genesis 49:1–2; and when he dies, he is called

Jacob in 49:33. Further, God never calls Himself "the God of Abram" but calls Himself the "God of Abraham" 15 times. On the other hand, while God is called "the God of Israel" 201 times, He is called "the God of Jacob" 25 times. Introducing his comments on Hosea 12:2–5, Charles Feinberg says,

> Those who have interpreted the account of the life of Jacob in the book of Genesis in such a manner that no good thing could be said of him, will find it difficult to understand the words of Hosea concerning the illustrious patriarch, with whose name God links His own—"the God of Jacob." It is easily discernable in the life of Jacob that he ever sought spiritual blessings throughout his life. He may have sought them before the appointed time or in the energy of the flesh, but he did long for the things of the Spirit of God and the spiritual life. This is undeniable.[24]

We must not miss the fact that even in Abraham's case, with a complete disconnect between the former name and the new name, the name change did not signify his conversion. It was as Abram that he was blessed by Melchizedek and paid tithes to him (Gen. 14:18–20). More significantly, it was under his old name that it is said of Abram that "he believed in the Lord; and he counted it to him for righteousness" (Gen. 15:6), which Paul cites as proof of salvation by faith (Rom. 4:3, 9). Since Jacob is given a new name without discarding the old, and since God is often called the God of Jacob, there is no way to argue convincingly that Jacob's name change signifies a spiritual transformation.

Abram's name was changed before the birth of Isaac in connection with God's pronouncing the covenant of circumcision (Gen. 17:5). Jacob's name was changed in relation to confirming the promise of blessing. In both cases the name change was intended to give assurance and confidence of God's blessing in the face of difficulty. God changed Abram's name to Abraham when Abraham had reason to believe that he and Sarah would have to be "revived" in order to have a son in their old age (one hundred and ninety respectively). God changed Jacob's name to Israel when Jacob had reason to believe that he might have to be "revived" to continue the promised line in the face of Esau's threats.

If we properly define the names, instead of letting Esau define Jacob with a pun, we find another significant parallel. In both cases, the name change represents an augmentation of the old, not an overthrowing of it. Abram's birth name means "exalted father," but with the clarification of the promise that he would have another son, this one by Sarah, God changed his name to Abraham, which means "father of a multitude." As I explained in chapter 1, Jacob's name does not mean "supplanter," which was a pun Esau made with a rhyming word that meant "heel-holder." "Jacob" actually means "God has protected him" or "God will protect him." Now, at this time of crisis, God names him "Israel," which means something like "one who fights victoriously with God" or "God's warrior." It is an exalted name indeed, implying that Jacob no longer needs God's protection or that he is one on whom the Lord can depend. As in the case of Abram's name change, this was not the moment of Jacob's regeneration. It was the moment of his exaltation.

After all this, Jacob asks the man with whom he wrestled to tell him his name. He receives only a question in reply—"Why do you ask my name?"—before the wrestler blesses him (Gen. 32:29). Jacob seems to have suddenly realized with Whom he has been wrestling. He knows His name without being told. He says, "I have seen God face to face," and names the place Peniel, which means "the face of God" (Gen. 32:30). When he adds, "and my life is preserved," Jacob/Israel is not marveling that he had not died from being so close to God. He is expressing confidence that God will spare his life in the coming confrontation with Esau. That has been what Jacob has pursued throughout the night, the events of which are recorded in this chapter. Earlier he had asked God to "deliver [preserve] me from the hand of my brother" (Gen. 32:11). Now he exults, "My life has been preserved [delivered]" (Gen. 32:30), using the same word in both instances.

So what really happened at Peniel? This is not Jacob's conversion, or even repentance and rededication. It is his entering into possession of a promise made by God long before. Obtaining the blessing of God has been his lifelong, single-minded focus. Through the prophet Hosea God commends Jacob for having pursued His blessing doggedly from before his birth and throughout his life and recommends that others follow his example instead of being distracted by worthless things and idols (12:2–5). That blessing had been pronounced by Isaac, once unintentionally and once intentionally. It had been confirmed at Bethel by God Himself, to be apprehended upon Jacob's return to the land. Well, he's back. Now he's prepared to meet Esau and "to enter the promised land to establish the foundations for the nation Israel."[25]

Lessons

One of the lessons of this chapter is to once again show how God is always present to help us, especially in times of crisis. He may be in the background, and His help may be unobserved, but He is always with us. However, His ever-present help does not relieve us of our responsibilities. Fathers must still care for their children, direct their families, and attend to business.

We can also learn from Jacob's example as a peacemaker. Jacob neither avoided the necessary confrontation nor behaved provocatively. His goal was reconciliation—he wanted peace with his brother, not conflict. We would all do well to approach those we have offended, or those who believe we have wronged them, with the same grace, humility, and generosity displayed by Jacob in his approach to Esau.

However, the primary lesson of this chapter is the need for the believer to learn perseverance in prayer. Sometimes the Lord wants us to demonstrate our dependence upon Him and our determination to do His will through strenuous prayer. Paul urges the Roman believers to "strive together with me in your prayers to God for me" (Rom. 15:30), using a word that means "to contend for victory in the public games"[26] or "to fight or wrestle."[27] Significant answers to prayer sometimes come only after we "wrestle" with God "until the breaking of the day" (Gen. 32:24).

9

Brothers Meet

Gen. 33:1–20

hen I was a high school junior, I got my first "real job" working at a fast-food restaurant. It was in some ways an eye-opening experience. Having grown up in a pastor's home and attended private Christian schools for the previous three years, I found myself in an environment for several hours at a time in which I was the only conservative Christian, and sometimes the only professing believer. Learning to get along with often antagonistic unbelievers without becoming like them was an important part of growing up in my faith.

One co-worker went out of his way to harass me about going to a Christian school and to church. When he found out I sang in the choir, he was merciless. On a couple of occasions when we were on break together, he challenged me with questions about what I believed or why I didn't do some of the things he thought were fun. One Friday night after the store had closed, as we were clocking out and getting ready to leave, he was taunting me for my unwillingness to party with the rest of them. He knew I wouldn't drink or smoke—tobacco or pot—like most of the rest of the crew. He asked me if I was going with the others, then sneered, "Oh, yeah, you don't do that so you won't go to hell."

He'd been on my case all week, and I'd had enough. I looked at him and said, "You know what? You could quit doing all that stuff and still go to hell. If you don't admit you're a rotten sinner and ask Jesus to forgive you, it doesn't really matter what you do. You're going to hell anyway."

The next couple of times I was working, I was glad he wasn't working the same schedule. I dreaded the confrontation I knew was coming. In less than a week we were both on the schedule again. The evening started without incident. He looked at me kind of funny but didn't say anything. I had no idea what he was plotting. Then the manager sent us both on break at the same time. I walked into the break room thinking, "OK, here it comes."

I decided to break the ice by apologizing for my rude comments. I started, "Look, about what I said the other day . . . " when he interrupted me.

He quietly asked, "Do you really believe that? I mean about it not really making any difference what I do, because I'm going to hell anyway?"

"Well, yeah," I said, "but I shouldn't have said it the way I did when I was mad."

He continued, "You go to church every Sunday, don't you? Would you mind if I came with you some time?"

"That would be great! Let me know when you want to come and I can either pick you up or meet you at the door."

"Are you sure it would be all right? What would your church people think about you bringing a black boy to church?" he asked. This was in Virginia in 1973, and lots of schools and churches were still segregated. My parents had long opposed racial segregation, so it hadn't occurred to me that it might matter.

I said, "You know what? My folks will be there, and they'll be glad you came. I can't promise that nobody will care, but what difference does it make?"

The next Sunday, he went to church with me. Once. A few weeks later he took another job, and I never saw him again. But that's not the point. God had transformed the confrontation I had dreaded into an opportunity to turn an enemy into a friend. I have no idea if he ever trusted Christ, but I've prayed for Bunion Hammond for over thirty years.

Jacob's parting from Laban had not been amicable, but it had at least been peaceable. He is now on the border of Canaan, and he knows that the first thing he has to do is face Esau, his brother. The thought of the looming confrontation terrified Jacob. He's been gone for at least twenty years, but there are four significant facts that he remembers well, even if he doesn't mention them. First, Jacob had caught Esau cooperating with Isaac to hijack the blessing God had conferred upon Abraham and Isaac and promised would be passed on to Jacob. Second, Esau had been so angry with Jacob for interfering that he planned to kill him after Isaac died. Third, Rebekah had advised Jacob to leave the area "for a few days," promising to send for him when Esau's anger had cooled. Twenty years have passed with no word calling him home, so Jacob has no reason to believe Esau has stopped plotting revenge. Fourth, before Jacob left home, Isaac confirmed upon Jacob the blessing and ordered Jacob to find a proper wife in contrast to the unsatisfactory wives of Esau. Jacob has no way of knowing how Esau responded to his father's repentance.

As if he didn't have enough reason to fear, the messengers Jacob sent to meet Esau have returned with word that Esau is approaching with four hundred men. No wonder Jacob is terrified! Esau may think Jacob is coming back to attack him for trying to take God's blessing by stealth and may have sent this large force to stop Jacob before he can penetrate all the way to Seir. Or maybe Esau is still furious enough with Jacob that he is bringing an armed band to attack him before he can get back home to claim his estate.

Reunion of Estranged Brothers (Gen. 33:1–7)

Jacob has just spent a sleepless night filled with strenuous activity. He has been weakened by the ordeal, but he has also been greatly encouraged. The Lord has given him a limp and assured him that his "life is preserved" (32:30). As the Lord departs, and Jacob heads back to camp, Jacob looks up. Esau is approaching with his four hundred men. The dreaded confrontation is upon him (Gen. 33:1). Does he run away like a coward? Does he collapse in shame or despair? No, he acts in a manner consistent with a godly and God-trusting man. He organizes his family for a formal introduction to his brother, treating Esau as a visiting dignitary.

Arranging the children with their mothers, he presents them in a specific order (Gen. 33:2). Bilhah and Zilpah, unnamed here and called merely "the handmaids," are presented first, each with their two sons. They are followed by Leah and her children—six sons and at least one daughter. At the rear are Rachel and Joseph.

The especially cynical assume that the purpose of this arrangement was to give Rachel and Joseph the greatest chance to escape should Esau attack. "Presumably, the purpose was to give the maximum possible protection to those he loved the most."[1] One writer calls Jacob's actions here evidence of "backsliding" immediately "after Peniel" because of his "needless fear."[2] Another describes this arrangement as "the inverse order of his affection for them:

concubines, Leah, Rachel,"[3] which more negatively than necessary suggests that those in front were the least loved, or even unloved. It is better to understand this as an order of presentation suitable for formal protocol, in ascending order of priority: his secondary wives and their children first; then Leah and her children, probably arranged so that the firstborn, Reuben, would come last; and finally Rachel and her son, Joseph.

Had Jacob feared Esau would kill them, he would have left them hiding in one of the canyons through which the Jabbok ran. His encounter with God had convinced him they would be fine, so he brings them out for presentation to his brother. He still does not know how he will be received, but he will not insult his brother or his family by acting either as a coward or as an aggressor. He has cast himself and his family on God's protection and sincerely hopes for peace with his brother.

Having arranged his family and instructed them on how to present themselves, Jacob takes the lead and goes to meet Esau (Gen. 33:3). He is not hiding behind his family. Having interpreted all Jacob's prior actions as craven or crooked, Hamilton calls this a "genuine change in Jacob's style of operation . . . from rearguard to vanguard."[4] Sailhamer sticks to his accusations and insists that this is still a "fearful approach,"[5] pointing to the fact that Jacob bows seven times as he advances to meet Esau. Rather than interpreting this as groveling, it may be that Jacob is showing a "deep reverence" for Esau in order "to win his brother's heart."[6] It is also possible that the Tel-el-Amarna tablets shed some light on this, indicating that when approaching a king the custom of the period demanded that one show proper respect by bowing seven times.[7]

The best and most straightforward way to interpret the entire scene is to understand Jacob to be acknowledging Esau's political superiority, as seen before in the messages addressed to "my lord" from "your servant." He behaves with the utmost decorum. He comes unarmed and bows seven times to show respect. He arranges his family for formal introduction, keeps them in the background until called for, then presents them without fanfare in ascending order of significance within the family. All of this is done to convince Esau that Jacob is neither a usurper who must be destroyed nor an invader who must be repelled.

Esau's response proves both the truth of God's promises and the wisdom of Jacob's actions. He apparently dismounts and runs to meet Jacob. Throwing his arms around him, he greets him with a kiss of welcome (Gen. 33:4).[8] Esau's enthusiastic, even energetically affectionate, greeting of Jacob surprises the reader almost as much as it must have Jacob. The last Jacob had heard, Esau was plotting his murder. However, that is not the last the reader has heard of Esau. What Jacob may not have known is that Esau learned that Jacob left with his parents' full blessing to find a wife that would meet their approval and that Jacob, unlike Esau, "obeyed his father and his mother" (Gen. 28:7). In response, Esau tried to please his parents by marrying a cousin descended from Ishmael (Gen. 28:6–9). Esau has had twenty years to mull over the consequences of his own rotten choices, how they contrasted with Jacob's choices, and how both of their futures were destined to reflect those choices.

Still, we assume too much if we conclude that Esau "had long since realized that Jacob had properly been entitled to the birthright and blessing, and that God had chosen Jacob to be the inheritor of the promises, and he was reconciled to this fact."[9] The first two statements are surely true, but the Esau we knew from the earlier account didn't care and was far from "reconciled to this fact." Had there been any obvious change of heart during the last twenty years, Rebekah would surely have sent for Jacob to return.

What caused Esau's apparent change of heart on this day? The obvious answer is that God did it in answer to Jacob's prayer (Gen. 32:11). While He often uses visible means, only God can change a heart. It's likely that Jacob's decision to shower Esau with gifts, to refuse to arm himself for defense, and to present himself in humility were inspired through his prayer and were used by God to soften Esau's heart. Esau may have left home intending to destroy Jacob, only to be "converted" in his feelings on the way.

The text doesn't tell us what emotions Esau was expressing when he embraced and kissed Jacob. Was it "an indication of forgiveness"?[10] That is possible, but in the absence of any confession or apology from Jacob, it seems unlikely. It assumes that Jacob was the offender and Esau was justly aggrieved. It's at least as likely that Esau was relieved to find "that Jacob no longer held any bitterness in his heart toward him."[11] Whatever the emotions, the outcome is clear. Jacob takes the initiative by indicating his desire to be reconciled, and Esau responds by expressing his own desire for the same.

The initial greeting past, Esau asks for introductions—"Who are these with you?" (Gen. 33:5a). Earlier, Jacob had credited God with giving him his flocks and herds (Gen. 31:5, 42). He had even credited God with having given him the "venison" he prepared for Isaac, a slip of the tongue that almost revealed his identity to his father (Gen. 27:20–21). Consistent with his habit, Jacob immediately credits God with having graciously bestowed upon him this family. Again referring to himself as "thy servant," Jacob presents his family in the prearranged order (Gen. 33:5b–7).

First comes a group of at least six—Bilhah and Zilpah with their four sons and any daughters that might have been born in the previous six years—who bow before Esau. Then comes a group of at least eight—Leah with her six sons and Dinah, with any other daughters born to Leah. Finally, Jacob presents his greatest treasure, Rachel and her son, Joseph. This order of presentation sets the stage for future jealousy among the brothers. Jacob may not yet have designated Joseph his primary heir, but every indication is that he will.

Reconciliation of Old Adversaries (Gen. 33:8–11)

Having met Jacob's family, Esau asks about the virtual avalanche of animals that met him on his way to Jacob's camp. What is the meaning of "all this drove which I met?" (Gen. 33:8a). What Jacob had communicated earlier through his messengers, he now explains in person. One writer says that "not only is the post-Peniel Jacob courageous ('he himself went on ahead of them'), but he is honest as well. Up until this point candor has not been one of Jacob's more distinctive traits."[12] Again, I fear this betrays a prejudice against Jacob not found in the text of Scripture. Except on the occasion in which he disguised himself before his father, which he did on his mother's orders and arguably for his father's protection, candor has in fact been one of Jacob's more distinctive traits. Impugning Jacob's character further, Hamilton adds, "He is forthright with Esau about his intention to buy Esau's forgiveness."[13] The text makes no mention of forgiveness, only of acceptance. Jacob honestly explains that the animals are a gift intended to influence Esau to look upon Jacob with favor (Gen. 33:8b). Jacob is wealthy and generous, so Esau need fear no threat to his security or his property. They should be able to get along. Jacob's gift is in no way sinister, dishonest, or inappropriate.

Esau's immediate response is to refuse the gift. Saying he has plenty ("enough," KJV), he urges Jacob to keep the animals for himself (Gen. 33:9). He can look around and see that Jacob still had large flocks and herds, but he will underestimate Jacob's wealth by more than half. Jacob has with him only one of the two encampments into which he had divided his property, and it was from this group alone that he had taken the 580 animals he sent ahead to meet Esau. Jacob was much better off than Esau realized.

What's more, we may be reading into Esau's initial refusal more than is warranted. This seems to be a large-scale example of a fairly routine practice in many cultures, including our own.

Something like this has probably happened to you. You are out to dinner with a friend and have finished your meal. The waiter leaves the bill on the table. You pick up the bill and say, "I'll take care of this." (I'll assume you are the generous one.)

Your friend responds, "No, that's not necessary."

You reply, "That's OK, I insist."

Your friend concedes, "OK, then, if you insist. Thanks."

If your friend accepted your initial offer, you might consider him greedy or presumptuous. If you accepted his first refusal without insisting, he might think your initial offer insincere. True, cultures differ, even regionally within our own country. However, Middle Eastern cultures practice far more elaborate social customs than these simply to show respect. Esau's initial refusal may have been nothing more than a customary initial reply to any gift.

Whether or not they are following a conventional conversational script, Jacob sincerely wants Esau to take the offered animals. He answers Esau's refusal of the gift by insisting that he take it. Exactly what Jacob means by his next statement is unclear: "I have seen thy face, as though I had seen the face of God, and thou wast pleased with me" (Gen. 33:10*b*). If it's in reference to his prayer for deliverance early the night before (Gen. 32:9–12), he may mean that he discerns in Esau's acceptance of him that God has changed Esau's heart—"In thy countenance I have been met with divine friendliness."[14] If it's in reference to his wrestling with the Lord in the wee hours of that morning (Gen. 32:22–30), he may mean that he has approached Esau in fear and hope just as he had approached God. He is as overjoyed to find himself vindicated in Esau's sight as he had been in God's. Whichever way we understand Jacob's comment, the point is that he is glad that Esau has welcomed him in peace.

Jacob then explains his twofold reason for insisting that Esau keep the gift (Gen. 33:11). For Jacob to feel reconciled to Esau, it is important that Esau take his gift as proof of acceptance. It will give Jacob both joy and peace of mind. Even if Esau doesn't need the gift because he has "plenty" ("enough" KJV), Jacob doesn't need it because he has "everything" ("enough" KJV). We should note that Esau says nothing about the source of his "plenty," while Jacob again credits his financial success to God's gracious provision.

Since Jacob had been accumulating property for only the last six of the previous twenty years, and Esau presumably began building his own wealth as soon as Jacob left, it's possible that Esau's wealth exceeded Jacob's. So why would Esau's insistence that he had "plenty" prompt Jacob to reply that he had "everything"? On one hand, it may be a statement of Jacob's confidence that with the Lord's presence, he would never need anything more—"For what is a man profited, if he shall gain the whole world and lose his own soul? or what shall a man give in exchange for his soul?" (Matt. 16:26). On the other hand, it may be a reference to the blessing God had promised through Abraham and Isaac. While thinking he was giving a blessing to Esau, Isaac had given Jacob "everything" (cf. Gen. 27:36). If the former is correct, Jacob is saying, "God is everything to me. With His presence and provision what I have is as good as if I owned the whole world." If the latter is correct, Jacob is telling Esau, "God blessed me with everything. It is important to me to be able to bless you with something." I believe we should probably understand Jacob's words on both levels.

Removal of Temptation to Compromise
(Gen. 33:12–17)

Having greeted Jacob, Esau makes an interesting offer. Assuming that Jacob plans to come all the way to the southern edge of Canaan and beyond, he offers to lead the way (Gen. 33:12). This offer may actually have been tempting. Jacob could relax a little, not worry about marauders or bandits, and let someone else take responsibility for the trip. He wouldn't have to think about where to settle or what to do. Esau has made the plans for him. All it would require is his surrender of control to Esau and the likelihood of his eventually intermingling his family with that of a brother that he knows cared nothing for God (Heb. 12:16–17).

Writers are quick to question Jacob's actions in this section but rarely if ever question Esau's. It is hermeneutically dangerous to attribute Esau's actions to "his own good nature"[15] while assuming the worst of Jacob. If we would be consistent with what God tells us about the character of these two brothers, we would do well to be more suspicious of Esau's motives than of Jacob's. Does Esau think Jacob has forgotten the way home? Surely Esau understands animal husbandry enough to know the pace Jacob would need to travel having flocks with their young. What does he really have in mind?

The text gives no indication of any sinister motives on Esau's part, but Jacob declines his offer. He explains truthfully that his children are "tender," or "frail" (Gen. 33:13). Remember that Reuben is barely twelve years old, and Joseph only six. Dinah is probably younger than that. Jacob adds that there are many newborn animals among his livestock. Both factors would require their moving at a snail's pace. Perhaps because he has no desire to be critical of his father-in-law, Jacob does not explain that they have pushed hard to get to this point, to outrun Laban. They desperately needed time to recover. To push his family harder would be heartless, and to over-drive his animals would risk losing the entire flock. Again using the language of humility and subordination, "my lord" and "thy servant," Jacob tells Esau to go on ahead. Jacob says he will lead his family and animals along at a pace appropriate to their condition, "until I come unto my lord unto Seir" (Gen. 33:14).

Rather than persist with his initial offer to lead Jacob to Seir, Esau reduces his offer. He says he will leave some of his men as an escort. Jacob's reply is essentially, "That is very kind, but not necessary. We'll be fine" (Gen. 33:15). Accepting that, Esau withdraws and returns to Seir (Gen. 33:16).

Still, many writers inexplicably persist in attributing evil motives to Jacob and a sterling heart to Esau. Victor Hamilton says,

> All of Jacob's concerns voiced at this point may be another subterfuge to distance himself once more from Esau. . . . The post-Peniel Jacob is not above making false promises and offering misleading expectations to Esau. . . . Esau is clearly concerned about his brother's safety. At almost every point in this story, Esau emerges as the more appealing, more humane, and more virtuous of the two brothers.[16]

I search the text in vain for any words explaining why Esau wanted to lead Jacob to Seir or at least place some of his men with Jacob on the trip. If we are going to read into the text what isn't there, as Hamilton has done, it seems just as likely that Esau is less interested in protecting Jacob than he is in keeping Jacob and his flocks from getting away. Perhaps he wants him close for his own benefit. Perhaps Jacob declines because he senses insincerity in Esau and thinks he, his family, and his property will be safer on their own than they would be with Esau's men shadowing their every move.

Once Esau has departed, Jacob moves his family and animals to Succoth, apparently called that because there Jacob made "booths" (Heb. *sukkot*) for his livestock. If this is the town later given to Gad on the east of Jordan (Josh. 13:27; cf. Judg. 8:5–7, 14–16; 1 Kings 7:46; 2 Chron. 4:17), Jacob has not continued southward toward Seir but moved back across the Jabbok, about two miles to the north. What's more, he builds a house there and stays for ten years or more.[17]

Most writers interpret this to mean that when Jacob tells Esau that he will come to him in Seir, he is lying to Esau to get rid of him. Never intending to go to Seir, he goes in the opposite direction.[18] While such a conclusion is possible, it is not required by the text. Several factors must be considered.

First, if Jacob suspects any sinister motives on Esau's part, putting the river between them makes good sense. More importantly, we should wonder where were the rest of Jacob's flocks and herds? Jacob has stayed with the group most likely to be discovered (which, by the way, points to courage, not cowardice). Esau has seen no sign of the other group on his trip up from the south. Therefore, they must have been left north of the Jabbok. Since Jacob has given away a significant portion of the flocks and herds with him, the other group is probably the larger of the two. It would make sense for practical reasons alone for him to move back to where the other animals are for the time being.

Furthermore, two generations earlier, Abraham and Lot had been forced to separate because the land could not support both their holdings in proximity to one another (Gen. 13:6ff.). After that time, Abraham's wealth grew before it was passed on to Isaac. Isaac, with Jacob's help, had increased his estate. Esau had moved his own center of operations south, actually outside "the land of thy fathers" to which God had told Jacob to return. Why would Jacob or Esau assume that the land could support them all living in the same area? It would make sense to establish his own operation at another location and then visit his parents and brother unencumbered by thousands of animals.

Accusing Jacob of lying ignores the significant fact that we have no idea what Jacob does or where he goes during the years of his sojourn in Succoth. Why assume he doesn't keep his word? He never said he would bring his family to Seir. What he actually says could be understood to mean that when he got his family and flocks settled, he (not we) would come to Seir (Gen. 33:14*b*). I believe Henry Morris's analysis is more on point.

Jacob no doubt also realized that he should remain separate and independent from Esau, as far as the future accomplishment of God's plans for his children was concerned; and it would be better to establish such a separation from the beginning. It was a great blessing and answer to prayer to be reconciled to his brother, but they were still of different natures and had different ways of life. They could, and no doubt did, continue to see each other frequently; but they must each live their own separate lives and accomplish their own independent purposes.[19]

Relocation to Shechem (Gen. 33:18–20)

Between Genesis 33:17 and 34:1 at least ten years pass. Since Jacob built a house in Succoth and "spread his tent" in Shechem, it is presumed that much of that time was spent in Succoth and that the events in Genesis 34 occurred shortly after Jacob's arrival. It's also possible that he spent several years at each place before the events in Genesis 34. All we know for sure is that when Jacob's children met Esau the boys were ages six to twelve, and Dinah was younger, but in the next chapter of the narrative Dinah is of marriageable age and the boys are young men.

Three important facts emerge from the closing verses of Genesis 33. The first is obscured by the transliteration of a word that probably should have been translated. The KJV reads that "Jacob came to Shalem, a city of Shechem" (Gen. 33:18). Shechem itself was a city, not a country, and there is no historical evidence that it contained within its territory a city called Shalem. The word *Shalem* means "peace." Had the word been translated rather than transliterated as a place name, the text would read that "Jacob came in peace to the city of Shechem." Such a reading is likely because of its prophetic significance in that it would amount to the initial fulfillment of the promise God made to Jacob to bring him "in peace" (Gen. 28:21) back "into this land" (Gen. 28:15; cf. 31:3). While living in Succoth, Jacob was not technically within the region identified with Abraham and Isaac. However, Shechem was clearly identified with Abraham, being the first city in Canaan described as one through which Abraham passed on his way to Bethel (Gen. 12:6). In coming to Shechem, Jacob is back in the land of his fathers.

The second important fact revealed in these verses is that when Jacob arrives in Shechem he purchases property (Gen. 33:19). He buys the land for what is apparently a large sum of money—the value of the "one hundred pieces of money" is impossible to determine—from the family of Hamor, Shechem's father. These men will be important in the next chapter. What is important now is that this is Jacob's first personal identification with the land of promise, indicating both his independent identity within the promise and his confidence in the Lord's intention to fulfill that promise. While this text does not say so, John 4:6 tells us that Jacob followed Abraham's and Isaac's example by digging a well there to provide his own independent water supply. It is this field that will eventually be the site of the burial of Joseph's bones when the nation of Israel emerges from four hundred years in Egypt (Josh. 24:32). By purchasing this field, Jacob is staking his claim on the land of Canaan by faith. Actually, it would have constituted a lack of faith for Jacob to have journeyed through Canaan southward to Seir, the region beyond Canaan occupied by Esau.

Finally, the chapter closes with the vital fact that on this land Jacob builds an altar and names it "El-Elohe-Israel," which means "El (God) is the God of Israel" (Gen. 33:19). This is important for several reasons. First, Jacob is following his father and his grandfather in worship, erecting an altar to the one true God. Second, Jacob is keeping the promise he made to God when he left the region. God had promised to be with him and bring him back safely. Jacob promised that God would be his God and that when he returned he would worship Him. Jacob also promised to give a tenth of whatever God gave him upon his return to the land. The fact that the text doesn't specifically mention Jacob's giving of a tithe doesn't mean he didn't keep his word. Given God's responses to broken vows in other men's lives, we should have expected God to bring it up if Jacob reneged. We should probably assume that either Jacob's gift to Esau was that tithe or that the purchase of the land is part of the tithe and that on the altar he offers the rest in unstated sacrifices.[20] In the naming of the altar, Jacob publicly identifies himself as a worshiper of God, and for the first time in the text, identifies himself by his God-given name—"A prince with God" or "God's warrior." His waiting until now to use that name in the written record shows its relationship to the covenant, not conversion. God had given him the name years before, but he hasn't appropriated it until he kept his word by building an altar in the land of his fathers.

There is no legitimate reason to find fault with Jacob for anything he says or does in this chapter. He starts the chapter in great confidence, having met with God and having been promised preservation.

He behaves with honor before Esau, treating him kindly and generously, but refusing to become entangled in his affairs or to be forced, even by kindness, to move beyond where God wants him to go. He has established himself in the land, identified himself with God and the promise, and kept his vow to honor the Lord upon his safe return to the land.

Lessons

Properly understood, Jacob's actions in greeting Esau provide a good model for evangelism when presenting the gospel to a potentially hostile individual. We should take the person's need to the Lord and ask God to change his heart. Then we should plan a presentation that is unapologetic but gracious, honest but humble, and approach the situation confident that the outcome is in the hands of the Lord. If the person to whom we witness is converted, the change of heart is God's doing. However, our careful preparation and presentation may be used by the Holy Spirit to effect that change (cf. Rom. 10:14–17).

Jacob's actions also show us how to reconcile with someone from whom we've been estranged. When there is a breach of fellowship, we should seek to repair the break. God calls us to unflinching kindness, even toward those who hate us. Esau was a rebel who cared nothing for God, but Jacob treated him with kindness and deference. Jacob may not have trusted Esau, but he treated him with respect. On the other hand, Jacob did not follow Esau home and subject himself to Esau's rule. That would have at least bordered on renouncing the birthright and forfeiting the blessing. Jacob did what he could to rebuild a relationship without entanglement or compromise.

Throughout this chapter, we've seen Jacob demonstrate his faith in God. He trusted God to protect him and his family as they approached Esau, and he trusted God to bless him in the land. He bought land in the region first identified by God as the land He would give Abraham. He built an altar there and gave it a name identifying himself as a worshiper of God. There is little he could have done that would have demonstrated more clearly his confidence in God's promises.

10

Jacob's Danger

Gen. 34:1–31

y wife and I recently attended a funeral in what used to be the small town of Alpharetta, Georgia. Alpharetta is still there, but it's difficult to identify. An atlas will tell you that Alpharetta is just over twenty-three miles north of Atlanta. The beautiful, upscale town of 35,000 residents has been swallowed up by urban sprawl. As you drive through suburban Atlanta, you can hardly tell when you transition from one community to another. There are busy highways, traffic lights, businesses, and residences everywhere in a steady continuum, mile after mile after mile.

The deceased whose funeral we were attending had been a well-known and well-loved lifelong resident of Alpharetta, and many who attended the service shared reminiscences of life before the town had been absorbed into metro-Atlanta. Most of the stories were told with a wistful longing for "the way things used to be," and some even expressed a sort of surprised realization at how much things have changed. Apparently, the changes have come gradually enough that many people had been too busy to notice until they stopped to remember times shared with an old friend. It was a bittersweet day, filled with laughter and tears. We came away with a sense of great loss, not just for the death of the father of our friend but for the passing of a community's identity.

In Genesis 34, Jacob and his family are offered an opportunity to merge with the community of Shechem. Had they done so, looking for potential economic benefit and stability, they would surely have been absorbed by the larger community. The loss would have been cause for much greater sorrow than simple nostalgia for "the good ol' days." There is a sense in which the very destiny of humanity is at stake here. Should Jacob's family lose its independent identity at the outset of its establishment as "Israel," what would happen to the messianic promise? While the story recounted here is brutal and ugly, and none of the central figures of the story behave with consistent honor (with the possible exception of Dinah), the events are recorded because the stakes are so high.

As we've studied the life of Jacob, we've seen that the Bible doesn't provide a complete biography. Decades often pass without mention. For instance, the period from Jacob's birth to his departure for Padan-aram in his midseventies is summarized in only two or three events. His twenty years with Laban are described only generally, punctuated by three significant events. Rather than giving us a thorough description of Jacob's life, God told us at the outset what kind of man Jacob is—blameless (Gen. 25:27)—so we will know how to interpret what we are told and how to fill in the gaps. The events that are included are significant to the developing history of God's people. The story told in this chapter tells us more about Jacob's sons than it does about Jacob himself.

At the end of the last chapter I said that, properly understood, Jacob's behavior in Genesis 33 is above reproach. Many commentators look to Genesis 33 for a reason for what happens in Genesis 34. A common accusation I've not yet addressed is that the tragedy in Shechem occurred at least in part because Jacob failed to fully obey the Lord's command to return to the land. Some advance this charge because he stayed for years in Succoth, which is not in "the land," being across the Jordan. The weakness of that argument is found in the fact that Succoth is part of the land allotted to the tribe of Gad under Joshua (Josh. 13:27). God always thought of that region as part of the land promised to Abraham, and there is no reason to assume that Jacob should think otherwise.

Others justify the charge of incomplete obedience on the basis that Jacob stopped short of Bethel when he bought property in Shechem. Theodore Epp says, "Jacob did not completely obey God, and he began to reap what he had sown. . . . One cannot stop short of God's will, purpose and place of service without reaping some bad fruit. . . . Jacob had compromised. He had settled in Shechem, not Bethel"[1] This charge requires that one assume that the text's statement that Jacob had come to Shechem "in peace" has no spiritual or prophetic significance. One must also assume that God expected

Jacob to go back to Bethel and that Jacob knew that. When Jacob first met God in Bethel, the Lord promised to be with him and bring him safely back into "this land" (Gen. 28:15) without specifying that he must return to "this place," a term used to identify Bethel several times in that context. Further, when the Lord spoke to Jacob in Padan-aram, He told Jacob to "return unto the land of thy fathers" (Gen. 31:3), without specifying Bethel. God does not specifically tell Jacob to return to Bethel until after the incident we are about to consider (Gen. 35:1), and then Jacob does exactly as he is told without hesitation.

The tragic events that occur in Shechem are included in the narrative for two reasons. Primarily, they illustrate for future generations of Israel the folly of commingling with the Canaanites. They also provide at least a partial explanation for Jacob's later prophecies concerning the future of his sons and their descendents (Gen. 49:5–7). I believe that the charge that this tragedy occurs because Jacob is in the wrong place is unjustified.

However, that does not mean that Jacob is completely blameless. His fault does not seem to be in a lack of personal piety. Neither does he fail to obey the Lord's specific instructions. Jacob's weakness is his apparent inattention to his family and his lack of sensitivity to the danger of close social contact with the Canaanites.

Dinah's Defilement (Gen. 34:1–4)

In the record of the birth of Jacob's children, Dinah is the only daughter identified by name (Gen. 30:21), while Genesis 37:35 and 46:7 refer to daughters in the plural. She may have been the first daughter born to Jacob, or even the only one born in Padan-aram, but her birth is mentioned earlier so we will know who she is at this point in the story.

How old is Dinah when these events occur? We can't say for sure, but we can come pretty close. We know she was born after Leah's sixth son, Zebulun (Gen. 30:20–21). We know that Joseph was the youngest of Jacob's sons born in Padan-aram. For all eleven of Jacob's sons to have been born within a seven year period, as the record indicates, Joseph must have been born shortly after Zebulun. Dinah had to be at least a few months younger than Joseph, and could have been as much as four or five years younger. When the family left Padan-aram, Joseph could have been no more than six years old, making

Dinah anywhere from one to five years old. The family apparently stayed in Succoth for several years, and the events in Shechem may not have happened as soon as they arrived. After these events, the family moves to Bethel, then to Ephratah, where Benjamin is born and Rachel dies, and then on to Hebron. While living in Hebron, Jacob's sons will be pasturing their flocks near Shechem when Joseph is sent to find them. Their jealousy will cause them to sell Joseph into slavery in Egypt. This happens when Joseph is seventeen (Gen. 37:2), and Dinah is between twelve and sixteen years old. If these events all happen within a single year, and if Dinah is no more than a year younger than Joseph, she could have been as old as fifteen when Genesis 34 opens. Given the nature of the events in Shechem, it is unlikely that Dinah was much younger than thirteen although she could have been as young as eleven.

This tragedy at Shechem begins when Dinah goes to "see the daughters of the land" (Gen. 34:1). Exactly what this means is open to some question. She may have gone out of curiosity to see what the local girls were like, or she may have gone socially to find companionship among the local girls. It's possible that she still is the only daughter in a family with eleven sons. Even if there are other daughters, she is almost certainly the oldest of them. Still, with four adult women in the family and many servants, she would not be without female companionship. We are probably safe in thinking that Dinah has recently come of age (perhaps thirteen?) and is beginning to go out on her own to socialize with some of the local girls.

Part of the reason this story is difficult to interpret is that while it revolves around Dinah, she never speaks to tell us what she is doing or thinking. Perhaps Dinah is rebellious, intentionally getting involved with people she knows she should avoid. Perhaps she is merely naïve, trusting people about whom she knows little. Perhaps Jacob or Leah should have taken care to supervise Dinah's activities. Whatever failure may have been Dinah's, Leah's, or Jacob's, the blame for what happens here lies squarely upon "Shechem the son of Hamor." He "saw" her, he "took" her, he "lay with" her, and he "defiled" (lit. "humbled") her (Gen. 34:2).

Since the text does not specifically say that Shechem "forced" her, he is sometimes described as having "seduced her."[2] Those who interpret the event that way assume that Dinah feels flattered by the attention of a man who is powerful and admired, essentially a prince, and that she falls victim to his charms. However, especially given Dinah's youth, she more likely falls victim to a powerful man's lust. Since both of the verbs "taken" and "humbled" imply force, this should be understood as an action that was against her will. Shechem did not "seduce" Dinah, but "violated,"[3] "raped,"[4] or "ravaged"[5] her.

In the Canaanite culture of that day women were often treated as property or merchandise. The sexual promiscuity so prevalent in Canaanite worship created a sexually charged social atmosphere, and the male dominance in society made unattached young women "fair game" for an adventurous young man.[6] Evidence of this is seen in the fact that the prince's taking a girl against her will for his own sexual pleasure is treated as rather commonplace from the Canaanites' perspective. The social climate alone should have warned Jacob and Leah that allowing Dinah to circulate among the "daughters of the land" might be dangerous.

Having had his way with Dinah, Shechem becomes so enthralled with her that he decides to keep her. Speaking "kindly" to her, he apparently tries to comfort her, even to woo her (Gen. 34:3). He then orders his father, "Get me this girl for a wife" (Gen. 34:4). For all his expression of a desire to marry Dinah, Shechem's selfishness is emphasized in the wording of his command. The word order places the indirect object before the direct object to make the "me" more emphatic. Had he wanted to emphasize Dinah as the object of his desire, he could have said, "Get this girl for me." By saying "Get for me this girl," the emphasis is placed on fulfilling his desire. Further, he never uses her name, referring to her disparagingly as "the girl" (Gen. 34:3) and "this girl" (Gen. 34:4). It's worth noting that no one in the story assumes that the sexual act alone constituted marriage. Shechem does not declare Dinah to be his wife but opens negotiations to make her his wife. Even among the heathen people of Canaan, marriages are arranged by the parents.

Israel's Dismay (Gen. 34:5–7)

It doesn't take long for Jacob to learn what Shechem has done to Dinah. Verse 5 uses the single verb "defiled" to summarize Shechem's action. While it can be used to mean "violation of chastity,"[7] it carries the spiritual significance of making a person "unclean." That does not mean that Shechem's action made Dinah sinful. It means "exclusion from the camp until cleanness is restored. Through being subjected to such an indignity by an outsider, Dinah is relegated to the status of an outcast."[8]

Jacob's feelings on learning this news are not revealed. He does not respond immediately but waits until his sons return from the field (Gen. 34:5). Jacob is sometimes faulted for his silence, as if he were afraid to take decisive action to make matters better. It's possible, though, that he refrains from speaking immediately to avoid saying or doing something he would later regret. Proverbs 14:29 says, "He that is slow to wrath is of great understanding: but he that is hasty of spirit exalteth folly." He has yet to hear what Hamor has to say about the matter. For that matter, Jacob either sends for his sons or has reason to believe they have received word and will come running.

A generation earlier, Abraham had sent his servant to find a wife for Isaac. He sent the man to Padan-aram, to the home of Bethuel, son of Nahor (Gen. 24:15). When Abraham's servant met Rebekah, Bethuel's daughter, he was convinced she was the young woman to whom God had led him as a bride for his master's son. When he met with her family to discuss Abraham's proposal to arrange this marriage, the agreement was reached between Abraham's servant and Rebekah's brother, not her father (Gen. 24:29, 50, 55, 60). Bethuel was present but was almost silent in the discussion as Laban made the arrangements. That event is in some respects similar to the one before us here. It was apparently customary, at least among Abraham's kindred, for brothers to take a more active or even decisive role in the disposition of their sisters than fathers did for their daughters.[9] This is the most likely reason for Jacob's initial silence on the matter of Dinah's rape. His sons' presence is required for the family council to decide what to do.

Hamor and the sons of Jacob apparently arrive at Jacob's headquarters about the same time. The text implies that Hamor intends to meet with Jacob alone since he comes to "commune with him" not "with them" (Gen. 34:6). It's possible that he realizes that Dinah's brothers will be displeased and wants to preempt their participation in the discussion. If that's what he's thinking, he's about to be disappointed.

The young men, maximum ages of sixteen (Joseph) to twenty-two (Reuben), arrive incensed (Gen. 34:7). The verb translated "grieved" is also used to describe God's feelings when He considered the chaotic wickedness of the earth in Noah's day (Gen. 6:6). It indicates a condition of deep "mental or physical discomfort."[10] This word will be used again to describe the feelings of these same young men when years later they are confronted with the knowledge that the Egyptian ruler who is treating them as spies is actually their brother Joseph

(Gen. 45:5). The sons are deeply distressed and absolutely furious over what has happened to their little sister, Dinah.

What Shechem has done to her is an affront to the whole family. The text says that he "wrought folly in Israel." The word rendered "folly" is used thirteen times in the Old Testament, and eight of those involve sexual crimes (Gen. 34:7; Deut. 22:21; Judg. 19:23, 24; 20:6, 10; 2 Sam. 13:12; Jer. 29:23). It's also used to describe Achan's sin in taking from Jericho that which had been dedicated to God (Josh. 7:15). The word refers to any kind of "serious disorderly and unruly actions resulting in the breakup of an existing relationship whether between tribes, within the family, in a business arrangement, in marriage or with God."[11] It should be thought of as a grievous vileness, an almost unthinkable wickedness because of the ripple effect of its impact. Shechem has done something that should not have been done, and what he has done will affect the entire clan.

Notice also that Jacob's family already thinks of themselves as a distinct people-group under God, using the covenant name God gave Jacob to identify themselves. Collectively, they are already becoming "Israel." Jacob must have been teaching his sons about his and their relationships with God. They have a lot to learn, but they understand that at least as far as their father is concerned they are God's people. We will find that they also understand at least the outward necessity of circumcision, if not necessarily its spiritual significance.

Hamor's Desire (Gen. 34:8–12)

Hamor finally arrives to address the fact that his son had raped Jacob's daughter. The Israelite clan has reason to expect Hamor to offer abject apologies, offer reparation for Dinah's and the family's loss of honor, and promise severe punishment for the perpetrator of the crime. Had he done so, the situation may have been resolved that day. However, it seems not to have occurred to Hamor that they might be unhappy about this. Either he hopes they haven't heard what happened, or he doesn't think what Shechem has done merits mentioning.

In verse 3, the text says that Shechem "loved the girl." The Hebrew word used there is *ahab*, which is a general word for a wide spectrum of emotion ranging from mild affection, as in the case of Isaac's "love" for Esau's venison (Gen. 27:4), to steadfast commitment, as in Jonathan's "love" for David (1 Sam. 18:1). It also says that his "soul clave" to Dinah, meaning either that his heart is clinging to her or that he has a strong desire for her.

When Hamor speaks in verse 8, he uses a verb translated "longeth for," which is "an expression denoting an intimate relationship based on loyalty and trust."[12] Shechem's own words were less definitive than those used by Hamor when he restates the request. The implication is that Hamor wants Jacob and Dinah's brothers to believe that Shechem's feelings for Dinah are more genuine, honorable, and permanent than Shechem himself has described them. Hamor is also more respectful in the way he speaks of Dinah than Shechem had been in private conversation with his father. He consistently refers to her as "your daughter," while Shechem had only called her "the girl."

While it may have been completely unintentional, Hamor has come to Jacob and his sons with an attitude that is deeply offensive. He comes, not with a proposal to arrange restitution but with a proposal to arrange marriage. Hamor actually seems to imply that the Israelite clan should be happy to make such a fine match for Dinah. Further, Hamor proposes intermarriage between his people and Jacob's (Gen. 34:9).

It is possible to infer from Hamor's mentioning Jacob's "daughters" to mean that Dinah was not his only daughter at this time. That is not conclusive, though, since he seems to be including the entire clan in his plan of intermarriage and may be speaking hypothetically of future daughters or generations of daughters. Bear in mind that Hamor's suggestion of intermarriage is not just an idle suggestion that would be nice if they could agree to allow their children to marry one another. Hamor is proposing that they formally arrange future intermarriage between the clans. Such an arrangement would be considered betrothals and would be contractually binding.

Hamor also suggests that Jacob make Shechem his permanent home, to live among them, move freely through the land, trade and become prosperous (Gen. 34:10). It isn't Hamor's fault that he's completely ignorant of God's promise to give all this land to Jacob and his descendents. God does not want Jacob to think of himself as "dwelling among" the Canaanite peoples—in Hamor's case, the Hivites. God wants Jacob to think of the land as his, albeit a future inheritance, and that the Hivites are temporarily dwelling among the Israelites. Hamor's suggestion is an insidious trap. For Jacob to agree to intermarriage with the Hivites would be to forfeit the blessing and undermine the promises of God, as it would have been for him to accompany Esau to Seir in the south.

Once Hamor has made his general proposals for intermingling the people of Shechem with the clan of Jacob/Israel, Shechem speaks for himself. Returning to his desire to marry Dinah, he speaks with some deference as he says, "Let me find grace in your eyes" (Gen. 34:11). He then offers a generous dowry, which would be a gift to Dinah, not to Jacob or the family (Gen. 34:12). He does not offer to purchase her but to make her rich. Once again, Jacob is presented with an offer to name his price. Shechem promises to give whatever Jacob and his sons require. However, for all his formal show of respect to Jacob and his sons, Shechem still comes across as arrogant and self-centered. He refers to Dinah as "the girl," emphasizes that he wants her for himself, and phrases it as in imperative—"Give me the girl as a wife."

Israel's Deception (Gen. 34:13–17)

Jacob does not respond to Hamor and Shechem's proposal. He leaves it to his sons to suggest an appropriate dowry, should they accept the offer of marriage. As I said earlier, this is probably consistent with regional customs. The brothers do not have the final say in the matter, but they are given great latitude in negotiating the dowry (cf. Gen. 24:53–60). We are not told if Jacob is "so distressed that he left the room altogether,"[13] or if the brothers confer on their own before coming in with this proposal. It may simply be a proposal put forward by Simeon and Levi and ratified by the rest. We know that Jacob is unaware of the treachery they are planning, but the text tells us nothing about his reaction to the offer his sons make.

Superficially, we might be able to interpret the suggestion of Jacob's sons as honorable, if misguided. They are telling him the honest truth when they say that "to give her to one that is uncircumcised" would be "a reproach unto us" (Gen. 34:14). Shechem's uncircumcised condition exacerbates Dinah's violation and makes it utterly defiling. However, they lie to Shechem when they say that if all the males of the city will be circumcised, they will accept not just the offer of Shechem's marriage to Dinah but the broader proposal of intermingling the clans to the extent that they will "become one people" (Gen. 34:15–16). That is something God could never allow to happen. Shechem and Hamor interpret this as a very generous offer. It will cost them no property and only brief misery.

We know that "they answered Shechem and Hamor . . . deceitfully" (Gen. 34:13), but we don't know if Jacob did. If he hears their suggestion, he may rationalize that the boys are requiring the Hivites to convert. After all, circumcision was the sign God gave Abraham of His covenant with him and his descendents (Gen. 17:9–14). Still, the proposal put forward by his sons would be unthinkable to Jacob if he is in a right relationship with God. Either he doesn't know what they are proposing, or he has fallen away from fellowship with the Lord to the extent that he is willing to risk the failure of the promise of God in order to maintain peace with the Hivites of this city.

Since the narrator tells us in advance that the brothers "answered . . . deceitfully," it is possible, even probable, that they deceive both the Hivites and their own father. Their deception of Shechem and Hamor is on two levels. First, they imply that the simple act of circumcision will bring the Hivites into the covenant and make intermarriage with them acceptable. Jacob has trained them well enough in the covenant promises and the worship of God that they know this is not true. Second, they have no intention of allowing Shechem to marry Dinah or allowing any other intermarriage between the clans.

To put more pressure on Shechem and Hamor, they add, "If this is not acceptable, we will take our daughter and leave." Again, they speak as a tribe—Dinah is their sister, but she is also the daughter of their clan.

Shechem's Destruction (Gen. 34:18–29)

As this section develops, we gain a little insight into why Jacob's sons think it's necessary to include the whole city in their plan of vengeance. No one in the city has spoken in Dinah's defense, nor even offered a word of protest or censure for Shechem's actions. Further, we discover that Dinah is still being held in Shechem's house (Gen. 34:26). Having raped her, he is holding her hostage while negotiating marriage. It seems that he plans to keep her one way or another and merely hopes to legitimize the relationship in the eyes of her family to avoid conflict. He never mentions letting her go if they do not agree to the marriage. Jacob's sons may think they will have to invade the city to rescue Dinah. To disable all the men of the city before mounting a rescue would be a militarily sound tactic.

But that's not all. We also discover that Hamor has ulterior motives of his own. He and the townsmen have no intention of allowing the proposed intermingling of Jacob's clan with the Hivites to benefit Jacob. They plan to absorb him into their culture and corporate economy (Gen. 34:21–23).

As the section opens, we are told that Shechem doesn't hesitate to agree to be circumcised because he "had delight in" or "took pleasure in Jacob's daughter." That may be why he was "more honorable," or "better respected," than all the other members of his father's household (Gen. 34:19). However, that phrase may simply indicate that he had greater influence or was more popular than the rest of the family.

As chief of the city, Hamor calls a meeting at the city gate, where legal and governmental matters were usually handled. He and Shechem have to convince the townsmen that this is a good plan. They don't start with the painful part. First, they give them part of the good news. Jacob and his family, the rich clan who just moved into the area with vast flocks and herds, are willing to make peace with the Hivites of Shechem. There is plenty of pastureland for them, and trade with them will provide a huge boost to the local economy. They are even willing to intermarry with the Hivites. There is only one minor condition. All the men of the city will have to circumcise themselves. Every member of Jacob's clan has been circumcised, so they aren't asking the Hivites to do something the Israelite clan are unwilling to do. Besides, look at all the animals they brought with them. Playing to the greed of their people, Shechem and Hamor add, "All their livestock, and all their wealth and every beast of burden will be ours" (Gen. 34:23a). They close with this: "If we will just agree with them, they will stay here among us" (Gen. 34:23b).

Notice that they say nothing about this plan being driven by Shechem's lust. He wants Dinah, and this is the only way to keep her peacefully. Further, no mention is made of Shechem's offense. Jacob and his sons haven't brought it up, so why worry about it? The only hard part is going to be cutting off their own foreskins without benefit of anesthetics or antibiotics. It will be painful, and the misery will increase for several days as almost inevitable infection sets in with its accompanying fever. They just don't mention that part of the deal again.

The men of Shechem agree. Work will have to stop for a few days, but the potential gain is worth it. The text says that "every male" is circumcised, then adds that this includes "all that went out at the gate of his city" (Gen. 34:24). The last phrase means that every man old enough to participate in government or commerce—every adult male—is circumcised, and it specifies that all the city leaders participate. It also means that no one will be capable of defending the city from attack.

The pain from this particular procedure is likely to be at its worst on the third day following the surgery.[14] On that day, when the men of Shechem are most vulnerable, Jacob's sons attack (Gen. 34:25). Simeon and Levi, two of Dinah's full brothers as the second and third sons of Leah, carry out the slaughter (Gen. 34:26). Apparently while the two of them are killing the men of the city and rescuing Dinah from Shechem's house, their brothers are rounding up the city's livestock, looting the city, and taking the women and children captive (Gen. 34:27–29).

The promises Hamor made to Jacob's family are fulfilled, but in a way that he certainly never imagined. The land is now open before Israel and they have gotten possessions in it (Gen. 34:10). The promises he had made to the people of Shechem have been turned upside down. Instead of absorbing Jacob's clan into the Hivite people and taking Israel's animals and wealth, this Hivite community has been destroyed and their animals and wealth have been taken by Jacob's clan. They have "sunk down in the pit that they made: in the net which they hid is their own foot taken" (Ps. 9:15).

Centuries later, God would order the nation of Israel under Joshua to slaughter all the Canaanites in the land, not even sparing the women and children. But those orders had not yet been given. Simeon and Levi have taken it upon themselves to preempt God's plan in their own time and their own way. Further, they have in effect trivialized their own faith by implying that their relationship with God was established merely by superficial surgery.

This situation is quite different from the one in which Jacob deceived his father to prevent Isaac's bestowing God's blessing on the wrong son, but the basic failure is similar. Neither Jacob then nor his sons now have been willing to wait on God to work out His plan. Their having adopted deceptive human means to accomplish what they considered a worthwhile end has resulted in bringing additional conflict and trouble into their lives that might have been avoided had they simply trusted God and behaved honorably.

Israel's Despair (Gen. 34:30–31)

Part of the blame for what happened that day in Shechem belongs to Jacob. He has brought his family to Shechem and has not properly supervised their activity. His family now faces a crisis. His daughter has been raped and is held captive, but where is the patriarch? Where is the spiritual and paternal leadership? Jacob abdicates his responsibilities and leaves the decisions and action to his sons, the oldest of them barely out of his teens. We could give him the benefit of the doubt and assume he doesn't know what they are up to, but why doesn't he know? How does he think the situation with Hamor is going to be resolved?

Jacob finally speaks up when the deed is done. His analysis is correct. What his sons have done will cause him "to stink," or "to be an abomination," among the people of the land (Gen. 34:30). He has tried to live at peace among them, as Abraham and Isaac had done, but Simeon and Levi have made him hated and vulnerable to attack. He is worried, because as strong as he is with his family and servants, the united force of the major people groups of the land, the Canaanites and Perizzites, could annihilate them.

Victor Hamilton says,

> It is ironic to hear Jacob venting his disgust over Simeon's and Levi's failure to honor their word, especially in terms of its potential consequence for Jacob, for he had done exactly that on more than one occasion. One need only recall events as recent as those in ch. 33, where Jacob gave Esau his word that he would follow Esau to Seir, only to take off for Succoth and Shechem.[15]

As I've explained, I believe Hamilton's analysis is incorrect. One of Jacob's strongest characteristics has been his commitment to keep his word.

The account of Jacob's life is better understood as a series of events in which he is the victim of broken promises, not the perpetrator of them. Isaac rewarded Jacob's decades of faithful service tending his father's sheep by never arranging his marriage and then trying to give God's blessing to the ungodly Esau. When Jacob promised Laban seven years of service for the right to marry his daughter, Laban rewarded him with a substitute bride. After fourteen years of service to Laban, Jacob agreed to work for any new striped, spotted, or discolored animals; and when the livestock produced an unexpectedly high percentage of such animals, Laban rewarded him by cutting his pay and then changing it often for six years. As far as the promise to meet Esau in Seir, there is no way to prove that Jacob did not go. He never promised to take his family or to move there, and to have done so would have been to leave the land to which God had told him to return. His only promise to Esau was that he would see Esau in Seir, and we have no reason to doubt that he did.

Yes, Jacob is incensed that his sons have lied, but there is nothing ironic about it. Integrity is the one trait that the inspired narrator attributes to Jacob at his introduction. It is one characteristic Jacob has in abundance and prizes above all others, and his son's actions have taken that away from him.

Those who suggest that Jacob is no longer confident of God's protection and needs to be revived may be correct. However, at the end of the last chapter, and possibly just weeks or months before, Jacob had built an altar and identified God as His God. It is probably better to think of him as so distraught over his sons' actions and his own failure to protect his family or guide them through this crisis that he now doubts that God will still act on his behalf. "God had delivered them from Laban and from Esau, both with relatively small bands of followers, when Jacob's cause was right. But how could they expect divine protection from the great host of ungodly Canaanites surrounding them when they themselves were in the wrong?"[16]

The narrator gives Simeon and Levi the last word. They had not been motivated by plunder but by a desire to protect their sister's and the family's honor. They ask a question Jacob can't answer: "Should he deal with our sister as with a harlot?" They interpreted Shechem's offer of whatever dowry they would demand as the price of a prostitute. Shechem probably didn't intend his offer to be taken that way, but his having raped her and kept her in his house, putting his sexual satisfaction first, makes Dinah's brothers' interpretation justifiable. It was their unauthorized actions that were not justified. "The sin of Shechem was an awful sin, but the sins of deceit and murder did not correct anything. One sin is not made right by committing another."[17]

Implied in their question is an accusation: "What was your plan, Dad? Where were you when Dinah needed you?" Jacob could say nothing in reply. He had failed his family and his God.

Lessons

Several spiritual lessons can be drawn from this passage. First, one should beware friendship with the world. Christians are often unwilling to recognize the danger posed by close friendship with or admiration of the world. Unbelievers' values are never thoroughly biblical, and all sorts of threats to one's safety or integrity can arise from too close an association with a skewed value system. This is true on both personal and corporate levels. Whether it is one person who compromises to get along with the world, or an entire congregation that does so to make "church" more compatible with the unbelieving community, the danger is the same (James 1:27; 4:4; 1 John 2:15–17).

A second lesson is that we must all beware the consequences of unbridled passion. Shechem's sexual lust dishonored Dinah, shamed Jacob, provoked Jacob's sons, and cost Shechem and his people their lives. Simeon's and Levi's vengefulness led to treachery, sacrilege, murder, robbery, and oppression. Seeking personal revenge causes more problems than it solves.

Believers throughout history have made a mistake similar to Simeon's and Levi's by trying to impose Christianity on unbelievers through military or political means. Those who would bomb abortion clinics are trying to stop a heinous crime by committing one themselves. They are no better than Simeon and Levi. Our knowing God and understanding His hatred of sin does not empower us to act as personal agents of divine justice.

I am speaking here of personal revenge, not judicial enforcement of law by legitimate government authority. In Romans 12:19, the apostle Paul says, "Dearly beloved, avenge not yourselves, but rather give place unto wrath, for it is written, Vengeance is mine: I will repay, saith the Lord." Just a few verses later, though, Paul says that God's vengeance is often executed on earth through the hands of proper governmental authorities. In Romans 13:1–5 he says that "the powers that be are ordained of God" to serve as "the minister [deacon] of God, a revenger to execute wrath upon him that doeth evil." Still, on a personal level, we are commanded to show mercy until Christ comes to act as righteous Judge, in the meantime deferring to appropriate governmental authorities. However righteous the cause, or however godly the man, it does not justify employing the ungodly means of personal revenge. Sin in the believer is more harmful than sin against the believer.

We also see in this passage an example of how God brings a reversal of fortune upon the people who plot evil against the people of God. A familiar theme in Scripture is that of the wicked man who digs a pit and falls in it, or lays a snare and is caught in it, being "taken in the devices that they have imagined" (Ps. 10:2).

Perhaps the most important lesson of all in this passage is a subtle one that is easy to miss. Religious ritual does not accomplish salvation. Circumcising the Shechemites did not make them God's people. Salvation was not accomplished by circumcision in Jacob's day any more than it is accomplished by church membership or baptism today. Salvation is by the grace of God through faith in Christ alone (Rom. 4:1–12; Eph. 2:8–10).

11

Jacob's Journey Home

Gen. 35:1–37:2a

ince World War II, the 3rd United States Infantry has been the army's official honor guard. One of the best known of their responsibilities is providing sentinels to "walk the mat" at The Tomb of the Unknowns in Arlington National Cemetery. The guard duty there has been honed to a specific ritual—twenty-one steps north at the pace of ninety steps a minute, pause for twenty-one seconds, turn, shift rifle to opposite shoulder (always the shoulder away from the tomb), stride twenty-one steps south, pause for twenty-one seconds, and repeat for anywhere from thirty minutes to two hours, depending on the season and time of day. They do this day and night, every day, in all weather. Even in severe conditions and when no one is watching, they do this for the sake of the honored dead. Contingency plans exist for keeping the tomb secure in weather conditions so severe that the sentinel's safety might be at risk, but as far as I can discover, the post has never been abandoned, even when Hurricane Isabel struck the capital in September 2003.[1] Someone has walked guard duty every minute since 1937.[2]

Guards on duty remain on post until relieved in a ceremonial changing of the guard. The relief commander approaches the sentinel on duty, salutes, and turns to face the visitors to ask for silence. The replacement sentinel approaches and submits to inspection by the relief commander. The two of them then march to the center of the mat on which the duty sentinel strides. The duty sentinel stops and faces his replacement. The relief commander says to the duty sentinel, "Pass on your orders." The duty sentinel replies, "Post and orders remain as directed," which indicates that he has faithfully stood his post and is prepared to relinquish it in the condition in which it was entrusted to him. The relieving sentinel then says, "Orders acknowledged." Having acknowledged the orders, the relief sentinel becomes the duty sentinel, and the duty sentinel is relieved from his post until his next duty cycle.

Soldiers who qualify for service at the tomb and are accepted for this duty are identified by a special badge. After serving for nine months, the badge becomes permanent. It is one of the rarest of army emblems, with only 567 having been awarded to date.[3]

As I said in the last chapter, it's possible to interpret the episode in Jacob's life at Shechem as evidence of God's judgment for Jacob's failure to fully obey God. He had returned to the land of Canaan but had not gone all the way to Bethel. Jacob had vowed that "this stone," which he erected at Bethel to mark the place where God had appeared to him in a dream, "shall be the house of God" (Gen. 28:22). That implies that he intended to return to Bethel to worship. Having made his home in Shechem, at least for a while, he had stopped fifteen miles short of Bethel. It is assumed that Jacob failed to arrive on post for duty.

However, we should not forget that Jacob has made a career of following orders, specifically the order to "arise and go" after a period of waiting at his post for just such an order. He stayed on duty, working the estate at home, until Rebekah told him to "arise and flee to Laban" (Gen. 27:43). Even then, he didn't forsake his post until Isaac confirmed the order, saying, "Arise, go to Padan-aram to the house of . . . Laban" (Gen. 28:2). This was further confirmed by God at Bethel, promising, "I am with thee, and will keep thee in all places whither thou goest" (Gen. 28:15). Jacob stayed on duty, doing exactly as his orders prescribed, until being relieved of duty and receiving alternate orders.

When Jacob arrived in Padan-aram, he joined himself to Laban's household and stayed at his post for twenty years, until God told him to "arise [and] get thee out of this land, and return unto the land of thy kindred" (Gen. 31:13). Again, Jacob followed orders. Then, having arrived in the land of "his kindred," he came to Shechem, the first place in Canaan with which Abraham was identified, and stayed on post there until God said, "Arise, go up to Bethel, and dwell there" (Gen. 35:1). Again, Jacob obeyed.

Called Back to Bethel (Gen. 35:1–4)

In the aftermath of the heartbreaking events at Shechem, God speaks to Jacob. He does not come with words of rebuke or censure. He reminds Jacob of his need for worship and close fellowship with God and calls him back to the place of his first real encounter with God (Gen. 35:1; cf. 28:10–22). It's possible that despite having spent as much as ten years in the land, this will be Jacob's first time going back to Bethel. That's the assumption of commentators such as Henry Morris,

> Though he had lived so close to it for about ten years, he had evidently never returned to see it again. This is all the more strange in view of the fact that Bethel is located almost directly between Shechem and Hebron, and Jacob certainly must have journeyed to Hebron on one or more occasions during this period to see his father Isaac. It almost seems that he had deliberately avoided Bethel. If this is so, it is probably because he knew he had not completely followed God's will, nor had he fully kept the promise he had made to the Lord at Bethel.[4]

As we will see, Morris is probably correct in assuming that Jacob had visited his father in Hebron (and, if so, probably Esau in Seir as well). Further, if Jacob has not been back to Bethel in all that time, Morris is almost certainly correct in suggesting that he seems to be avoiding it. However, it isn't necessary to assume that. Jacob may well have often traveled the fifteen miles up to Bethel for worship without moving his family there.[5]

God commanded Jacob at this time to go to Bethel. He adds that Jacob is to "dwell," or settle, there. He also tells him to build an altar there, or to construct a place of worship. Abraham had built altars at Shechem (Gen. 12:6–7) and at Bethel (Gen. 12:8) when he first arrived in Canaan. He also built one in Mamre (Hebron, Gen. 13:18) after returning from Egypt and separating from Lot. Much later, he built an altar in Moriah (Gen. 22:9) on which to offer his son Isaac. Isaac had built an altar in Beer-sheba (Gen. 26:23, 25), where the Lord appeared to him to confirm the covenant. Imitating Abraham, Jacob had built an altar at Shechem when he returned from Padan-aram (Gen. 33:18–20). The verse before us now (Gen. 35:1) is the only instance in which God instructs one of the patriarchs to build an altar. While Jacob may have visited Bethel during his years at Shechem, the fact that he had not yet built an altar there implies that he may not have fully kept his vow. It's possible, though, that he thought he had kept his vow by building an altar and offering sacrifices at Shechem. God never accuses Jacob of negligence. He merely says, "Arise, go up to Bethel, and dwell there, and make there an altar unto God."

In giving Jacob his instructions, God identifies Himself as the One "that appeared unto thee when thou fleddest from the face of Esau thy brother." This is not a reminder of an earlier failure but of an earlier fear. Hamilton points out that "God's word to Jacob is a reminder of his distant past, rather than of his immediate past. It is not Jacob's reconciliation with Esau that is recalled (ch. 33), but his earlier flight in terror from Esau (28:10ff.)."[6] God wants Jacob to remember that it was He Who had protected and kept Jacob when Esau was planning his destruction. Because of his sons' slaughter of the people of Shechem, he is facing at least as much danger from the neighboring peoples who are planning his destruction. God does not want Jacob to fit in with the people of the land, much less to be assimilated by them. Since He wants him to remain separate, He emphasizes His power to protect, not His power to reconcile.

As we have learned to expect, Jacob responds to these instructions by doing exactly as he is told. He gathers his household and everyone in his entourage, which now includes all the women and children taken from Shechem. He issues three commands that amount to an order for spiritual revival or conversion of the newcomers (Gen. 35:2). The first is that they are to get rid of their "strange gods." It's possible that Jacob has become so complacent in his status as "God's fighter" (Israel) that he has tolerated idolatry among his family and servants. However, we don't have to infer that from this statement. First, God did not tell Jacob to do this—he does it on his own. Second, there is no evidence that these "strange gods" were being worshiped by his family or servants. Surely the refugees from Shechem had some of their teraphim with them. Besides, in the looting of the city, his sons and their servants almost certainly brought out objects worshiped by those who practiced the Canaanite cult. Further, Jacob may be aware by now that Rachel had been responsible for Laban's missing household gods. Whether or not these images were being worshiped, their presence was inappropriate. Rather than being evidence of a lapse into idolatry otherwise unmentioned, it's better to see this as evidence of Jacob's piety. If he is to take his family and all those now with him to Bethel, he is not about to let any of them take their cultic objects with them.

Jacob's second and third orders are related to the first but can be performed only after all traces of idolatry have been removed. They must "be clean"—"purify" or "wash" themselves—and change their clothes. Joshua would later demand the same of the Israelites before they crossed the Jordan River into the Promised Land (Josh. 3:5; 4:1). There is a sense in which this has its parallel in New Testament baptism, though it's not baptism, nor even a primitive form of it. It does, however, foreshadow baptism in its signification of wholeheartedly identifying with God, leaving behind their former selves, and moving forward on a fresh start with God as their Master.

Jacob explains to everyone that they are going to move to Bethel, where Jacob will erect an altar to God, "who answered me in the day of my distress, and was with me in the way which I went" (Genesis 35:3*b*). While God's description of the situation had been more specific—"when thou fleddest from the face of Esau thy brother"— Jacob's words accurately describe for his people that this was "the day of my distress," or "the moment of my dire need."[7] Jacob actually expands on God's words, adding that He "was with me in the way which I went." He is crediting God with having brought him to Padan-aram, given him his family and property, and protected him to this point in his life.

The clan responded positively. They brought "all the strange gods" they had, and they also brought their "earrings" (Gen. 35:4). The root of the word translated "earrings" actually seems to refer to the nostril, which would make it more likely that it refers to jewelry worn in the nose than in the ear.[8] Jacob hasn't asked for the jewelry, but it is brought along with the gods. Again, we don't know who brought these things. It may be that the people from Shechem are the only ones in view. Whoever had them, though, apparently attached some cultic significance to the jewelry. Taking the gods and the jewelry, Jacob buried them under a tree in Shechem. Hamilton points out, "The parody on such gods continues from ch. 31 into ch. 35. Such gods may be stolen, sat on, stained with menstrual blood, and now buried."[9]

The KJV identifies the tree under which they were buried as an oak, but that is in some question. A related word is more accurately rendered "oak" in verse 8, which tells of the burial of Deborah. The translators of the KJV may have wanted to tie the two "burials" together, although the word "hid" in verse 4 and the word "buried" in verse 8 are not the same. It is more likely that the reference to burying the cult objects under this tree is intended to tie the passage to Abraham's initial visit to the region. Genesis 12:6 says, "And Abram passed through the land unto the place of Sichem [Shechem], unto the plain of Moreh." The word translated "plain" in Genesis 12:6 is translated "oak" in Genesis 35:4. In both cases it might be better rendered "terebinth tree" and both verses probably refer to the same tree. It was at the terebinth tree of Moreh, near Shechem, that the Lord appeared to Abram and promised him the land, and where Abram built his first altar to the Lord. That may well be why Jacob settled there, having returned to the very spot at which God had promised Abram the land. After Abram worshiped the Lord in Shechem, he moved on to Bethel and built another altar. Jacob again emulates his grandfather. Having already built an altar in Shechem, and upon being called of God to move from Shechem to Bethel and build another altar there, it is fitting for Jacob to bury the things associated with idolatry under the terebinth tree before going to build another altar.

Returning to Bethel (Gen. 35:5–8)

Moving to Bethel would be a risky venture. A man traveling with his property is more vulnerable to attack or other misadventure than when established in a place. In Jacob's case the danger is even more acute. He has been made an abomination to the people of the land, and they are seeking retaliation for what his sons had done to Shechem (Gen. 34:30). Jacob's only hope would be God's protection. God had just reminded him of His power to protect him. Now the Lord sends "the terror of God" upon all the cities of the region, keeping them from pursuing Jacob (Gen. 35:5). Jacob and those with him are able to travel unmolested to Luz, still the Canaanite name of the place. They had arrived at Shechem in peace (Gen. 33:18), and they are allowed to leave Shechem in peace.

As soon as they arrive, Jacob builds the altar, which he names "El-Beth-el," meaning "the God of Bethel"[10] or "The Strong God of the House of God"[11] (Gen. 35:7). Why add God's name to the beginning of the name he had already given the place? Jacob is honoring his vow to worship Abraham's God as his God. He is not building a mystic shrine that would be thought to have special powers of its own. He is not worshiping a place, but a Person. He does this to emphasize the God of the place, not the place itself.

At this point, the narrator jarringly interrupts the account of Jacob's worship at Bethel to tell us of the death of Deborah, Rebekah's nurse. This is the first time she has been mentioned by name anywhere in Scripture although she had been mentioned by title in negotiation with Laban for Isaac's right to marry his sister, Rebekah. Genesis 24:59 says, "And they sent away Rebekah their sister, and her nurse, and Abraham's servant, and his men." She had come with Rebekah from Laban's household. She had probably been Jacob's (and Esau's) nanny, assisting Rebekah in rearing the twins. Her presence with Jacob now implies several things.

It indicates that Rebekah is probably already dead. Surprisingly, her death and burial are never mentioned. When Jacob and his mother are parted, they are never reunited, and she is never heard from again. Her complete disappearance from the record may be evidence of God's having judged her, not Jacob, for lying to Isaac. When Jacob had objected to the plan, she said, "Upon me be thy curse, my son: only obey my voice" (Gen. 27:13).

Second, Deborah's presence proves that Jacob has had contact with his father's household since his return to the land. It's possible that she joined them at Bethel only to die immediately. However, her arrival at the camp is not mentioned, only her death. She had probably been with him for some time before dying when he returned to Bethel. If so, the accusations that Jacob lied to Esau about his intention to visit him in Seir are baseless. Since he obviously visited his father in Beer-sheba without any contact having been mentioned, there is no reason to assume Jacob failed to keep his promise to visit Esau.

Further, Deborah had probably joined Jacob's clan at least partly because she loved Jacob as she knew her mistress had loved him. Perhaps before her death Rebekah had charged her to watch for Jacob's return and expressed her regret at not seeing him again. She may have given Deborah items to take to Jacob as mementos of his mother. Deborah may also have joined him because two of his wives were Rebekah's nieces. Deborah would welcome news from Laban's daughters.

Deborah was clearly loved by the family. Other than those who became wives—Hagar, Bilhah, and Zilpah—she is the only female servant in the narrative to be named. Even her burial is recorded, and Rebekah's is not. She is buried with honor under an oak tree. Her death brought such great sorrow to Jacob and his family that her burial site was named Allon-bachuth—"The Oak of Weeping" (Gen. 35:8).

Confirmation of the Promise (Gen. 35:9–13)

The wording of the text suggests that some time has passed between Jacob's arrival at Bethel and his hearing from God. It's unlikely that Jacob arrived, built an altar, dug a grave, and then God appeared, all within a couple of days. God had told him to "dwell," or "settle," at Bethel. On the other hand, no more than a year or so could have gone by. Jacob's children are still getting older, and Joseph will be sold into slavery at age seventeen. Most of the time between leaving Padan-aram and Joseph's sale had to have been spent at Succoth and Shechem, or Dinah would have been too young to be considered of marriageable age and Jacob's sons would have been too young to exact vengeance on the city of Shechem. After arriving in Bethel, Jacob builds the altar. While there, Deborah dies. After she dies, God speaks.

This is the fifth time God speaks to Jacob, and the third time He appears to him (see Gen. 28:12–17; 31:3; 32:24–30; 35:1). God will later speak to Jacob a sixth time, in Genesis 46:2–4, after Jacob has learned of Joseph's survival in Egypt and while he is considering moving there at Jacob's request.

When God appears to Jacob at Bethel, lest we think God is now going to judge Jacob for something, we are told from the first that His appearance is for the purpose of blessing Jacob (Gen. 35:9). He reminds Jacob of his name change (Gen. 35:10). Ten years may have passed since Peniel. Jacob has been nearly overwhelmed by great distress over the injury to his daughter, the vengeance of his sons, and the enmity with the Canaanites. He desperately needs to be reminded of his relationship with God. While the name is not explained here, we know it signifies Jacob's dedication to God, his fervent desire for God's blessing, and his victorious importunity with God. For this, God had called him "God's warrior." God is on his side, and he is God's representative. He has no need to fear. The significance of the name change was not to show a change in Jacob's character. It was to show an enhancement in Jacob's relationship with God to give him confidence, first for courage to face Esau's anger, and now to persevere in the face of the Canaanites' anger.

God now identifies Himself by a name He had used with Abraham (Gen. 17:1) and Isaac (Gen. 28:3), El Shaddai (Gen. 35:11a). The name means "almighty God," especially in the sense of being "all-sufficient." Since God is with Jacob, Jacob will never need anything more. Jacob is a prince who has power with the God Who is the

almighty, all-sufficient One. If Jacob is to weather the storms still to
come, he needs to be absolutely confident of this relationship. His
life has been filled with conflict, heartache, betrayal, and grief. It will
only get worse. Jacob needs to know that he can trust God to be all he
needs and to be powerful enough to protect him.

God tells Jacob to "be fruitful and multiply" (Gen. 35:11*b*). Since
Jacob has four wives, eleven sons, and an undisclosed number of
daughters, I wonder, "How much more fruitful does God want Jacob
to be?" In fact, in a few verses, we see that his favorite wife dies in
childbirth. As a direct result of his obedience to this command, Jacob
will lose his beloved Rachel. Jacob has faced injustice at the hands of
his father and his father-in-law. Now he must face what must feel like
injustice at the hand of God. Jacob's steadfast faith in the face of such
tragedy, misery, and apparent injustice is hardly less astounding than
the persevering faith of Job.

Nevertheless, God probably isn't telling Jacob to have more sons
and daughters. He ties this promise to the original instructions to
mankind. He wants Jacob and the reader to realize that God is still
developing His plan to bring blessing to all humanity through Jacob.
He also promises that Jacob's family will multiply to become "a nation
and a company of nations" (Gen. 35:11*c*). God indicates that in their
national existence, there will be perpetual tribal identifications within
the one nation of Israel. For only the second time in history, God
also says that kings will come from this line. That's a promise He had
made to Abraham (Gen. 17:6) but had never repeated to Isaac. God
also reiterates that His promise to give Abraham and Isaac the land
of Canaan would be guaranteed to Jacob and his future descendents
(Gen. 35:12). "Thus within these brief words several major themes
of the book have come together. The primeval blessing of mankind
was renewed through the promise of a royal offspring and the gift of
the land."[12] After making this absolute, irrevocable, unconditional
promise, God "went up from him" (Gen. 35:12), which reminds us of
Jacob's vision of the stairway reaching to heaven at this place.

Consecration to God (Gen. 35:14–15)

Having received confirmation of God's promises, Jacob erects a
pillar at the place where God had appeared (Gen. 35:14). This monument is not to be confused with the altar but is a different structure.
Jacob pours oil on it, as he had on the pillar he had erected on his

first contact with God at Bethel (Gen. 28:18). The drink offering that he also pours on the pillar is the first such offering on record. When the system of Levitical offerings was established centuries later, drink offerings would be auxiliary and optional. Never offered alone, they are additional offerings brought to show special gratitude, devotion, or consecration to the Lord (Lev. 23:13–37; Num. 15:5–24; 28:7–31; 29:6–39).

The point of this whole section has been to show Jacob's consecration to the Lord. As soon as God tells him to go to Bethel, he goes. Before leaving for Bethel, he makes sure that everyone in his household, including family, staff, servants, and captives have removed any trace of idolatry from their belongings. He also requires their personal consecration to the Lord. When he arrives, he builds the altar God had told him to build and worships Him there. Then he stays at Bethel until God appears to him again with renewed promises of blessing, after which he builds yet another structure for worship and makes an additional offering to God. If Jacob's faith and commitment had slipped while he was at Succoth and Shechem, it has been bolstered at Bethel.

More Heartache (Gen. 35:16–22*a*)

Having heard from God at Bethel, Jacob can now continue southward toward his father's home in Mamre (Hebron). It seems as if he wants to get his family there in time for the birth of Rachel's second child. It has been a long time between children. Her first child, Joseph, had been born after nearly seven years of pining for a child. At his birth, she had expressed a longing for another son: "The Lord shall add to me another son" (Gen. 30:24). That was nearly seventeen years ago. God's promise has been confirmed and renewed. A child is on the way. Jacob is coming home to reclaim his position as Isaac's heir. This was shaping up to be an especially joyous homecoming.

As has so often been the case in Jacob's life, the rejoicing was to be tainted with grief. I wonder, "How much trouble, conflict, betrayal, and heartache can one man bear in a lifetime?" Apparently a little more. Along the way to Mamre, as they approach Ephrath, later named Bethlehem, Rachel goes into labor (Gen. 35:16). The baby's birth is probably premature, since they are still traveling when she delivers the child. The text tells us twice that she had "hard labor." The assisting midwife is probably the same one who delivered Joseph. She tries to comfort Rachel with the assurance that she is having another son, reminding her of Rachel's own words on that earlier occasion (Gen. 35:17). Yet Rachel's travail in childbirth is so severe that she will not survive. As Rachel is dying, she names her son Ben-oni (Gen. 35:18*a*).

Jacob, however, gives his newborn son a different name, calling him Benjamin (Gen. 35:18*b*). This is surprising for a couple of reasons. First, of his twelve sons, this is the only one Jacob names. All the others were named by their mothers. Second, while many people in Scripture have their names changed in connection with some key event in their life, this may be the only example in the biblical record of a child being given one name at birth only to have it changed immediately. Another for whom that might have been the case will be Solomon, who was named Jedidiah by the Lord through the prophet Nathan (2 Sam. 12:24–25). Another possible example is found in the New Testament. When Elizabeth bore a son in her old age, relatives and neighbors thought he should be named Zachariah, like his father (Luke 1:59), but Elizabeth and Zachariah insisted that his name was John (Luke 1:60).[13]

Commentators do not agree on exactly what these two names signify. One common explanation is that Ben-oni means "son of misfortune" while Benjamin means "son of my good fortune" by contrast. A slight variation on this sees Ben-oni meaning "son of my sorrow" and Benjamin meaning "son of my right hand" (as in the KJV). The "right hand" reference could refer either to strength or honor of position in the family or to Jacob's joy at having a young son to lean on in his old age now that he has a permanent limp. Citing D. Cohen, Victor Hamilton makes an interesting alternate suggestion. Ben-oni could mean "son of my wickedness" while Benjamin could mean "son of my oath." If that is the case, Rachel could be naming her child as a deathbed confession of her sin of stealing her father's gods and lying about them, and Jacob could be renaming him in reference to the oath he made at the time that whoever was found with Laban's gods would surely die (Gen. 31:32).[14] This latter explanation would make the names more complementary than contrasting. The weakness of that explanation is in the absence of any reference in the text for either Rachel or Jacob believing that Rachel's death was sin related.

After Rachel's death, she is buried along the way to Bethlehem (Gen. 35:19). The text anticipates the future importance of this little city. Events both great and tragic would occur there. The greatest would be the birth of Jesus Christ (Luke 2:4–7). The most tragic would be Herod's subsequent slaughter of all male children age two and younger (Matt. 2:16–18). The text at that point even describes "Rachel weeping for her children and would not be comforted, because they are not."

In the same way that he had marked the locations of his communion with God at Bethel, Jacob marks the location of Rachel's grave with a pillar (Gen. 35:20). Saying that it remains there "unto this day" is probably a reference to the days of Moses in his compilation and editing of the final form of this text. Moses wanted the descendents of Israel to enter the Promised Land looking for this marker.

Leaving this place of both joy and grief, Jacob and his family continue southward to Hebron. They stop for a while at a place called the "tower of Edar" (Gen. 35:21). Its exact location is uncertain but may have been a watchtower "for the protection of flocks against robbers"[15] erected not far from Bethlehem, toward Jerusalem. While there, a troubling event takes place. Jacob's firstborn son, Reuben, has sexual intercourse with Bilhah, Rachel's handmaid and Jacob's wife or concubine (Gen. 35:22a).

Reuben cannot be over twenty-three years old at this time. Since Leah had four children before Jacob took Bilhah as his wife (Gen. 29:32–30:3), Reuben would have been about three years old by then. While she may have been older, Bilhah could have been as young as thirteen or fourteen, which could make the age difference between the two only ten years or so. However, the disparity in their ages is not the real issue.

What would prompt Reuben to do this? Henry Morris might be right in suggesting that "there was little opportunity for him to find a wife or even to meet any prospective girl friends" other than servants and Canaanites, who were "off limits to him in view of his position."[16] Surely those servants and Canaanites were not more "off limits" than was Bilhah! Since the text does not hint at rape, the act is apparently consensual. The probable reason for this is not simply sexual gratification, which would have been bad enough. It is more likely a power grab, to establish himself as Jacob's primary heir.

There are several examples in the Old Testament in which a new king would claim the wives of his predecessor as his own. Sometimes a usurper attempting to overthrow a king would take his wives or concubines as a part of his coup attempt (see 2 Sam. 3:7; 12:8; 16:20–22; 1 Kings 2:22). Even David seems to have taken a wife of Saul in retaliation for Saul's having given David's wife Michal to another man

(1 Sam. 25:43–44; cf. 14:50) and other of Saul's wives later (2 Sam. 12:8a).

Why would Reuben do this? Perhaps Jacob's recent failure to even respond to Dinah's rape at Shechem had something to do with it. This and a couple of other incidents that will follow almost immediately afterward may indicate that his sons have lost respect for his leadership. Further, Jacob has already demonstrated that Rachel's oldest son, Joseph, is his favorite, having presented him to Esau last of all his sons. As the firstborn son, Reuben may be trying to take control. The fact that Jacob knows Reuben had relations with Bilhah and does not respond may have reinforced his sons' disrespect for his authority. Still, while Jacob does not confront this sin, neither does he forget it (cf. Gen. 49:4).

Finally Home (Gen. 35:22b–37:2a)

What we have in these verses is in many ways the finale of Jacob's story. The final sentence in the text above—"Now these are the generations of Jacob"—is usually understood to introduce the next section of the text running all the way to the end of Genesis, as if what follows is "the account of Jacob" (NIV). The chapter and verse divisions, added by translators many centuries after the originals were written, testify to a long-standing tradition of seeing this and other similar statements as introductory to the subsequent narrative. Commentators routinely treat it the same way, even though many express surprise. John Sailhamer says, "The formal title of the section is 'This is the account of Jacob' (v. 2a). As v. 2b suggests, however, the remaining narrative is not about Jacob as such but about Joseph."[17] Similarly, Victor Hamilton says, "Although everything in 37:2b and following is titled as the story of Jacob (37:2a), it is obvious that the data is preponderantly about Joseph."[18]

Henry Morris makes an alternate suggestion that makes a lot of sense. He argues that the *toledoth* ("generations") formula, oft repeated in Genesis, constitutes in most cases a closing signature rather than an introduction.[19] Instead of identifying the theme of the subsequent text, which it never does effectively (the only exception being Genesis 36:1 and 9 which bracket the list of Esau's descendents), it identifies the original author of the preceding narrative. While Jacob will live for many more years, the focus of the text will shift to the next generation. Jacob's sons will become the main characters, with two emerging as contenders for being next in the line of God's promised blessing.

As Jacob approaches home, we have another roster of his sons (Gen. 35:22b–26). This time, the list is not arranged chronologically but by families. They are apparently listed in the order in which he will present them to his father: the six sons of Leah in their birth order, the two sons of Rachel in their birth order, the two sons of Rachel's handmaid in their birth order, and the two sons of Leah's handmaid, in their birth order. Strictly speaking, Benjamin was not "born to him in Padan-aram," actually having been born near Bethlehem. However, Isaac had told him to go to Padan-aram to find a proper wife. While Jacob has visited Isaac since returning to Canaan, he is bringing his family and property home for the first time. This is the official end of his trip to Padan-aram, so we don't have to consider it an "error" for the narrator to present this as a list of the sons "born to him in Padan-aram" (Gen. 35:26b).

Finally, Genesis 35:27 tells us that Jacob settles in his father's homeland. He has followed Abraham's footsteps home without duplicating Abraham's disobedient side trips into Egypt and the land of the Philistines. Abraham had built an altar at Shechem, then at Bethel, then at Mamre and had settled more or less permanently in Hebron. Upon his return, Jacob had built an altar at Shechem, then at Bethel, and now has moved to Mamre, particularly Hebron. He has done as God instructed in returning to the land of his fathers. The heir to the birthright and the promise has come home.

The final two verses of the chapter briefly recount Isaac's death and burial. His age of 180 at the time of his death is interesting. This means Isaac doesn't die until twelve years after Joseph is sold into Egypt. While the calculations are not really complicated, they can be confusing. Joseph was thirty years old when he was elevated to Pharaoh's court in Egypt (Gen. 41:46). Jacob moved to Egypt after the second year of famine, which came after seven years of plenty, so he got to Egypt when Joseph was thirty-nine (Gen. 45:6) and Jacob was 130 (Gen. 48:9). That means Joseph was born when Jacob was ninety-one. Since Joseph was born during Jacob's fourteenth year with Laban (Gen. 30:25), Jacob must have been seventy-seven when he left home to go to Padan-aram. Isaac was sixty years old when Jacob was born (Gen. 25:26), making him 137 when Jacob left home. If Joseph is sold the year Jacob gets home, Jacob has been gone for no more than thirty-one years, making Isaac no more than 168 when Jacob arrived back at Hebron. For a man who claimed he was dying and tried to give Jacob's blessing to Esau, he sure has held on for a long time—another forty-three years.

Following Isaac's death, Jacob and Esau work together to bury him. They are apparently on friendly terms even though this signifies the final stage of Jacob's ascendancy over Esau. With Isaac's death, Jacob inherits the birthright.

With these verses, the essence of Jacob's story has been completed. He has received everything God promised to give him in this life, and the stage has been set for future blessings. Despite his consistent faith and fidelity, he has endured his father's neglect and disrespect. Finally permitted to marry, he was sent out with nothing and had to earn his own bride-price. He was cheated by his father-in-law. In his absence, his beloved mother had died. On his return home, his daughter had been raped, two of his sons have become murderers, another has slept with one of his wives, and his favorite wife has died.

On the other hand, when Jacob left home with nothing but his staff in his hand, he went with the promise of God's constant presence, provision, and protection. He has heard from God five times and met him three times. He has received specific instructions from God, which he has followed to the letter, and has received specific promises from God, many of which have already been fulfilled. He is now dwelling in the land where his father had sojourned, awaiting and anticipating the complete fulfillment of God's promises.

Jacob's critics often describe the hard parts and tragedies in his life as just recompense for his own wickedness. They call him grasping, sneaky, deceptive, cowardly, and just plain evil. But because at the end of the story he is worshiping God and elevated with a significant new name, they say that he has learned his lesson, repented of sin, turned back to God, and been converted. That analysis has three serious flaws. First, it ignores the good things God has said about him throughout Scripture. Second, it overlooks the fact that God never has any word of rebuke for Jacob, but only words of encouragement and honor. Third, it fails to note that Jacob never confesses sin or asks forgiveness from God or anyone else, so there is no evidence of "conversion."

As I said at the outset, I think the far better way to look at Jacob's life is to see him as a man with a consistent passion for God's blessing despite hardship, abuse, misunderstanding, and betrayal. Like any other great man of faith, he is not perfect, but he does have a heart for God. Jacob has kept his word, and so has God. No wonder God so often calls Himself "the God of Jacob." Jacob is God's man, and the Lord is Jacob's God.

Lessons

In this chapter Jacob provides an important example in worship. Before going to Bethel to worship God, Jacob had his family and all the people appertaining to them divest themselves of anything connected with false worship. I fear that much of what is called worship in today's churches, particularly in the United States, falls short of the worship God demands. I was recently discussing this with a friend I met in our local choral society. His attitude toward contemporary worship is a lot more tolerant then mine. He told me of his recent visit to a church in town, which he described as a little "over the top" when they turned on the laser lights and fog machine. Worship styles are often patterned after the world's entertainment, intentionally trying to duplicate it. Rather than setting aside the false gods of pleasure, entertainment, and wealth, contemporary worshipers often bring them along and give them preeminence.

Further, once Jacob got to Bethel, he emphasized the importance of the God they worshiped, not the place they met Him. The place itself is not sacred. It is God alone Who is to be worshiped.

This chapter also provides additional evidence of the central theme of Jacob's life—trusting God when life is hard. God seems to be telling us all the horrible things that happen to Jacob, with occasional episodes of encouragement. Jacob will eventually give Pharaoh an honest description of his life: "Few and evil have the days of the years of my life been" (Gen. 47:9), but then he will bless Pharaoh (Gen. 47:10). When you and I are faced with trials, we tend to be quick to doubt or even accuse God. We would do well to be more like Jacob. Despite the hardships, ill treatment, and misfortune that he endured, Jacob remains confident in God's leadership and goodness.

12

Jacob's Later Years

Gen. 37:2b–48:22

y wife's parents had dreamed for years of moving to the beach when they retired. Preparing for it for years, they purchased a lot on Oak Island, near Wilmington, North Carolina. They built a modest home with an ocean view, part of the third row of houses from the beach in a quiet residential community. Summer rentals paid much of the mortgage until they were ready to move in permanently. When they were finally able to retire, they joyfully sold their home in north-central South Carolina and moved to their dream house at the beach. They anticipated living out their days in restful contentment to the sound of the surf.

Life rarely works out the way we plan. Living at the beach was not as simple and carefree as they had expected. They missed the familiar surroundings of their hometown, including their family, friends, and church. Then hurricanes forced them to board up and evacuate three times in two months. The first two storms just brushed their property and did little damage, but the third struck almost head on. When they returned after that storm had cleared, they found their third-row house on the second row. Their house hadn't moved, but the first row of houses was gone, and part of one of those houses was in their front yard. It took months to clean up. Then their insurance costs nearly tripled. Staying at the beach had become very costly and not much fun. It was certainly neither restful nor carefree. Realizing that their dream had been less fulfilling than expected, they decided to sell their beach house and move back to their hometown.

Even that had its disappointments. Rather than living in town, they were out a few miles, so it was harder to see their friends than they had expected. My father-in-law took a part-time job to help with the bills and the boredom. Then they developed health issues, the most serious of which was the discovery that my mother-in-law had a brain tumor that was causing weakness and a loss of coordination. The tumor was removed, and proved to be benign, but learning to walk again was a struggle. After two years of slow progress, her condition began to worsen. Recent tests have indicated that the radiation therapy used to keep the tumor from regrowing has caused permanent brain damage that will produce classic Alzheimer's symptoms but will be untreatable.

When we got this word, my wife was understandably distraught. We drove to meet them and took them to dinner. Expecting them to be distressed and fearful, we were a little surprised to find them peaceful and confident. They know God is capable of making her better, but that is not their expectation. They are realistically discussing the coming difficulties, as caring for her will become more demanding. They are already considering the possibility of needing to find an assisted living facility in the near future. Their retirement has been less enjoyable than they expected, but they know the Lord of life and are confident of His promise of eternal glory. As Paul said, in this life we "groan within ourselves, waiting for the adoption, to wit, the redemption of our body" (Rom. 8:23), knowing that "the sufferings of this present time are not worthy to be compared with the glory which shall be revealed in us" (Rom. 8:18).

The bulk of Jacob's story has been told. A thorough discussion of the remainder of Genesis would have to focus primarily on Jacob's sons and go well beyond the scope of this study of Jacob. However, at the close of the last chapter, we left him alive and well in Hebron. He will live for many more years, and there are events yet to come in his life and death that are worthy of our notice.

Jacob is in position to inherit Isaac's estate. When combined with his own property, this will make him extraordinarily wealthy. He probably hopes to live out his years in uneventful, domestic tranquility. He will soon be disappointed. It has been no more than two years since the awful events at Shechem, and no more than a year since the death of his beloved Rachel. He is barely settled in Hebron before conflict among his sons disrupts his peace.

Jacob's Despair (Gen. 37:2*b*–35)

Jacob's favoritism toward Rachel's firstborn son, Joseph, has been described as "the central problem that initiated the action of the story, for it angered Joseph's brothers and turned them against him."[1] However, that assumes Jacob's favoritism of Joseph was unfounded and, I believe, misses part of the narrator's point. While Jacob's unabashed favoritism of Joseph was likely to cause contention, it does not necessarily follow that he was wrong to favor Joseph. The story is more about the sins of jealousy and envy than about the consequences of favoritism.

Jacob's sons' jealousy of Joseph focused on the special coat (Gen. 37:3) Jacob made for him. What the coat looked like is debated. Traditionally, it is thought of as "many colored" (KJV), based on the reading of the LXX and the Vulgate. Making different assumptions on the etymology of the word *passim*,[2] more recent scholarship tends to describe it as "an upper coat reaching to the wrists and ankles, such as noblemen and kings' daughters wore."[3] Combining the two ideas, the NIV says Jacob made "a richly ornamented robe." Whether it is "varicolored" (NASB) or "long sleeved" (RSV), the point is that the coat designated Joseph as Jacob's heir, the intended inheritor of the birthright—a double portion (two-thirteenths for Joseph and one-thirteenth for each of the others). The brothers are jealous of Joseph's position, not his wardrobe.

The common assumption is that Jacob was wrong to do this, that he should have learned a lesson from the friction caused in his own family by his father's favoritism toward Esau. In Jacob's defense, we must remember that he doesn't publicly identify Joseph as his heir until after the three eldest sons of Leah have disqualified themselves by actions that were both unrighteous and traitorous. Simeon and Levi had usurped Jacob's position in their vengeance upon Shechem. Not much later, Jacob's firstborn son, Reuben, had usurped his father's prerogative by having sexual relations with Bilhah. Now we learn that the four sons of the handmaids are also involved in some activity that threatened Jacob's testimony or the family's security in some way (Gen. 37:2). Other than the infant Benjamin and his older brother, Joseph, the only sons who have not been specifically indicted for something are Judah, Issachar, and Zebulun. It's also possible that of the sons Jacob brought out of Padan-aram (all but Benjamin) Joseph alone had not been involved in the looting of Shechem. Jacob makes this coat for Joseph shortly after he becomes aware of Reuben's mutinous affair. He has not disowned his other sons, but he has demonstrated his profound disappointment in Reuben in particular by making this public declaration.

As the story of Joseph progresses, we find that he, more than any other of Jacob's sons, exhibits a desire to honor God. Jacob's choice of Joseph as his heir actually indicates that he learned a very important lesson from Isaac's favoritism. Jacob was determined not to make the same mistake his father had made. He would not disregard the son of his favorite wife. Neither would he bestow honor upon an unworthy son. He would honor the son who would tie him most closely to his beloved wife and who would be most likely to honor God.

A day comes when Jacob's sons are tending his flocks fifty miles north of Hebron near Shechem (Gen. 37:12). Why are they in Shechem, of all places? Jacob has good reason to fear for their safety. It has been no more than two years since their slaughter of the Shechemites, and they are surely still hated by the other inhabitants of the region. If so, his willingness to send Joseph alone to find them may imply that Joseph was known to have been innocent of slaughter and pillage. Furthermore, Jacob may fear for their piety. The last thing he did before leaving Shechem was bury the false gods collected from among those with him. Had they, like Lot's wife, been unwilling to leave those things behind? Have they returned to retrieve those cult objects? Jacob sends Joseph to check on his brothers (Gen. 37:13).

Joseph may be wearing his special coat on this occasion simply to lord it over his brothers, but the narrator never accuses him of that. It's just as likely that he is wearing it for protection. Anyone he might encounter will know from his coat that he is an important individual and that he acts as his father's surrogate. Whatever the reason, when his brothers see him coming wearing that coat, they are provoked into plotting his murder (Gen. 37:18–20). When Judah suggests that it might be better to sell him to a passing band of Ishmaelites (Gen. 37:23–28), the others agree. They take his special coat, cover it with goat's blood, and return it to Jacob for identification (Gen. 37:29–32). When he sees the coat, Jacob says, "It is my son's coat; an evil beast hath devoured him; Joseph is without doubt rent in pieces" (Gen. 37:33).

On its surface, Jacob seems to have concluded that Joseph had been attacked by a wild animal. However, since there is no evidence that the coat was torn and no body or part thereof had been recovered, he may be implying that he suspects his sons had killed Joseph and were themselves "evil beasts." If so, it would help explain the depth of Jacob's despair. He was inconsolable. He refused to take any comfort from his sons and daughters[4] and expressed his intention to mourn Joseph's loss until his own death (Gen. 37:34–35).

We shouldn't miss the fact that Jacob is confident of life after death. When he says, "I will go down into the grave unto my son mourning," he indicates his expectation of reunion with his beloved son in the afterlife.

Jacob's Doubt (Gen. 42:1–38)

Twenty-one years pass before Jacob is mentioned again. Joseph has spent a combined thirteen years behaving honorably in the house of Potiphar and in an Egyptian prison. After that, Joseph was exalted in Egypt to a position second only to Pharaoh's. He has spent seven years storing the surplus from bountiful harvests and another two managing grain distribution during the first two of the seven years of famine. During all this time, Jacob continues to grieve for Joseph.

Jacob has felt the famine's impact in Canaan, apparently to the point of threatening the lives of his livestock and even his family. Yet his sons have done nothing about the situation. Having heard that there is grain to be had in Egypt, Jacob asks his sons, "Why do ye look upon one another?" (KJV), or "Why are you standing around looking at each other?"[5] In words "that foreshadow the final outcome,"[6] Jacob says, "Get you down thither . . . that we may live, and not die."

This is the third famine in that region, one affecting each of the three patriarchs. In the two earlier famines, both Abraham and Isaac had moved out of the region promised by God. Abraham went to Egypt, where he lied about Sarah's identity, and Isaac moved in among the Philistines, where he lied about Rebekah's identity to save his life. We shouldn't miss the fact that when Jacob is faced with a severe famine, he doesn't even consider moving from the place God told him to settle.

Instead, Jacob sends ten sons to Egypt to buy grain (Gen. 42:1–3) but keeps Benjamin at home. Jacob refuses to send him with his ten brothers, saying, "Lest peradventure mischief befall him" (Gen. 42:4). Benjamin is no longer a child, being about twenty-two years old. I suspect this is further evidence that Jacob thinks his sons had been responsible for Joseph's death. Does he think a wild animal will attack all eleven and overcome Benjamin alone? It is not circumstance that he mistrusts; it is his sons.

When Jacob's sons arrive in Egypt, they have no idea that the government official they meet there is Joseph. The story is a fascinating one, but most of it is not germane to our study of Jacob. What is significant is that when Joseph decides to test his brothers, apparently realizing that Reuben had tried to spare him all those years ago, Joseph kept Simeon, the second son, as prisoner (Gen. 42:24). The nine remaining sons of Jacob are forced to return without Simeon with the promise that Simeon would be released only if they return to Egypt with Benjamin. When they arrive home and explain the situation to Jacob, he cries, "Me have ye bereaved of my children: Joseph is not, and Simeon is not, and ye will take Benjamin away: all these things are against me" (Gen. 42:36).

Two important thoughts emerge from Jacob's statement. First, Jacob comes very close to making an outright accusation against his sons for killing Joseph, further supporting the idea that he has always at least suspected their collusion in his death. He may even imply that he doesn't believe their story about Simeon. He may think they have killed Simeon and that they are now plotting to get Benjamin away from him so they can kill him too. Second, it implies that Jacob is on the verge of giving up hope of the fulfillment of God's promises. Having transferred his hopes for the future from Joseph to Benjamin, and believing his sons are plotting Benjamin's death too, he doubts that any of his surviving sons could possibly qualify to carry on the line of the promised Messiah.

Therefore, Jacob refuses to allow his sons to take Benjamin to Egypt, implying that he fears what they might do to him on the way: "My son shall not go down with you; for his brother is dead, and he is left alone: if mischief befall him by the way in the which ye go, then shall ye bring down my gray hairs with sorrow to the grave" (Gen. 42:38). Having read the end of the story, we can't help but sense the irony in his despair. Just as circumstances are converging to produce an outcome better than he could have imagined, Jacob wails, "All these things are against me!" He is still ignorant of what God is doing. He has no idea that "all these things" are actually working "together for good" (Rom. 8:28).

Jacob's Revival (Gen. 43:3–46:28)

Despite the worsening famine, Jacob still doesn't consider moving and resists allowing Benjamin to leave his estate, apparently willing to sacrifice Simeon, if need be. Jacob's fourth-born son, Judah, emerges as a leader at this time. Twenty-one years before his intervention had saved Joseph's life (Gen. 37:26–27). He unwittingly expands on Jacob's earlier prophetic statement that by going into Egypt they would "live and not die" (Gen. 42:2), indicating this would be for the salvation of the entire clan, "we, thou, and our little ones." Judah offers himself as surety for Benjamin's safety (Gen. 43:8–9) if his father will let him go. Basically, his argument is "You can let him go and risk his life, or you can keep him here and we'll all die. Which will it be?"

Jacob finally relents. Before sending his sons to Egypt, Jacob says, "And God Almighty give you mercy before the man, that he may send away your other brother, and Benjamin. If I be bereaved of my children, I am bereaved" (Gen. 43:14). Not fully trusting his sons, Jacob has decided to trust El Shaddai—the God Who had promised him eternal possession of the land, nations of descendents, and kings among his progeny (Gen. 35:10–12). Jacob's faith has been weakened but not destroyed. At what may have been the lowest point in his life emotionally, his faith is beginning to be revived. Significantly, his prayer that "God Almighty give you mercy before the man" will guide our understanding of the rest of the narrative to the conclusion of Genesis. God answers this prayer at the close of the story. "In these subtle and indirect ways the writer informs the reader of the power of God in directing the lives of his people and in carrying his plans to completion."[7]

Further evidence of Judah's rise to leadership is seen on this trip to Egypt. Joseph engineers a situation to justify his arresting Benjamin and sending the other brothers home. Believing Benjamin to be guilty of theft, Judah responds by offering himself in exchange for Benjamin (Gen. 44:18–34). In an eloquent plea for understanding, Judah explains that he offers himself specifically for his father's sake. He cannot bear to see what will happen to his father if he returns without Benjamin. It's this aspect of his plea that sets Judah apart from Reuben, who had earlier expressed despair over Joseph's disappearance because he didn't know what would happen to himself (Gen. 37:30). In Judah's act of self-sacrifice for the sake of his father we see the first hint of a division within the promises of God between two sons of Jacob. Joseph, the favored son, will receive the birthright, but Judah will receive the most significant part of the blessing and be the son through whom the Messiah will come.

In the dramatic events that follow, Joseph reveals his identity to his stunned and terrified brothers. Inadvertently acting in answer to Jacob's prayer that God would give them mercy before the Egyptian official, Joseph treats them mercifully. Loading them with gifts, he sends them back to fetch their father and their families so they can survive the famine in comfort in Egypt (Gen. 45:1–25).

When Jacob gets the news that Joseph is alive and essentially ruling Egypt, his initial response is a numb heart and disbelief (Gen. 45:26). His sons then tell him "all the words of Joseph," which meant they had to confess their own sin against their brother and their father. When he hears their words, Jacob's "spirit . . . revived" (Gen. 45:27), and he believes them. Realizing he will no longer have to wait until he dies to be reunited with Joseph, he says, "I will go and see him before I die" (Gen. 45:28).

Jacob has not forgotten his family history. Abraham and Isaac had both gotten in a lot of trouble by leaving the land God had promised them to escape a famine (Gen. 12:10–20; 26:1–3). Now, despite another famine, Jacob has steadfastly resisted moving to Egypt. Even in his despair and doubt, he has obeyed the directive of God to settle in the land of his fathers and assumed the earlier prohibitions about moving to Egypt were still in effect. He has purchased Egyptian grain, but he has stayed on post in the land where God told him to dwell. He even consented to risking Benjamin rather than leave the land God told him to occupy.

Now, his son Joseph has invited him to move. Should he go? He makes preparation, and relocates his family a few miles south to Beersheba, where God had last appeared to Isaac (Gen. 26:23–25). When he gets there, Jacob offers sacrifices to God, and God speaks to Jacob for the seventh and final time.[8] We should note that the text says, "God spoke to Israel," then, when God speaks, He calls him "Jacob." Once again, the two names are being used interchangeably without positive or negative spiritual connotations. In this vision, God tells Jacob not to be afraid to go to Egypt (Gen. 46:1–4). This, too, was part of God's plan. In Egypt, Jacob's descendents will become a great nation, but they won't stay in Egypt forever. God will bring them back to the land He had promised to Abraham, Isaac, and Jacob. Not only that, Jacob will live the rest of his life in Joseph's presence, and Joseph will personally minister to him in his death.

Once before, God had sent Jacob from his homeland, promised to bring him back safely, and kept His word. When Jacob hears similar instructions on this occasion, it's good enough for him. Never having made any move without full confidence of God's blessing, Jacob now has what he needs. He packs up his entire family and property and moves to Egypt, fully believing God will keep His word (Gen. 46:5–27). Acknowledging Judah's leadership among his sons, Jacob sends Judah ahead to point the way to the place where they would settle in Egypt (Gen. 46:28). Just when it seems that "all these things are against" Jacob, he discovers that God has been working all along for his benefit.

Jacob's Final Days (Gen. 47:9–48:22*a*)

Shortly after arriving in Egypt, Jacob is taken to meet Pharaoh. He is often criticized for being pessimistic and for ignoring God's blessing when he describes the days of his life as "few and evil" (Gen. 47:9). However, given everything that has happened to him, the description seems apt. Still, that fact is often thought to prove that Jacob was a scoundrel. Admitting that the Bible contains not a single word from God that censured Jacob, Sarna says, "An explicit denunciation could hardly be more effective or more scathing than Jacob's unhappy biography."[9] Such an interpretation is consistent with the popular Jewish misunderstanding of blessing and reward. Like Job's friends, their view is that wealth and happiness are signs of God's blessing while poverty and misery are signs of God's displeasure. Even in Jesus' day, the Jewish leaders assumed that Jesus' crucifixion was proof of God's displeasure. We should not make the same mistake but recognize that God often has His own purposes for giving comfort or misery. Jesus shocked all His critics when He said that the miserable beggar Lazarus went to "Abraham's bosom" while the comfortable rich man went to the torments of hell (Luke 16:19–31).

When Jacob says his days have been "few and evil," he is not denying God's work or blessing. He is merely telling the truth. He has not lived as long as his father or his grandfather, and his life has been filled with conflict and pain. It's significant that Jacob immediately proceeds to bless Pharaoh (Gen. 47:10). For all his so-called pessimism, Jacob believes himself to hold a position superior to Pharaoh's, at least in terms of fellowship with God. In pronouncing a blessing on him, Jacob is acting toward Pharaoh as a priest of Yahweh.

After living and prospering in Egypt for seventeen years, Jacob realizes that his death is imminent (Gen. 47:28–29a). He calls Joseph to him and makes him promise not to bury him in Egypt but to take his body and bury him with his fathers (Gen. 47:29–31). The promise of the land was central to God's promise to Abraham, Isaac, and Jacob. By demanding that he be buried with Abraham and Isaac, Jacob expresses his confidence that God will keep His word. By making Joseph swear an oath to do so, he is reminding Joseph of the significance of the land. Joseph has spent most of his life in Egypt. His memories of the land are not all pleasant. Jacob wants to be sure Joseph's own heart will be oriented toward the land God promised.

Not much later, Joseph receives the report that Jacob is gravely ill (Gen. 48:1). Joseph takes his two sons, Manasseh and Ephraim, to see their grandfather. The scene is reminiscent of the day when Isaac sought to bless Esau without the rest of the family's knowledge. However, three vital distinctions must be noted. First, Jacob begins by invoking the name of El Shaddai—almighty God (Gen. 48:3). Isaac merely spoke of God in a general way and may have invoked the names of pagan deities. Second, this time the birthright is being intentionally passed on through a son who was not his firstborn to a grandson who was also not the firstborn. Third, unlike Isaac before him, Jacob is here pronouncing the birthright, not the "blessing" that God had given to Abraham. He explicitly makes no attempt to dispossess his other sons, much less make them Joseph's servants. He is merely exercising his prerogative in assigning to the most obviously pious of his sons the double portion of the birthright. Given Joseph's role in saving the family from the famine despite his brothers' attempt to be rid of him, it would be difficult for any of his brothers to object.

Essentially adopting Joseph's children as his own, Jacob gives each of them a share of the estate equal to what he will give each of his other sons without disinheriting anyone. At the end, he explains this to Joseph, saying that in blessing his two sons he had given him "one portion above thy brethren" (Gen. 48:22)—one more portion and only one more portion, not even close to what Isaac tried to give Esau (Gen. 27:37).

In pronouncing this blessing, Jacob states that Ephraim will be greater than Manasseh, but he does not make Manasseh Ephraim's servant. Neither does he make Joseph's sons superior to his other sons. Further, this blessing is limited to Ephraim and Manasseh. Realizing Joseph could have other sons, "they would share in the inheritance of Ephraim and Manasseh, and would be assigned to either of these two tribes. Joseph would receive a double portion, but only a double portion."[10] The character of this "blessing" is far different from the one Isaac tried to give Esau (Gen. 27:28–29). Jacob is fully aware of God's program and is not trying to subvert it. Rather, he is communicating and exercising submission to it.

Especially significant in this blessing is Jacob's prayer (Gen. 48:14–16). There are three particular points of interest. First, the wording implies that Jacob has at least a rudimentary understanding of a triune God. His invocation identifies God in three ways: "God before whom my fathers Abraham and Isaac did walk, the God which fed me all my life long unto this day, the Angel which redeemed me from all evil." The first could be thought of as the Father, the second as the Spirit in His leading and nurturing role, and the third as the Son in His redemptive role. Second, Jacob's prayer indicates a life of faith directed by God. Contrary to how his critics have presented him as selfish and driven by personal ambition, Jacob says that God had "shepherded" him "all my life long unto this day." Third, the prayer contains two significant terms used here for the first time in Scripture: God is described as a "shepherd" (translated "fed" in the KJV), as in Psalm 23:1, and He is described as having "redeemed" Jacob, making this the first reference to the primary work of Christ. Jacob's understanding of God and his own dependence upon Him is apparently greater than any patriarch before him. He has truly become "A Prince" who has "power with God" (Gen. 32:28).

Lessons

All sorts of lessons could be drawn from this chapter, but I want to mention just two. First, we see some of the consequences of the terrible sin Jacob's sons commit against their brother. Years pass while they vainly think that they have gotten away with it, but it eats away at their consciences and erodes their relationship with their father. Jacob is brought to the brink of despair. Yet God always knew the truth, and he didn't let them rest. When confronted with their sin, they did the right thing. They asked forgiveness of their brother and confessed to their father, resulting in improved relationships and revived spirits. Sin will do that to you too. God offers forgiveness and restoration of fellowship to the repentant.

Second, we have seen Jacob allow himself to be almost consumed by the pain of his losses and the conflict within his home. His faith ebbs to the point that he begins to doubt the very promise of God on which his entire life has been based. Just as God is about to change his circumstances from agony to joy, he cries in despair, "All these things are against me." But even in distress, he has not abandoned the promise. Like the man who said to Jesus, "Lord, I believe; help thou mine unbelief" (Mark 9:24), Jacob clings to the last scrap of his faith and stays in the land of his fathers rather than leaving for Egypt. He steadfastly refuses to leave until God tells him to go. Even if all his sons disqualify themselves from the blessing of God, he will not do so.

What a tremendous example for us! When life doesn't go as we planned, when circumstances look dark and we are tempted to despair, God is still in control. He hasn't lost His grip, and He's not unaware. He's working for our glory, even in "all these things" that seem to be against us. He hasn't told us everything we must endure, but He has told us the end of the story. We have no reason to doubt. "If God be for us, who can be against us?" (Rom. 8:31b).

13

Jacob's Legacy

Gen. 49:1–50:14

ne of the most effective ways to guarantee contention among your children is to die without having made out a detailed will. I've seen families fracture over property disputes involving items outside observers might have thought worthless. Often, the strife could have been avoided by having a family meeting in advance in which you made your intentions clear. However important such a meeting could be, we tend to consider such conversations morbid. I suppose we like to think of ourselves as immortal, which may explain our reluctance to discuss our final arrangements in advance.

As the end of Jacob's life approaches, he has more on his mind than simple property distribution. A lot of that will actually be left for Joshua to deal with some four hundred years later when the land of Canaan is divided among the children of Israel/Jacob. The previous chapter examined how Jacob began the process of setting his affairs in order. In a semiprivate ceremony involving Joseph and his two sons, he designated Joseph as the recipient of the birthright. Unlike his father before him, Jacob handles the birthright and the blessing separately, and he has no intention of pronouncing God's blessing upon one son in private. Even in his designation of Joseph's younger son Ephraim as the recipient of a "greater" future than Manasseh, Joseph's firstborn, he does it in the presence of Joseph and explains his intentions, something Isaac never did. The time for pronouncing the blessing has come, so Jacob calls all his sons together. I can't help but wonder how much pain and turmoil Rebekah, Jacob, and Esau might have been spared had Isaac been wise enough to handle things the way Jacob does.

Jacob's Oracle (Gen. 49:1–28)

For the pronouncing of the blessing, Jacob calls his sons together and recites what must have been a laboriously prepared poem with prophetic statements about each of them (Gen. 49:1–28). He addresses them in more or less maternal birth order, starting with the sons of Leah, proceeding to the sons of the handmaids, and concluding with the sons of Rachel.

All the prophecies seem to have at least a degree of temporal fulfillment in the future history of Israel. In examining the sometimes partial, obscure, or even unidentifiable ways in which these prophecies have been fulfilled historically, we must keep in mind that Jacob's emphasis is consciously on the eschatological future fulfillment in the kingdom. Jacob says that this prophecy has to do with "that which shall befall you in the last days" (Gen. 49:1*b*). His deathbed pronouncement is far more than near-term wishful thinking. Since the focus of our study is still Jacob, not his sons, I will not deal with all the nuances of interpretation of the prophecies included in Jacob's blessing. Still, we need to take a look at the gist of what Jacob says to each son.

Jacob is aware that he is speaking a divine oracle, a prophecy of things to come. This is something no prior patriarch had done. Jacob's use of the term "last days" implies prophetic insight well beyond any of his predecessors. Not only is this the first time this phrase appears in Scripture, but it doesn't appear again until Isaiah 2:2, which, incidentally, is one of the passages whose context refers to the Lord as "the God of Jacob":

> And it shall come to pass in the last days, that the mountain of the Lord's house shall be established in the top of the mountains, and shall be exalted above the hills; and all nations shall flow unto it. And many people shall go and say, Come ye, and let us go up to the mountain of the Lord, to the house of the God of Jacob.

Even at the end of time, when God's kingdom is established, people will still be calling the Lord "the God of Jacob."

Quite naturally, Jacob begins his prophecy with Reuben, his firstborn, "the beginning of my strength" (Gen. 49:3). Having occupied a position excellent in dignity and excellent in power, he will no longer excel. Comparing him to dangerous, turbulent waters, Jacob publicly acknowledges for the first time that he knows of Reuben's attempt to disrupt Jacob's leadership by defiling his "father's bed" (Gen. 49:4). For this treachery, Reuben will not receive the birthright, nor will he enjoy the respect of his brethren. "Reuben no longer had the right of the firstborn of the household of Jacob because he violated the honor of his father."[1] While his tribe would be the first to receive their inheritance on the east side of the Jordan (Num. 32), they would also lose the respect of the nation by not responding to the call to arms under Deborah and Barak in the Canaanite wars (Judg. 5:15b–16). "His tribe attained to no position of influence in the nation."[2]

Next, Jacob addresses Simeon and Levi together (Gen. 49:5–7). They are "brethren" both in parentage and disposition, "not merely as having the same parent, but in their modes of thought and action."[3] He describes them as cruelly violent and willfully angry. Presumably, this is a reference to their murder of the Shechemites, but it may have included a veiled reference to what might have been their leadership in the plot to kill Joseph. Jacob announces that he wants nothing to do with their behavior or even their company, and he pronounces a curse upon their cruel wrath. To prevent them from organizing united efforts in the future, he says they will be "divided in Jacob and scattered in Israel" (Gen. 49:7b).

This would be fulfilled in different ways for these two tribes. Simeon will be given an inheritance within the territory of Judah (Josh. 19:1) and will be mostly assimilated into Judah or scattered outside Israel among the Edomites and Amalekites (1 Chron. 4:39–43). After the kingdom is divided, many of the Simeonites will defect from the northern kingdom to join Judah (2 Chron. 15:9). This tribe will be virtually unknown after King Asa.

Levi will assume the responsibility for the priesthood. The tribe of Levi will be scattered among numerous cities throughout Israel (Josh. 21:1–3) as they serve a vital role in Israel's worship during the Old Testament period. They will be elevated to this position because they alone will stand with Moses against the idolatry of the golden calf (Exod. 32:26). It isn't insignificant, though, that the descendents of Levi will spend their history slaughtering innocent lambs for the sake of the guilty as a constant reminder of their own blood-guiltiness. It's also worth noting that in his remarks about Simeon and Levi, Jacob speaks in the first person as God, saying, "I will divide them in Jacob and scatter them in Israel" (Gen. 49:7). In this case, Jacob is so closely identified with God that he speaks with divine authority in a way that is rare, even among the prophets.

Next in line is Judah (Gen. 49:8–12). For the first time in this speech, Jacob has a prophecy with some good news. He describes Judah as strong and courageous. He will be praised by his brothers and victorious over his enemies. He is described as a lion (Gen. 49:9). "The lion, having recently eaten, has retired to its sleeping quarters to digest its meal. Even while it is reposing, nothing else tries to invade its territory, so powerful is the lion."[4] In words consciously reminiscent of Joseph's dreams many years before, Jacob shifts their focus by saying that Judah's brethren "shall bow down before thee [Judah, not Joseph]" (Gen. 49:8; cf. 37:5–11). That ascendancy, which had happened to Joseph in his own lifetime, will ultimately be transferred to Judah. "Those who reign from the house of Judah will do so in anticipation of the one to whom the kingship truly belongs"—Shiloh (Gen. 49:10).[5] This promise will find its initial fulfillment at David's coronation 640 years later. Judean leadership will be maintained throughout Israel's national history. Even during the Babylonian captivity, the most prominent Israelite is Daniel, from the tribe of Judah (Dan. 1:6). When Rome sacked Jerusalem in AD 70, the "scepter" seemed to fall from the hand of Judah. However, that historic fact is indirect proof that the Messiah had already come. Christ Jesus had been identified as the coming King (Matt. 2:2; 27:37; cf. Mic. 5:2–5). The promise will see its ultimate fulfillment when Christ Jesus, "the Lion of Judah" (Rev. 5:5), returns to rule as King.

Concerning the next six sons—the last two of Leah's sons, taken in reverse order, and the four sons of Bilhah and Zilpah—there is little or no specific information in Genesis about their lives on which to base any assumptions about the reasons for the prophecies. Zebulun's promise is difficult (Gen. 49:13). He will "dwell at the haven of the sea," but when the land is distributed by lot under Joshua, his territory will not be coastal. He is told that his territory will border Sidon, but the land apportioned to him will not do that either (Josh. 19:10–16). However, if Sidon is "taken as a collective term for Phoenicia,"[6] then the statement is accurate. This should probably be understood as a promise of future conquest, expansion, and trade (cf. Judg. 1:30; 5:18) and may well have to wait for Christ's return to be fulfilled literally.

The prophecy concerning Issachar is usually understood to mean that he will be strong and hard working, but without ambition (Gen. 49:14–15). Content with "material good," he "would rather submit to the yoke and be forced to do the work of a slave, than risk his possessions and his peace in the struggle for liberty."[7] It's possible, however, that this should not be taken so negatively. Deborah praises the valiant contributions of the descendants of Issachar (Judg. 5:15). Further, Judges 1 lists the territories of tribes that failed to drive out the Canaanites: Manasseh (v. 27), Ephraim (v. 29), Zebulon (v. 30), Asher (v. 31), and Naphtali (v. 33). Although some of those territories bordered Issachar's, Issachar is not mentioned. For these reasons, Hamilton may be right to translate the final clause, "[he] became a servant unto tribute" (KJV), as "he became a farmer" and to argue that the prophecy means that he would "not shy away from assuming tasks of some physical magnitude."[8]

Lest anyone wonder if the sons of the handmaids will have a share in Jacob's estate, Jacob now moves to them. First among them is Dan to whom Jacob promises that he will "judge his people" (Gen. 49:16–17). This does not mean that he would condemn his people, but that he would defend, or "plead their cause." There's a sense in which this is fulfilled in Samson, who was from this tribe (Judg. 13:2ff.). It's more difficult to interpret the imagery of his being a serpent lying by the wayside to cause destruction by biting at a horse's heels. Interpreting it positively, Hamilton suggests that it means "that Dan, although small, will be quite capable of holding his own. His strength will be greater than his size."[9] Similarly, Morris says, "While apparently unimpressive . . . [Dan] nevertheless was a dangerous adversary, well able to protect Israel's northern boundary against invaders."[10] It's also possible, however, that it should be understood negatively. Idolatry would be officially introduced to the land of Israel through Danites (Judg. 18:30–31). Jeroboam, who rebelled against the Judean king Rehoboam and split the kingdom, would later set up one of his two golden calves in Dan (1 Kings 12:28–30). Morris suggests that "this is why Dan is not listed among the tribes in Revelation 7:4–8 (note Deuteronomy 29:16–21)."[11]

Jacob exclaims, "I have waited for thy salvation, O Lord" (Gen. 49:18), following his remarks to Dan. He expresses his confidence that protection and deliverance will ultimately come from the Lord. Significantly, this is the first use of the word *salvation* in the Bible, and the Hebrew word is *yeshuah*. Transliterating that word to Greek, as a proper name it becomes Jesus. Perhaps understanding more than we realize, Jacob may be indicating that his expected salvation would come through a Person—"I have waited for Your Jesus, O Lord."

Jacob tells Gad that he will be "overcome" by a "troop" but that "he shall overcome at the last" (Gen. 49:19). Gad's territory would be on the east of Jordan and would be vulnerable to attack, particularly by the Ammonites (Judg. 11:1–12:7). Early in their history, they are rebuked by Deborah for failing to come to the aid of their brethren on the west of Jordan (Judg. 5:17). Later, though, they are lauded for valiance (1 Chron. 5:18) and compared to lions in their ferocity (2 Chron. 12:8–15). While they will often be overrun, they will be victorious in the end.

Asher, whose name means "blessedness," or "happiness," is promised agricultural bounty: "his bread shall be fat, and he shall yield royal dainties" (Gen. 49:20). Asher will be allotted "one of the most fertile parts of Canaan, abounding in wheat and oil, with which Solomon supplied the household of king Hiram (1 Kings 5:11)."[12] Jacob is probably promising that Asher "will be blessed by God with abundance and prosperity and will produce food luxuriant and rich enough for royalty."[13]

Naphtali is described as "a hind let loose: he giveth goodly words" (Gen. 49:21). The simplest explanation is that this is a promise of swiftness and success in battle and eloquence in song. The most distinguished future descendant of Naphtali is Barak (Judg. 4:6–15). The victory song of Deborah and Barak may be an example of his eloquence (Judg. 5:1–31).

Jacob's final prophetic words are addressed to the sons of Rachel. He addresses Joseph first (Gen. 49:22–26). The initial reference to his fruitfulness has already been fulfilled by the time Jacob recites his oracle. Joseph's two sons will each receive a full share of Jacob's estate as if they were his own sons—the double portion constituting the birthright. From them two tribes will descend. The statement that he is hated and wounded by archers has also already been fulfilled. His brothers had sold him into slavery, and Potiphar's wife had him imprisoned on false charges. Yet he had been "made strong by the mighty God of Jacob" (Gen. 49:24).

We see again Jacob's genuine confidence in God in the way he speaks of the Lord. He calls Him "mighty," pointing to His strength. He calls him "the shepherd," referring to His tender provision. He calls Him "the rock," referring to his steadfast reliability. Not content with that, Jacob calls him "the God of thy father, who shall help thee," and "the Almighty, who shall bless thee with blessings of heaven above, blessings of the deep that lieth under, blessings of the breasts, and of the womb" (Gen. 49:25). The fulfillment of this is seen in the future prosperity and prominence of the two tribes, from whom come some of Israel's greatest future leaders. From Ephraim come Joshua, Deborah, Samuel, and Jeroboam. From Manasseh came Gideon and Jephthah.

Jacob saves his last prophetic remarks for Benjamin, whom he describes as a ravenous wolf that devours prey in the morning and

divides the spoil at night (Gen. 49:27). At times this warlike quality will be manifested positively and at other times negatively. Early
in the period of the Judges, Ehud of Benjamin will rescue the nation from Moabite oppression (Judg. 3:15–30). Later, through their
despicable behavior in the case of the rape of the Levite's concubine
they will incite a civil war. In that conflict, they will hold their own
for a while before being almost annihilated (Judg. 19–20). Later still,
they will have a reputation for being mighty warriors and archers
(1 Chron. 8:40; 12:2). Saul, the first king of Israel, will be a Benjamite
(1 Sam. 9:1). He will start out as a valiant warrior (1 Sam. 11:1–11)
but end in ignominious defeat (1 Sam. 31:2–13).

Significantly, "Jacob's blessing centered especially on Joseph
and Judah . . . [and] only physical blessings were promised Joseph,
whereas the spiritual blessing of being the ancestor of Messiah was
promised Judah, in addition to physical blessings and political leadership."[14] In the future of Jacob's sons, Joseph's descendants will dominate during the period of the conquest and the judges. Benjamin
will dominate briefly under Ehud and, later, Saul. Ultimate political
and spiritual supremacy will go to Judah, through David, during the
monarchy. Precisely how these prophecies might be fulfilled in the
kingdom is impossible to say. We do know that the ultimate King,
Jesus Christ, comes from Judah.

The closing words of Jacob's speech make two important points
(Gen. 49:28). First, he is already thinking of his sons and their
families as "tribes" within the larger nation of "Israel." Second, he
has included all twelve sons in his blessing. Granted, some of his
statements don't sound particularly "blessed," but he asserts that they
have each received that which is appropriate to the individual. Jacob
wants his sons to understand that they are all participants in God's
prophetic future. While Isaac had tried to give the entire blessing to
Esau, Jacob had been the God-intended recipient. In the generation
to follow, however, no son will be left out. They will not share equally,
to be sure—Joseph and Judah have received the broadest promises—
but all will participate.

Jacob's Last Words (Gen. 49:29–33)

Before ending this family meeting, Jacob repeats for all his sons
a charge he had earlier issued to Joseph (cf. Gen. 47:29–31). On the
earlier occasion, Joseph may have spoken more for Egypt than for

the family in promising to bury his father with Abraham and Isaac. Now, Jacob wants a commitment from all his sons. Jacob also wants his other sons to receive his burial instructions from him, not Joseph, so there will be no confusion. Anticipating both his death and his future resurrection, he says he is going "to be gathered unto my people" (Gen. 49:29). He tells his sons that he expects them to bury him in Canaan as a testimony to all succeeding generations of his faith and of the faith of his forebears. I find it intriguing that at some point since he returned to Canaan, Jacob seems to have decided that he had been wrong to favor Rachel. She is not the wife that he buried in his ancestral plot. It is Leah with whom Jacob intends to be buried (Gen. 49:31).

Most importantly, Jacob wants to be sure his sons won't forget the significance of the land they had left behind. He firmly believes God will keep His promise to Abraham and Isaac by giving the land to Jacob's offspring forever. Many prosperous years in Egypt could make a future generation less eager to go home. Jacob is doing what he can to make sure his sons and grandsons for generations to come never forget that Egypt is not their home. There is a land promised by God to which they must return, and to which God will one day take them.

Having made clear his intention to be buried in Canaan, Jacob lies down and dies (Gen. 49:33). As has also been said upon the deaths of Abraham (Gen. 25:8), Ishmael (Gen. 25:17), and Isaac (Gen. 35:29), and in fulfillment of Jacob's expectation, he "was gathered to his people" (Gen. 49:33). This is not a statement about his plan to be buried in the family burial ground. It refers to his continued existence after death in the presence of those faithful ancestors who have died before him.

Jacob's Funeral (Gen. 50:1–14)

In reading of Jacob's funeral, we gain some fascinating insights into Egyptian culture, but that is not why this account is so remarkable. We notice, first, that Jacob was afforded an Egyptian state funeral. His body was embalmed by a process that took forty days (Gen. 50:3). The Egyptians held official mourning for him for seventy days (Gen. 50:3). By contrast, Moses was only mourned for thirty days (Deut. 34:8). When taking Jacob's body to be buried, the procession included "all the servants of Pharaoh, the elders of his house, and all the elders of the land of Egypt, and all the house of Joseph, and his brethren, and his father's house. . . . And there went up with him both chariots and horsemen: and it was a very great company" (Gen. 50:7b–9). Only their little ones and livestock were left behind. Once they arrived in Canaan, they "mourned with a great and very sore lamentation" for another seven days (Gen. 50:10), making a total mourning period of seventy-seven days. The event was so significant that the Canaanites, who were not participating and were probably not particularly sorry to see Jacob dead, said, "This is a grievous mourning to the Egyptians," and they named the place Abel-mizraim—"the mourning of the Egyptians" (Gen. 50:11).

Second, this account is remarkable simply for its length. Funerals of other significant individuals are far more concise. Abraham's burial is described in two verses (Gen. 25:9–10). Isaac's is described in one verse (Gen. 35:29). Joseph's is described in two verses (Gen. 50:26 and Josh. 24:32, when his bones are reburied in Canaan four hundred years later). Moses' is described in three verses (Deut. 34:6–8). Joshua's is described in one verse (Josh. 24:30). Samuel's is described in half a verse (1 Sam. 25:1a). David's is described in one verse (1 Kings 2:10). All told, ten-and-a-half verses are dedicated to the burials of Abraham, Isaac, Joseph, Moses, Joshua, Samuel, and David. No less than thirteen-and-a-half verses are dedicated to Jacob's funeral—30 percent more space than is devoted to all those other funerals combined. The only other burial in Scripture to get similar attention is that of Jesus Christ, the longest account of which is found in Matthew 27:59–66—eight verses long. Mark gives it two verses (15:46–47), Luke four (23:53–56), and John five (19:38–42). Combined, the gospel accounts of Jesus' burial take only 50 percent more space that the account of Jacob's. Taken singly, the account of Jacob's funeral exceeds the longest account of Jesus' funeral by 50 percent.[15]

Some commentators struggle to find a reason for this. Sailhamer expresses some angst over it.

> The question naturally arises why such detail over the burial of Jacob is given when in the death of the other patriarchs we are simply given the bare facts that they died and were buried. Even the account of the death of Joseph, which is also recorded in this chapter, consists only of the brief notice that he died and was embalmed and entombed in Egypt (v. 26). Was his burial of any less magnitude than Jacob's? Surely it was not, but virtually no attention in the narrative is devoted to it. Why, then, the emphasis

on Jacob's burial? Perhaps such a description is intended merely as a concluding flourish at the end of the book, or does it play a part in the ongoing strategy of the text? In light of the writer's careful attention to his larger themes throughout these narratives, it is appropriate to seek a motive for such an emphasis within the narrative.[16]

I believe the answer is actually quite simple. Despite the opinions of a majority of commentators, Jacob was a great man. His funeral is given so much space to draw attention to that fact.

Lessons

One lesson to be drawn from the closing episodes of Jacob's life is simply that we see the wisdom of setting our affairs in order before we die. Writing our will and final communications to our children can have great value. Related to that, and even more important, we should see that much of Jacob's focus was on the consequences of his sons' past actions and the importance of their future relationship with God. Each of us should do what we can to encourage our children in the faith, even to issuing deathbed challenges to keep their hearts and minds fixed on fulfilling God's will. Their future relationship with God is much more important than any property we might leave them.

Further, we see that Jacob counts on and lives for the promise of God even to the very end of his life. Each of us should have our hearts so firmly established upon God's promise that we will be able to face our own death with the same confidence, grace, and steadfast faith that Jacob demonstrates. Jacob has endured much. Paul might as well have had Jacob specifically in mind when he wrote these words:

> Who shall separate us from the love of Christ? shall tribulation, or distress, or persecution, or famine, or nakedness, or peril, or sword? As it is written, For thy sake we are killed all the day long; we are accounted as sheep for the slaughter. Nay, in all these things we are more than conquerors through him that loved us. For I am persuaded, that neither death, nor life, nor angels, nor principalities, nor powers, nor things present, nor things to come, nor height, nor depth, nor any other creature, shall be able to separate us from the love of God, which is in Christ Jesus our Lord. (Rom. 8:35–39)

Summation

I realize that the account of Jacob's life is usually treated quite differently than I have described it. Many will find in my analysis a blatant bias in favor of Jacob. I readily admit that to be true, but I must also admit that it's a bias I adopted reluctantly. Many passages would have been easier to interpret negatively. However, I believe that the text of Scripture is much kinder to Jacob than most commentators and Bible teachers have been. God calls him *is tam* (Gen. 25:27), unfortunately translated "plain" rather than its otherwise uniform translation as "perfect," "spotless," or "blameless." God repeatedly identifies Himself as the God of Jacob, using the name Jacob that most consider indicative of a corrupt character. After changing his name to Israel, the narrator continues to use the two names interchangeably, regardless of context, right up to his death and burial, and in later passages of Scripture as well. There is no way to distinguish between the significance of the names' contextual usages in any coherent way. Further, God speaks to Jacob directly seven times (Gen. 28:12; 31:3, 11; 32:30; 35:1, 9; 46:2) and appears to him on three of those occasions. Every time God speaks to Jacob, it is with words of promise, encouragement, and blessing. He never has a word of rebuke, and Jacob never demonstrates repentance. Finally, at the time of Jacob's death, God gives more space in the text of Scripture to the description of Jacob's funeral than to all other significant Old Testament burials combined, comparable only to the New Testament accounts of the burial of Jesus Christ.

I believe that the only way I could be faithful to the text of Scripture in my interpretation of the person of Jacob required that I reexamine the story of Jacob's life in the light of God's consistently positive presentation of Jacob's character. While Jacob was not without sin, and his life shows occasional lapses of confidence, I've concluded that the Bible presents Jacob as a saint, not a scoundrel. He was a man we would do well to emulate. His faithfulness in the face of abuse, heartbreak, and betrayal, believing steadfastly in the good intentions of God and the reliability of His promises, should inspire all of us to greater service and greater trust. By God's grace, may each of us be worthy sons and daughters of Jacob as we endure the difficulties of life while waiting for the appearing of our Savior. On that great day we will fall before Him and worship "the God of Jacob."

NOTES

INTRODUCTION

1. Henry Morris, *The Genesis Record* (Grand Rapids: Baker, 1976), 415.
2. Theodore Epp, *The God of Abraham, Isaac, and Jacob* (Lincoln, NE: Back to the Bible, 1970), 211, 212.
3. There is some question which "god" Laban had in mind in his oath, since Joshua says that Terah, father of Abraham and Nahor, was an idolater. That is probably why Jacob responded to Laban in the name of "the fear of his father Isaac" to avoid any confusion.
4. Those are the only two times the title "servant" is used for Isaac.
5. Paul was, of course, called the servant of Christ frequently, but that was not relevant to this search.
6. Howard G. Hendricks, "Foreword," in *Jacob: Following God Without Looking Back*, Gene A. Getz (Nashville: Broadman, 1996), ix.

CHAPTER ONE

1. Isaac was forty when they married (Gen. 25:20) and sixty when the twins were born (Gen. 25:26).
2. Martin Sicker, *The Ordeals of Isaac and Jacob* (New York: iUniverse, 2007), 16. Sicker cites as his source the Midrash Rabbah, Gen. 63:5.
3. C. F. Keil. *Biblical Commentary on the Old Testament, The Pentateuch*, vol. 1, trans. James Martin (Grand Rapids, MI: Wm. B. Eerdmans, 1968), 267.
4. Victor P. Hamilton, *The Book of Genesis: Chapters 18–50, New International Commentary on the Old Testament* (Grand Rapids, MI: William B. Eerdmans, 1995), 176.
5. Keil, 267.
6. The prophecy of the elder serving the younger would not be fully realized for nearly one thousand years, when David, the descendent of Jacob, subjugated the Edomites, descendents of Esau (2 Sam. 8:12–14) and "all they of Edom became David's servants" (8:14*b*).
7. John H. Sailhamer, "Genesis," in *The Expositor's Bible Commentary*, ed. Frank Gaebelein, vol. 2 (Grand Rapids, MI: Zondervan, 1990), 183.
8. Gene A. Getz, *Jacob: Following God Without Looking Back* (Nashville: Broadman & Holman, 1996), 8.
9. The exact derivation is obscure. The word for red (*admoni*) sounds more like Edom than Esau. The word for hairy (*se'ar*) sounds more like Esau's eventual home (Seir) than his name. The main point of the text is not the source of the name but a description of Esau that will be important later.
10. Keil, 268.

11. Nahum M. Sarna, *JPS Torah Commentary: Genesis* (Philadelphia: The Jewish Publication Society, 1989), 180.

12. Morris, 414.

13. Charles L. Feinberg, *The Minor Prophets* (Chicago: Moody Press, 1948), 58.

14. Getz, 8.

15. Joyce C. Baldwin, *The Message of Genesis 12–50* (Downers Grove, IL: Inter-Varsity Press, 1986), 105.

16. Hamilton, 178.

17. Sarna, 180.

18. Ibid., 179.

19. Gen. 32:10; Exod. 32:13; Deut. 9:27; 1 Chron. 16:13; Isa. 41:89; 44:12, 21. (twice); 45:4; 48:20; 49:3, 56; Jer. 30:10; 46:27–28; Ezek. 28:25; 37:25.

20. Epp, 218.

21. James I. Packer and Carolyn Nystrom, *Never Beyond Hope* (Downers Grove, IL: Inter-Varsity Press, 2000), 39.

22. Getz, 10.

23. Sarna, 181.

24. Ibid.

25. Benno Jacob, *The First Book of the Bible: Genesis*, abr. and trans. Ernest J. Jacob and Walter Jacob (New York: KTAV Publishing House, 1974), 168.

26. Victor P. Hamilton, *The Book of Genesis: Chapters 1–17* (Grand Rapids: William B. Eerdmans, 1990), 461.

27. Ibid., 277.

28. Sarna, 50.

29. Layton Talbert, *Beyond Suffering: Discovering the Message of Job* (Greenville, SC: BJU Press, 2007), 59.

30. Ibid. In footnote 6, p. 300, the internal quote is identified as from "J. Barton Payne in *Theological Wordbook of the Old Testament*, vol. 2, ed. R. Laird Harris, Gleason L. Archer, Jr., and Bruce K. Waltke (Chicago: Moody Press, 1980), 974."

31. Hamilton, *Chapters 18–50*, 181. (Unless otherwise noted, future citations from Hamilton will be from the source cited here.)

32. Ibid. I cannot explain why, after drawing this conclusion, Hamilton persists in treating Jacob as negatively as does anyone else.

33. Sicker, 24.

34. Morris, 415.

35. Benno Jacob, 168.

36. Ibid.

37. Sicker, 28, citing Midrash Rabbah, Gen. 63:11.

38. Sicker, 28.

39. Benno Jacob, 168.

40. Sicker, 32.

41. C. I. Scofield, *The Scofield Reference Bible* (New York: Oxford University Press, 1917), footnote 2 on Gen. 25:31, 38.

42. Ibid.

43. Getz, 18, 19.

44. Baldwin, 106.

45. Keil, 269.

46. Avraham Yaakov Finkel, *The Torah Revealed: Talmudic Masters Unveil the Secrets of the Bible* (San Francisco: Jossey Bass, 2004), 54.

CHAPTER TWO

1. Since at least seventy-five years pass between Abraham's contact with Abimelech and Isaac's, this is clearly not the same man. It is worth noting that the title of Ps. 34 is "A Psalm of David, when he feigned madness before Abimelech" yet the account of that event in 1 Sam. 21:10–15 identifies the Philistine king as Achish. Abimelech was either a common name assumed by royalty among the Philistines or a general title for all kings of the Philistines, like Pharaoh was to the Egyptian kings. It is likely that this Abimelech was either a son or grandson of the earlier Abimelech, and he may well have remembered the stories of events when Abraham had visited.

2. Hamilton, 195.

3. Morris, 421.

4. Sailhamer, 187.

5. Hamilton, 197.

6. Ibid., 198.

7. Hamilton, 201.

8. Hamilton, 207–8.

CHAPTER THREE

1. Morris, 428.

2. For comments that treat the blessing as stolen, see John Sailhamer, p. 189; Theodore Epp, p. 230; the *Scofield Reference Bible*; the *Hebrew-Greek Key Study Bible* (Spiros Zodhiates), the NASB, and the HCSB. Exceptions include Henry Morris, *The Genesis Record*, pp. 427–42, whose treatment of this event is similar to my own. Also, C. F. Keil uses the neutral "Isaac's Blessing" (p. 273). While Victor P. Hamilton's treatment is just as negative as most others, he uses the more moderate heading, "Jacob Receives Blessing Through Deception" (*The Book of Genesis: Chapters 18–50*, p. 211). The *Nelson Study Bible* (NKJV) and the ESV title this chapter simply "Isaac Blesses Jacob."

3. Homer A. Kent Jr., *The Epistle to the Hebrews* (Winona Lake, IN: Baker Book House, 1972), 268.

4.   Bayha ben Asher, *Biur al haTorah*, 3 vols., ed. Charles B. Chavel (Jerusalem: Mossad Harav Kook, 1966), on Gen. 27:19.

5.   Sicker, 55–59.

6.   Sarna, 190.

7.   Sarna, 190.

8.   Hamilton, 212.

9.   H. C. Leupold, "Isaac," *Pictorial Encyclopedia of the Bible*, vol. 3 (Grand Rapids: Zondervan, 1975–76), 312.

10.   Hamilton, 216.

11.   Sailhamer, 191.

12.   Epp, 232.

13.   Alan P. Ross, *Creation and Blessing* (Grand Rapids: Baker Book House, 1988), 440–41.

14.   Baldwin, 115.

15.   I realize that there are later places in the narrative that are sometimes identified as evidence of repentance, but I intend to show as we go that there is never an explicit or implicit admission of guilt or request for forgiveness from Jacob. That is in marked contrast with the statements of Joseph's brothers, with Judah as spokesman, that their troubles had befallen them because they had sinned against their brother (Gen. 42:21).

16.   Sicker says, "Jacob may have been convinced by his mother that the only way to produce the proper outcome was to deceive Isaac. To allow Isaac to transfer Abraham's legacy to Esau would have been a travesty and would probably have brought the entire covenantal enterprise undertaken by his grandfather to an ignominious end. Indeed, Isaac conferring it on Esau was an irresponsible act, knowing his son as he did, and Rebekah and Jacob were fully justified in subverting it; commission of a lesser moral transgression by them justified by the prevention of a much greater one by Isaac" (p. 52).

17.   Hamilton, 217.

18.   Sicker says, "Some have understood this response to Isaac's question as stating, 'It is I,' followed by the unrelated assertion, 'Esau is thy firstborn.'" He argues that such a reading is consistent with the usual usages of two different words for "I" in Hebrew. One word, *ani*, "is intended as a straightforward self-identification without any implicit nuance, such as in the statement, 'I and no other.' However *anokhi*, which is employed here, is normally used when 'I' introduces a distinction as in 'I am sitting here but my desk is over there.'" He argues that if this is correct, Jacob could have considered his words truthful, even if misleading. Alternatively, he suggests that it could "be understood as saying that for the purposes of the birthright, which Esau had long ago transferred to me, I stand in place of your first-born Esau, making the response deceptive but not untruthful" (p. 54).

19.   Hamilton, 220.

20. Keil, 275.
21. Morris, 434.
22. Benno Jacob, 181.
23. Hamilton, 221.
24. Ibid., footnote 18.
25. Ibid., 221.
26. Morris, 439.
27. Sarna, 104.
28. Morris, 440–41.
29. Hamilton, 228.
30. Morris, 441.
31. Hamilton, 228.
32. Epp, 238.

CHAPTER FOUR

1. Sailhamer, 193.
2. Spiros Zodhiates, *Hebrew-Greek Key Study Bible* (AMG Publishers, 1984, 1991), paragraph heading at Gen. 27:41.
3. Hamilton, 242.
4. Sailhamer, 194.
5. Hamilton, 234.
6. Sailhamer, 195.
7. Hamilton, 235.
8. Morris, 444.
9. There is considerable confusion surrounding the names and identities of Esau's wives. "Mahalath the daughter of Ishmael" (28:9) is called "Bashemath Ishmael's daughter" in 36:3. However, 26:34 identifies one of his wives as "Bashemath the daughter of Elon the Hittite," while 36:2 calls her "Adah the daughter of Elon the Hittite." Another wife identified in 26:34 is "Judith the daughter of Beeri the Hittite," who is apparently called "Aholibamah the daughter of Anah the daughter of Zibeon the Hivite" in 36:2. Either Esau had more than three wives, and one (Judith) had died before 36:2, or they each had more than one name and Judith's father was known by more than one name. The latter is more likely.
10. The text will explain how Jacob names the place. The narrator used the new name to refer to this place in Abraham's day over 150 years before the name is given to the place so that we won't miss the connection.
11. Hamilton, 240.
12. J. P. Fokkelman, *Narrative Art in Genesis* (Sheffield: JSOT Press, 1991), 51–52.
13. Morris, 448.

14. E.g., Hamilton, 244.
15. Hamilton, 246.
16. Getz, 56.
17. For an example of this interpretation, see Theodore H. Epp, p. 254. Also see J. Gerald Janzen, *Abraham and All the Families of the Earth: Genesis 12–50* (Grand Rapids: Wm. B. Eerdmans, 1993), 111–12. Many others share this view.
18. Benno Jacob, 191–92.
19. Sailhamer, 196–97.

CHAPTER FIVE

1. Epp, 256.
2. Keil, 235.
3. Morris, 458.
4. Hamilton, 255.
5. Keil, 285.
6. D. Daube and R. Yaron, *Journal of Semitic Studies* (Oxford University Press, 1956), 61–62, cited by Hamilton, 258.
7. Hamilton, 258, footnote 6.
8. Hamilton, 259.
9. Ibid.
10. Hamilton, 262.
11. Morris, 463.
12. Hamilton, 263.
13. Sailhamer, 199.

CHAPTER SIX

1. Sailhamer, 200.
2. See Hamilton, pp. 266–67, for a brief discussion.
3. Hamilton, 268.
4. Hamilton observes, "It is ironic that Rachel, who believes she will die if she mothers no children and who is not satisfied with adopted children, dies while trying to mother a second child (35:16–19)," p. 270.
5. Keil, 288.
6. Hamilton, 271.
7. Morris, 467.
8. Ibid. Also, Keil (p. 289) and Hamilton (p. 273) provide concurring opinions.
9. Morris, 467.
10. Keil, 289. Morris says that he was probably seven, but his chronology

assumes the children were born during a span of ten to twelve years rather than the seven years implied by the text (p. 468).

11. Sarna, 209.

12. See Ps. 127:3—"Lo, children are an heritage of the Lord, and the fruit of the womb is his reward ['sakar]."

13. Hamilton, 276, and Kiel, 290.

14. Morris, 469.

15. Hamilton, 281.

16. Many modern translations use the word "divination" here (i.e., NASB, HCSB, ESV).

17. Hamilton, 282.

18. See Epp, who calls this section "Jacob Schemes to Deceive Laban," 263–65.

19. Hamilton, 283.

20. Keil, 294.

21. Hamilton, 284.

22. Ibid., 293.

23. Sarna, 212. See Morris, 476, for a similar suggestion.

24. Benno Jacob, 206.

25. Sarna, 212.

26. Sailhamer, 203.

CHAPTER SEVEN

1. Hamilton, 287.

2. Eleven sons were born during the second seven-year period of Jacob's sojourn with Laban. Dinah is the only daughter named and was probably born during the six years of Jacob's working for wages. The only other son to be born to Jacob would come later. However, it is possible that other daughters were born during Jacob's final six years in Padan-aram.

3. Hamilton, 288.

4. For instance, Hamilton says, "in ch. 30 Jacob prospered because he was crafty and adept at sympathetic magic."

5. Keil, 296.

6. Morris says, "Laban had become an idolater. . . . Rachel seems to have been influenced by him in this regard. Though she trusted Jacob's God, she also was reluctant to completely give up her previous superstitions" (p. 482). Hamilton says, "Rachel possibly stole the hearth gods for protection on her journey to Canaan" (p. 295).

7. See Hamilton, 294, and Morris, 483.

8. Hamilton, 300.

9. The word rendered "sons" refers to any subsequent generation. In this case it refers to Laban's daughters' sons, who were Laban's grandsons.

10. Epp, 271.

11. It is possible to hear in Jacob's words an unintentional prophecy. Shortly after returning to the land of Canaan, Rachel will die in childbirth (35:2–4, 16–20).

12. Hamilton, 292.

13. Hamilton, 306.

14. As I mentioned earlier, there is the possibility that in Isaac's initial blessing of Jacob he invoked the names of some of the Canaanite gods of the region near Hebron. If so, that should be seen as the temporary influence of his poor judgment in favoring Esau rather than a pattern of worship. Since Laban would have no knowledge of it, there would have been no point in introducing that to this conversation. God had called Himself "the God of Isaac" (Gen. 28:13), so Jacob's use of this name to identify God to Laban is appropriate.

15. Morris, 492.

CHAPTER EIGHT

1. Morris, 494.

2. Keil, 301.

3. Hamilton, 320.

4. These are the generally assumed proportions on the basis that the birthright constituted two shares. If Jacob and Esau are the only two sons of Isaac and Rebekah, then Jacob would receive two-thirds and Esau one-third. If, however, Jacob and Esau had younger brothers as the text implies, the proportions would be reduced.

5. Keil speculates that perhaps Esau's property had increased so much since Jacob left that he "severed himself more and more from his father's house, becoming increasingly convinced, as time went on, that he could hope for no change in the blessings pronounced by his father upon Jacob and himself, which excluded him from the inheritance of the promise, viz. the future possession of Canaan" (p. 302).

6. Sarna, 225.

7. Morris, 496.

8. Hamilton, 323.

9. Keil says that the phrase "to smite me, mother with children" "is a proverbial expression for unsparing cruelty" (p. 303).

10. Morris, 496.

11. Hamilton, 325, 326.

12. Sailhamer, 209.

13. Epp, 284, 285.

14. Hamilton, 328.

15. Sailhamer, 210.

16. Morris, 499.

17. The *JPS Torah Commentary* gives a radically different interpretation. After a lengthy discussion, it concludes, "The mysterious creature who assails Jacob . . . is none other than the celestial patron of Esau—Edom, who is the inveterate enemy of the people of Israel. . . . The change of name from Jacob to Israel . . . constitutes Esau's acquiescence in Jacob's right to the paternal blessings" (Sarna, 404). Dan. 10:13 refers to a celestial "prince of the kingdom of Persia" who "withstood" Gabriel on his way to deliver a message to Daniel. Gabriel had to call on Michael in order to get through with his message. Presumably on the basis of that passage, Sarna has extrapolated the existence of "celestial patrons" for all nations. He does not base it on the New Testament references to "principalities, powers, etc." since he rejects the validity of the NT. Further, his view is also shaped by the Jewish belief that there are no fallen angels. Satan did not rebel against God but is an ally of God sent out to oppose God's people to test them. Therefore, the reasoning goes, a celestial opponent representing Edom could be thought to oppose Jacob, then pronounce a divine blessing upon him when Jacob prevails. While I will grant the possibility that such angelic patrons exist for various nations, I reject the view that we have no spiritual opponents that desire our destruction and the overthrowing of God's throne. If Sarna is right about the identity of Jacob's opponent, he is wrong about the result. I suspect he is wrong on both counts. (For information on the Jewish doctrine of Satan and fallen angels, see two articles available online: "Jews Believe in The Satan, and Not in the Devil," by Rabbi Stuart Federow [www.whatjewsbelieve.org, accessed 2/6/2008] and "Does Judaism Believe in Satan?" [www.beingjewish.com/basics/satan.html, accessed on 2/8/2008].)

18. Sarna, 228.

19. Epp, 294.

20. Hamilton, 328.

21. Similar theophanies appear in the Old Testament. For instance, Joshua is confronted by a man with a drawn sword whom he does not recognize at first as the Lord but proves to be the Lord as the story progresses (Josh. 5:13–6:2*a*).

22. Hamilton, 333.

23. Epp, 294.

24. Feinberg, 58.

25. Morris, 502.

26. Zodhiates, 1759.

27. Ibid., 1682.

CHAPTER NINE

1. Morris, 503.

2. Epp, 301.

3. Hamilton, 343.

4. Ibid.

5. Sailhamer, 212.

6. Keil, 307.

7. Morris, 503.

8. Several writers point out that the Hebrew phrase translated "and he kissed him" is marked with dots above each consonant, an enigmatic marking that appears fewer than a dozen times in the Masoretic text. The most common assumption is that the dots are "intended to mark the word as suspicious" (Keil, 308). Some consider them to "represent the erasure of letters" (E. Tov [*Textual Criticism of the Hebrew Bible* (Assen and Maastricht: Van Gorcum; Minneapolis: Fortress, 1992), 55–57] cited by Hamilton, 340, footnote 5). However, that conclusion is far from certain. Treating the words as authentic does no harm to the text.

9. Morris, 503.

10. Hamilton, 344.

11. Morris, 503.

12. Hamilton, 345.

13. Ibid.

14. Keil, 308.

15. Hamilton, 345.

16. Hamilton, 347.

17. After leaving Succoth for Shechem, where he pitches a tent rather than building a house, we find his children acting as adults in the next chapter.

18. For an example of this opinion, see Epp, 305.

19. Morris, 506.

20. For a concurring opinion see Keil, 283.

CHAPTER TEN

1. Epp, 308, 314.

2. Keil, 311; Morris, 510.

3. Hamilton, 355.

4. Ibid., 356.

5. Sailhamer, 214.

6. Morris, 509.

7. Hamilton, 356.

8. Ibid.

9. In the case of Jacob's negotiations for Rachel with her father, Laban, rather than her brothers, it is likely that her brothers were younger,

perhaps not of legal age, since Rachel was the one in the field with the flocks, not her brothers.

10. Zodhiates, 1647.

11. A. Phillips, "Nebalah," *Vetus Testamentum 25* (1975), 241, cited by Hamilton, 357.

12. Hamilton, 358.

13. Morris, 512.

14. Keil, 314; Hamilton, 368; Morris, 515.

15. Hamilton, 371.

16. Morris, 516.

17. Epp, 315.

CHAPTER ELEVEN

1. An urban legend has circulated online claiming that as Hurricane Isabel approached Washington, DC, the tomb sentinels were ordered to stand down but refused. That is not true. No such order was given, and they remained on post. See www.tombguard.org, the official website of the Society of the Honor Guard, Tomb of the Unknown Soldier.

2. Ibid.

3. As of October 27, 2008. Ibid.

4. Morris, 518.

5. While we tend to think of moving southward as going "down" as it would appear on a map, Scripture tends to use the words "up" or "down" in reference to relative elevation, not compass points. Speaking cartographically, we would have said Jacob was going down to Bethel, but since Bethel's elevation was about 1000 feet higher than Shechem's, it was topographically correct for God to tell Jacob to "go up to Bethel."

6. Hamilton, 374.

7. Ibid.

8. The same is true in Gen. 24:22, 30, 47; Exod. 32:2, 3; 35:22; Judg. 8:24, 25, 26; Job 42:11; Prov. 25:12; and Hosea 2:13.

9. Ibid., 375.

10. Keil, 316.

11. Morris, 519.

12. Sailhamer, 218.

13. Victor Hamilton suggests another possible example in Isa. 7:14 and 8:3 if Immanuel is the name given by the child's mother and Maher-shalal-hash-baz is the name given to the same child by his father, but that is far from certain (p. 385).

14. Hamilton, 384–85.

15. Keil, 319.

16. Morris, 523.

17. Sailhamer, 226.

18. Hamilton, 405–6.

19. This formula appears twelve times, demarking eleven sections: Gen. 2:4; 5:1; 6:9; 10:1; 11:10, 27; 25:12, 19; 36:1, 9; 37:2; and Exod. 1:1. If Morris is correct, each marks a conclusion, not an introduction. The first, being the only one with no human name attached, says, "These are the generations of the heavens and of the earth," and concludes God's account of creation. The second, "This is the book of the generations of Adam," concludes Adam's account of creation and the establishing of his family. The subsequent texts conclude the sections written by Noah, Noah's sons collectively, Shem in particular, Terah, Ishmael, Isaac, Esau, Jacob, and the sons of Jacob. See Morris, pp. 26–30, for his detailed explanation.

CHAPTER TWELVE

1. Sailhamer, 226.

2. The contention is that *passim* is more likely related to the word for the "flat of one's hands or feet" or to the word for one's "extremities" than to the word for "colors." For a discussion of the issue, see Victor Hamilton, 407–9.

3. Keil, 335.

4. This is the first mention of daughters other than Dinah. Some believe this to be a reference to daughters-in-law (e.g., Hamilton, 427). However, there is no more evidence that any of his sons were married at this time than there has been of other daughters born to Jacob. Since daughters are mentioned again in Gen. 46:7, 15 as moving with him to Egypt, it is better to assume he had other daughters not previously mentioned in the text.

5. Hamilton, 514.

6. Sailhamer, 244.

7. Sailhamer, 250.

8. Morris counts eight, but he includes the time the angels appeared to Jacob after his encounter with Laban (Gen. 32:1). The text says nothing about God's presence on that occasion.

9. Sarna, 398.

10. Morris, 646.

CHAPTER THIRTEEN

1. Sailhamer, 275.

2. Keil, 390.

3. Ibid.

4. Hamilton, 658.

5.   Sailhamer, 276.

6.   Hamilton, 664.

7.   Keil, 403.

8.   Hamilton, 668.

9.   Hamilton, 670.

10. Morris, 658.

11. Ibid.

12. Keil, 405.

13. Hamilton, 674.

14. Morris, 660.

15. Of course the death, burial, and resurrection accounts concerning the Lord Jesus are much longer than the descriptions of His burial alone.

16. Sailhamer, 281–82.

ALSO BY PAUL W. DOWNEY

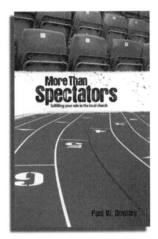

More Than Spectators–212340

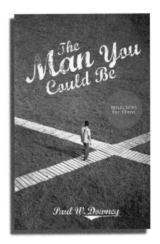

The Man You Could Be–247874

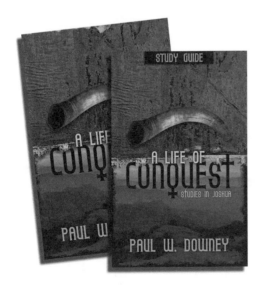

A Life of Conquest–230029

A Life of Conquest–241034
Study Guide